2004

ETHNIC IDENTITY GROUPS AND U.S. FOREIGN POLICY

ETHNIC IDENTITY GROUPS AND U.S. FOREIGN POLICY

Edited by Thomas Ambrosio

PRAEGER

Westport, Connecticut
London

Library of Congress Cataloging-in-Publication Data

Ethnic identity groups and U.S. foreign policy / edited by Thomas Ambrosio.
   p. cm.
   Includes bibliographical references and index.
   ISBN 0-275-97532-0 (alk. paper)—ISBN 0-275-97533-9 (pbk. : alk. paper)
      1. United States—Foreign relations.   2. Minorities—United States—Political activity.
3. United States—Ethnic relations.   4. Pressure groups—United States.   I. Ambrosio,
Thomas, 1971–
JZ1480 .E87   2002
327.73—dc21   2002070960

British Library Cataloguing in Publication Data is available.

Library of Congress Catalog Card Number: 2002070960
ISBN: 0-275-97532-0
ISBN: 0-275-97533-9 (pbk.)

First published in 2002

Praeger Publishers, 88 Post Road West, Westport, CT 06881
An imprint of Greenwood Publishing Group, Inc.
www.praeger.com

Printed in the United States of America

♾

The paper used in this book complies with the
Permanent Paper Standard issued by the National
Information Standards Organization (Z39.48-1984).

10   9   8   7   6   5   5   4   3   2   1

Copyright Acknowledgment

A version of Paul Y. Watanabe's chapter in this volume, "Asian-Americans and U.S.-
Asia Relations," was previously published as "Global Forces, Foreign Policy, and Asian
Pacific Americans," in *PS: Political Science & Politics* 34, no. 3 (2001): 639–44. Permis-
sion kindly granted by the American Political Science Association, Washington, D.C.

Contents

Preface

This book has its origins in a panel at the 2000 American Political Science Association's annual conference in Washington, D.C. While doing the research for my conference paper (which, incidentally, was on a related, but different topic than my contribution to this book, chapter 8), I noticed that there was a dearth of post–Cold War materials on the subject of ethnic identity groups and U.S. foreign policy. Some time after the conference, I contacted members of the panel and suggested the creation of an edited volume. After the panelists concurred, prominent scholars in the field—including Michael Jones-Correa, Yossi Shain, and Paul Watanabe—were contacted and asked to contribute chapters to the volume you are now holding in your hands.

Progress on the book was interrupted by the devastating events of September 11, 2001, when we all saw the United States attacked and two mighty symbols of American ingenuity, risk taking, and power collapse. That day fundamentally changed the lives of countless millions and, yes, the relationship between ethnic identity groups and U.S. foreign policy. Not only was there a new national mission, guiding Washington through the fog of post–Cold War uncertainty, but these events infused American politics with a renewed sense of patriotism and unity. How this will effect the ethnic influence on U.S. foreign policy remains to be seen. But one thing is certain: this volume is as timely now as it was on September 10.

The editorial process was helped tremendously by the contributors, whose patience with frequent updates, queries, and editorial changes was greatly appreciated. Also, Tony Smith provided some helpful suggestions at the beginning stages of the process. Jim Sabin and the staff at Greenwood Publishing Group have made my second book with Praeger a pleasure. Last, but certainly not least, my wife, Beth, has been a bedrock of support and understanding, without whom none of this would have been possible.

Finally, I would like to dedicate this book to my great-grandfather, Henry Heissenbuttel—an immigrant from Hamburg, Germany, who truly became an American in the wake of Pearl Harbor when he sent two of his sons off to war against the Axis—and my grandfather, Henry L. Heissenbuttel, who dropped the proverbial "hyphen" and has always been simply an American. Both would consider my love of the politics of ethnicity ironic.

Thomas Ambrosio

Chapter 1

Ethnic Identity Groups and U.S. Foreign Policy

Thomas Ambrosio

There has been an explosion in ethnic group participation in politics in
this city.
—Representative Lee Hamilton (D-Ind.)[1]

ETHNIC IDENTITIES AND "FACTION"

In *Federalist* 10, James Madison considered the problem of "faction" and how
the proposed new republic would ameliorate the negative consequences of internal divisions. Just as during the founding of the United States, controversies
over faction remain politically meaningful today. Current attention has shifted
from ideological or economic divisions to those based on racial, ethnic, religious,
or national identities. In order to include all of these different bases of identity
under one conceptual framework, this book uses the term *ethnic identity
groups*—politically relevant social divisions based on a shared sense of cultural
distinctiveness.[2] Some scholars see the rise of multiculturalism as inherently
dangerous to the internal cohesion of the United States and potentially threatening the very survival of the country.[3] In foreign policy, the United States is
sometimes seen as increasingly unable to define its national interests with any
degree of consensus, largely because of identity-based divisions.[4]

Like other societal interest groups, ethnic identity groups establish formal organizations devoted to promoting group cohesiveness and addressing group concerns.
Although many of these groups are apolitical, others are created for explicitly political purposes. Interest groups in general seek to influence policy, either domestic
or foreign. As the line between international and domestic politics becomes blurred,
so too does the permissible range of interest group activities. The phrase "politics
ends at the water's edge" is commonly cited but is often irrelevant because foreign
policy is increasingly driven by parochial concerns. Likewise, the interests of domestic actors are becoming more and more a product of events overseas. When it
comes to ethnic identity groups, this phrase becomes completely meaningless.

Nearly all ethnic identity groups have connections outside of the United States. Either they are part of a diaspora, with ethnic kin in their historical homeland or scattered among numerous countries, or they perceive similarities between themselves and other ethnic groups (e.g., southern whites and Afrikaners in South Africa or African-Americans and black South Africans). Ethnic identity groups often attempt to advance the interests of their ethnic kin through the formation of ethnic interest groups or, as they are commonly known, ethnic lobbies. Like all interest groups, ethnic interest groups seek to influence U.S. policy abroad in line with a specific agenda. But unlike, for example, business or environmental interest groups, which are concerned with profits and social values, respectively, ethnic interest groups are concerned with the well-being of members of the self-defined ethnic group, wherever they reside.[5] Consequently, one can define *ethnic lobbies* as political organizations established along cultural, ethnic, religious, or racial lines that seek to directly and indirectly influence U.S. foreign policy in support of their homeland and/or ethnic kin abroad. Stephen Garrett's observation about ethnic lobbies during the Cold War is equally true today: "Their stated *raison d'être* is to influence American policy."[6] Among some of the best-known ethnic lobbies are the Polish-American Congress, the Cuban-American National Foundation, TransAfrica, the National Association of Arab-Americans, the American Israel Public Affairs Committee, the Armenian Assembly of America, and the American Hellenic Institute Public Affairs Committee.

Ethnic lobbies primarily seek to influence policy in three ways: framing, information and policy analysis, and policy oversight. Framing refers to the attempt by interest groups to place an issue on the government's agenda, shape perspectives of that issue, and influence the terms of debate. This is closely connected to the role of interest groups as information provider: given the large number and diversity of the issues confronting a congressional staff, it is impossible for staffers to invest sufficient time to research issues themselves. Consequently, they are forced to rely on outside sources of information; interest groups provide this information, most likely with an analysis (or "spin") beneficial to their agenda. Finally, interest groups closely monitor government policies pertaining to their agenda and react to those policies through the dissemination of supplementary information, letter-writing campaigns, calls for hearings or additional legislation, support or opposition of candidates during elections, and so forth. While interest groups in general face a number of constraints on their ability to influence U.S. foreign policy, "[t]hese three roles allow interest groups to have an impact on the early stages of the decision-making process."[7]

In 1975, Nathan Glazer and Daniel Patrick Moynihan observed that the "ethnic composition" of the United States is "the single most important determinant of American foreign policy."[8] Although they may have overstated the case, there is certainly some truth to their observation. Being a country founded and populated by immigrants, the United States has always contained groups with significant affective and political ties to their national homeland and their ethnic kin throughout the world. Individuals within these groups are routinely assimilated to varying degrees into an overarching and separate "American" national identity. However, their connection to peoples outside of the United States may lead to a situation in which they suffer from dual, divided, or conflicted loyalties. Under these circumstances, a discordance arises between the interests of their *state* (the political-territorial entity where they reside) and the interests of their *nation* (the political-cultural entity that is fundamentally emotional in nature).[9] In other words, the foreign policy adopted by their country may conflict with a foreign policy that would benefit their ethnic kin.[10]

The notion of divided loyalties has long been a bogeyman for those who wish to call into question the allegiance of certain ethnic groups to the United States and its interests. For example, during World War II, Japanese-Americans on the West Coast were interned because of fears that they would act as a fifth column in support of Japan. The use of a hyphen to designate one's ethnic identity as well as one's citizenship—for example, Italian-American—has historically been seen as representative of divided loyalties.[11] However, the rise of multiculturalism during the 1970s and 1980s has led to greater acceptance of multiple identities within the American body politic without calling into question the loyalty of those holding multiple identities.[12] Moreover, there has been a growing acceptance that ethnic identity groups have the right to mobilize politically for the purpose of influencing U.S. policies at home and abroad. Consequently, there has been a rise in the number of ethnic lobbies and their influence.

A FRESH LOOK

During the 1970s and 1980s, a number of books and articles were published on the role of ethnic identity groups and U.S. foreign policy.[13] Since the end of the Cold War, the media and politicians of all stripes have increasingly turned their attention to this issue. Unfortunately, few books have been published on the subject in the past decade. Changes in the international system provide heightened opportunities for ethnic identity groups to influence U.S. foreign policy, although recent examinations of this phenomenon are scarce.[14] Two classic edited volumes, *Ethnicity and U.S. Foreign Policy* and *Ethnic Groups and U.S. Foreign Policy,* were published prior to the end of the Cold War.[15] The present edited volume aims to make a contribution by presenting a fresh look at this subject. It includes a number of case studies of ethnic identity groups in the United States, hailing from regions as diverse as Africa, North America, Eastern Europe, and Asia. Although some chapters provide a historical perspective on the relationship between ethnic identity groups and U.S. foreign policy, the volume's primary emphasis is on contemporary cases.

One question that the present work leaves open is whether ethnic identity groups *should* play a role in the U.S. foreign policy process. Some have argued that America's foreign policy has been "captured" by parochial interest groups and no longer serves American state interests. Although certainly recognizing that the potential for conflict exists between broader interests of the United States and the more narrow interests of certain substate actors, the contributors to this volume do not believe that the influence of ethnic identity groups on foreign policy is illegitimate. Instead, our position is that the rise of identity politics in U.S. foreign policy is a natural outcome of the changes in the American polity that have opened the policy process to greater influence by societal interest groups, some of which mobilize along ethnic, racial, or religious lines.

The question, however, is too important to be ignored and goes right to the heart of theories of democratic governance, citizenship, political loyalties, and identities. It is a difficult question without an easy answer. The case studies in this volume tackle the question from the other direction: not who *should* speak for America, but rather who *does* speak for America. We seek to understand how ethnic identity groups fit into the U.S. foreign policy process and the scope of their influence, rather than argue for or against ethnic identity group influence on U.S. foreign policy. Nevertheless, one must not disregard the moral or philosophical question. Consequently, the final chapter of this volume, "Legitimate Influence or Parochial Capture? Conclusions on Ethnic Identity Groups and the Formulation of U.S. Foreign Policy," provides an overview of the advantages and disadvantages of ethnic identity group influence on U.S. foreign policy.

The remainder of the present chapter serves as a primer to the role of ethnic identity groups and U.S. foreign policy. It is divided into four sections. In order to provide a historical context, the first section presents a brief history of ethnic identity groups and U.S. foreign policy. Because the sea change in America's grand strategy following the end of the Cold War has heightened opportunities for ethnic identity groups to influence the foreign policy process, the second section separately examines the post–Cold War factors affecting ethnic identity group influence. However, greater opportunities for ethnic identity groups in general have not led to an equal level of influence among all ethnic lobbies. The third section provides an overview of the factors that determine the relative strength of ethnic identity group power in the formulation of U.S. foreign policy. The final section of this chapter introduces the volume's case studies.

A BRIEF HISTORY OF ETHNIC IDENTITY GROUPS AND U.S. FOREIGN POLICY

Since the founding of the United States, ethnic identity groups have played a role in U.S. foreign policy. Despite pressures to assimilate into an exclusive American national identity, many individuals retained strong ties to ethnic kin and homelands outside of the United States. Alexander DeConde, for example, argued that U.S. foreign policy was markedly pro–Anglo-Saxon until World War I.[16] This was in line with the dominant sense of American national identity at the time, which identified the United States with the larger Anglo-Saxon world and, through that identity, with the dual notions of civilization and progress.

However, waves of immigration, especially during the Irish potato famine of the 1840s, altered America's sense of itself. The Fenians, an Irish-American revolutionary movement that resolved to liberate Ireland from British rule, launched two invasions of Canada from American soil (1866 and 1870) in an effort to weaken the British and drag the United States into war. While pro-Anglo-Saxon and pro-Irish foreign policies illustrate two instances in which ethnic identity groups shaped U.S. foreign policy, it was not until the massive waves of immigration during the late nineteenth century and early twentieth century that the "ethnic factor" really became a matter of significant public concern.

American ethnic identity groups were deeply concerned with U.S. involvement in World War I. As Tony Smith cites, roughly one-third of the American population was somehow connected to the conflict: some 13 percent of the population were born in countries actively involved in the war, and an additional 17 percent were native-born Americans with at least one parent who was born in a country that was directly involved in the war.[17] On the one hand, those of Irish and German ancestry sought American neutrality; on the other, Italians, Poles, English, Czechs, Slovaks, Armenians, and southern Slavs pushed for early and deep U.S. involvement in the conflict. Moreover, foreign leaders and nationalist activists looked toward their ethnic kin in America to help influence U.S. foreign policy. DeConde nicely summarizes the interactive relationship between World War I and American ethnic identity groups: "The World War quickened the ethnic consciousness of minority groups. They promptly created organizations to help the causes of their old European homelands that had become belligerents. Through whatever means possible, the ethnic activists among them sought to give direction to Washington on matters of policy that affected their overseas kin, making the United States a lobbying battleground between rival interest groups emotionally entangled in the war."[18]

In the waning years of the war and afterward, ethnic identity group mobilization continued. Those nations without territorial independence urged the United States to help secure statehood for their ethnic kin in the postwar settlement. For example, Jewish-Americans were particularly interested in the Balfour Declaration of late 1917, which promised a Jewish homeland in Palestine, and Armenian-Americans were disappointed that the United States failed to protect the nascent Republic of Armenia from Soviet occupation.

World War II was a watershed in the United States foreign policy and national identity. During the war, America was united as never before. Afterward, the global conflict against the Soviet Union gave U.S. foreign policy a sense of national purpose. Ironically, it also generated substantial changes in the role of ethnic identity groups and U.S. foreign policy: the shift from isolationism to internationalism arising out of American resistance to the Soviet Union and communism meant that the United States would take an active role in the international system. This role would be shaped and reinforced by ethnic identity groups in the United States. For example, Americans of both East European and West European ancestry united in opposition to Soviet occupation of Eastern

Europe and in support of the fledgling democracies of the West. In particular, East European ethnic lobbies coordinated their influence through the Assembly of Captive European Nations (ACEN), which urged the United States to take a hard line against the Soviet Union.[19] Because American national interests and the interests of the members of the ACEN coincided so closely, it is somewhat difficult to gauge the influence of the ACEN on U.S. foreign policy. Nonetheless, pressure from the ACEN certainly helped to dampen any chance for a rapprochement with the Soviet bloc.

Despite their significant activity during the Cold War, Stephen Garrett has questioned the real impact of East European lobbies on U.S. foreign policy for a variety of reasons:

- the relative exclusivity and insulation of the foreign policy establishment;
- the domination of the executive branch in the foreign policy process;
- a general wariness of interest group influence on foreign policy;
- questions surrounding the degree to which these lobbies had general American interests at heart or whether they were simply supporting their own parochial interests;
- the relative strength of WASP cultural dominance and historic prejudice against Southern and Eastern Europeans; and
- the geopolitical importance of Europe for American security and U.S.-Soviet relations.[20]

According to Garrett, each of these factors limited ethnic identity group influence during the Cold War.

America's Cold War foreign policy was largely formulated by a "small, cohesive club of academics, diplomats, financiers, lawyers and politicians that ascended to power during World War II."[21] Most of the foreign policy elite were concentrated in the executive branch, which was highly insulated from congressional oversight and less influenced by ethnic politicking because ethnic groups tend to be less effective in presidential elections.[22] In addition, the stakes of the Cold War were extremely high, especially within Europe. Consequently, the public tended to grant foreign policy elites the widest latitude and deference in policymaking. Although the Vietnam War, Watergate, and the consequences of the civil rights movement helped to erode the Cold War consensus and the elite-centric foreign policy process, the basic trajectory of U.S. foreign policy was largely set during the first two decades of the Cold War. As a result, ethnic identity groups found it difficult to fundamentally redefine American interests.

While the influence of special interest groups on U.S. foreign policy in general was largely considered illegitimate—American foreign policy was supposed to serve the general interests of the country as a whole—the risk of illegitimacy was seen as being an especially acute problem for ethnic groups. The well-established notion that the "hyphen" symbolized divided loyalties or even disloyalty to American national interests persisted throughout most of the Cold

War. Moreover, those groups who migrated to the United States during the period of "new immigration" (late nineteenth and early twentieth centuries) were still perceived as outsiders by the already-established Western and Northern Europeans who believed that only *they* had the right to define American national interests.

All of this is not to say that ethnic identity groups had no influence during the Cold War. In fact, their influence expanded throughout the 1960s and 1970s to the point that the press, scholars, and policymakers began to pay increasing attention to the issue. Glazer and Moynihan's statement already noted—that the "single most important determinant" of U.S. foreign policy is ethnic composition—illustrates that concern over the role of ethnic lobbies existed during the mid-1970s. A 1981 article by Maryland senator Charles McCurdy Mathias, Jr., in *Foreign Affairs* bemoaned what he perceived as the harmful effects of ethnic group lobbying.[23] In addition, *Foreign Policy* published a special three-article overview entitled "New Ethnic Voices."[24] Despite the limitations identified by Garrett, a number of ethnic identity groups had a significant impact on U.S. foreign policy even during the Cold War. From the founding of Israel to the formation of a close alliance between Israel and the United States, Jewish-Americans have long been the most influential ethnic lobby in the United States. The Intifada uprising of the 1980s, which pitched Israelis against Palestinians, further mobilized Jewish-American organizations and also led to the belated creation of Arab-American associations. The awakening of African-American consciousness, the successes of the civil rights movement in facilitating African-American organizational ability and access to the U.S. policy process, and the intensification of international condemnation of South Africa's apartheid regime all led to a growing role for African-Americans in the foreign policy process. Cuban-Americans helped to ensure that the United States' anti-Castro Cuban policy would be unchanging throughout the Cold War. Finally, the Cyprus conflict mobilized Greek-Americans in order to push for an arms embargo against Turkey.

During the Cold War, the influence of ethnic identity groups was limited by the nature of both the international system and the U.S. foreign policy process. By the early 1980s, however, there were clear signs that ethnic identity groups were playing a more significant role in U.S. foreign policy and would continue to do so in the future. The end of the Cold War served as a catalyst for a profound change in the relationship between American national interests and the interests of American ethnic identity groups.

POST–COLD WAR INFLUENCE OF ETHNIC IDENTITY GROUPS

The collapse of the Soviet Union in December 1991 fundamentally altered the international system and America's grand strategy. The logic of the Cold War was relatively simple: despite periods of greater or lesser confrontation, and despite some misguided policies arising out of Washington's containment policy, the United States and its allies were pitted against the perceived communist threat from the Soviet Union and its allies. Although ethnic identity groups had some role in fostering and reinforcing an enemy image of the Soviet Union, the relative inflexibility of U.S. foreign policy reduced the range of ethnic lobby influence. In many cases, moreover, the interests of ethnic identity groups and American national interests coincided—this was most clearly seen in regard to the U.S. alliance with Israel and American opposition to Soviet domination of Eastern Europe.

By contrast, the post–Cold War international system is highly fluid, with few guideposts to help determine American national interests. The Clinton administration's December 1999 report *A National Security Strategy for a New Century*, which attempted to define the premises of American foreign policy, was understandably vague given that no clearly identifiable, serious threat to U.S. national security existed at that time.[25] In the post–Cold War period, the United States has been forced to confront unforeseen situations and challenges, all the while attempting to construct a coherent foreign policy. Moreover, America's dominance in the international system provides it with greater latitude to pursue unilateral politics. Thus, U.S. foreign policy has moved squarely into the domestic political debate. The end of the Cold War created unprecedented opportunities for interest groups in general, and ethnic identity groups in particular, to influence the formulation and implementation of U.S. foreign policy. Ethnic lobbies have been adept at exploiting this upheaval in order to promote the interests of their ethnic kin and national homeland. As Ross Vartian, the former executive director of the Armenian Assembly of America, put it: "The object is not just to win the Cold War, but to win the post–Cold War."[26]

The greater opportunities afforded to ethnic identity groups by the fluidity of the international system is bolstered by a growing acceptance of ethnic identity group influence on U.S. foreign policy. Especially during the 1990s, the multiethnic nature of the American polity acquired increased political salience. Although Americans of European descent remain the dominant group demographically, the number of non-Europeans has grown considerably and is expected to grow in the future.[27] This movement adds more voices to what Yossi Shain has called America's "multicultural foreign policy."[28] More important than numbers, however, is the increasing rejection of cultural assimilation and, in its place, growing support for expressions of ethnic diversity. Regardless of whether this is a positive or negative development for American national identity, the massive demographic changes are a reality and have the effect of promoting a national identity that is more tolerant of individuals celebrating their ethnic heritage. More important for the purposes of this book, Americans are less willing to make charges of disloyalty against those who retain ties to their ethnic kin abroad and who advocate positions in line with the interests of their homeland.

The proliferation of ethnic conflicts throughout the world since the end of the Cold War has also heightened the stakes for many ethnic identity groups. Attempts to expand influence over U.S. foreign policy will increase as the independence, survival, or general welfare of a group's ethnic kin or homeland is threatened. Although interstate war has been rare in the past decade, intrastate conflicts have given many ethnic identity groups a reason to be active. The collapse of the former Yugoslavia pitted American-based Muslims, Croats, and Serbs against each other.[29] The U.S.-led North Atlantic Treaty Organization (NATO) war over Kosovo caused a split between many Orthodox Christians and the American government.[30] The second Intifada in the Israeli Occupied Territories and Israel itself has mobilized both Arab- and Jewish-Americans.[31] The conflict in the Transcaucasus between Armenians and Azeris has also increased lobbying activities by both groups.[32] Even a crisis such as the coup and refugee crisis in Haiti during the 1990s, though clearly not an ethnic conflict, has also energized African-Americans.[33]

Factors within the U.S. foreign policy process itself have also provided ethnic identity groups with greater opportunities to influence that process. The last decade has witnessed radical changes in the foreign policy establishment, including the decline of both the traditional, insulated foreign policy elite and the executive branch domination of the foreign policy process.[34] The following statement by John Dietrich provides a good overview of these changes:

Beginning in the early 1970s and continuing into the post–Cold War era, the U.S. foreign policy-making system has been transformed from the relatively closed and presidentially dominated system of the early cold war into a more open, contentious, and pluralistic system. The president remains the most powerful actor, but he now must contend with an active Congress, oversee a complex executive bureaucracy, and respond to pressures and ideas generated by the press, think tanks, and public opinion. During this period, there also has been a sharp increase in the number of interest groups actively seeking to influence U.S. foreign policy. These interest groups have mobilized to represent a diverse array of business, labor, ethnic, human rights, environmental, and other organizations. Thus, on most issues, the contemporary foreign policy-making system has become more similar to its domestic policy-making counterpart, with multiple interest groups using multiple channels to try to influence policy choices.[35]

All of these forces have been heightened since the end of the Cold War because, absent a coherent, identifiable threat, America's post–Cold War grand strategy is largely up for grabs.

Although ethnic identity groups must compete with a plethora of other special interest groups, increased pluralism expands these opportunities to influence policy. Moreover, increased congressional oversight and clout in foreign policy matters are beneficial to ethnic lobbies.[36] Demographically concentrated ethnic groups have a disproportional effect on members of Congress, who, in turn, become advocates for their constituents' ethnic kin outside of the United States. Members of Congress and other segments of the foreign policy establishment, according to Representative Lee Hamilton, "don't see much difference between lobbying for highway funds and slanting foreign policy toward a particular interest group."[37]

In addition, the growth of "intermestic" policy issues has also eroded the relative autonomy of the president in foreign affairs and opened the formulation and implementation of foreign policy to domestic forces.[38] During much of the past decade, the often acrimonious conflict between Republican Congress and the Democratic White House fueled congressional activism: "Republican lawmakers—and presidential candidates—are actively soliciting foreign affairs proposals that differ from the Clinton administration's positions."[39] This situation was exacerbated by President Clinton, who was initially focused on domestic issues and less interested and experienced in foreign policy matters.[40] The pattern has continued with his successor: George W. Bush's controversial election and lack of foreign policy experience, when combined with the narrow balance between Republicans and Democrats in the Congress, will likely prevent a coherent foreign policy vision from emerging.[41] Consequently, interest groups will be well positioned to exploit the opportunities presented by divided government.

These factors have together led to an environment in which ethnic identity groups possess greater access, more legitimacy, and a heightened ability to influence the foreign policy process in the United States. Like interest groups, however, all ethnic lobbies do not possess the same strength. The next section outlines the conventional wisdom on the relative effectiveness of ethnic identity groups.

VARYING STRENGTHS OF ETHNIC IDENTITY GROUPS

In their review of the literature on ethnic interest groups, Patrick Haney and Walt Vanderbush distill a list of factors that affect the relative strength of such groups.[42] These include the following:

- *organizational strength*—"organizational unity, a professional lobbying apparatus that provides useful information, and financial resources";
- *membership unity, placement, and voter participation*—based on the group's electoral implications;
- *salience and resonance of the message*—the ability to influence public opinion;
- *push on an open door*—"ethnic interest groups will be more successful if they promote policies that the government already favors";
- *strength of opposition*;
- *permeability of and access to the government*—"ethnic interest groups are more likely to be successful when the policy in question requires a congressional role since it is usually more porous than the executive";
- *mutually supportive relationships*—"while groups need policymakers to do something for them, policymakers also need the ethnic interest groups. Ethnic interest groups may provide a host of valuable resources to policymakers, including information, votes, and campaign contributions."

Each of these factors plays an important role in determining the influence an ethnic identity group has over the foreign policy process.

Organizational Strength

Interest groups in general are better organized, are more effective, and possess greater influence than ever before.[43] Moreover, changes in technology and access to members of Congress have lowered the costs of lobbying.[44] Several decades of active lobbying by a variety of ethnic identity groups have created a road map for new entries in the process. The literature is unanimous in identifying the American Israel Public Affairs Committee in particular, and the Jewish lobby in general, as the quintessential ethnic lobby in the United States.[45] Its success is often seen as a model that other groups could hope to emulate. Other powerful ethnic lobbies, such as the Cuban American National Foundation and the Armenian Assembly of America, are also held up as models.[46]

Electoral Implications

Many of the ethnic identity groups involved in the foreign policy process are concentrated in states rich in congressional districts and electoral college votes: for example, New York, New Jersey, California, Florida, and Illinois all play a significant role in ethnic identity group politics and together possess nearly a third of all members of Congress. Although as a percentage of the overall population in a congressional district, state, or the country as a whole, many ethnic identity groups may be relatively small, bloc voting and the potential for grassroots mobilization can provide these groups with influence disproportionate to their numbers. Targeted campaign contributions for or against a specific candidate can have a significant impact on the outcome of any given election. Moreover, as Tony Smith has observed, "ethnic money buys political influence" and "political influence solicits ethnic money."[47] Politicians often appeal to the interests of key ethnic identity groups in order to tap into the "ethnic money" and to garner more votes. For example, ethnic politics played at least some role in President Clinton's election-year decision to support NATO expansion.[48]

Public Opinion

Ethnic identity groups often benefit from the general population's lack of knowledge of foreign affairs. On many of the issues that ethnic lobbies care about, the average American either does not know enough to form an opinion or cares so little that the issue has no significant political impact with the wider populace. Consequently, American policy can be disproportionately influenced by a committed minority without much fear of a public backlash. "Most of the issues that recently excite ethnic lobbies, not one person in a thousand has ever heard of.... So a lot of members (of Congress) regard a vote on an ethnic issue as almost a throwaway vote."[49] In other words, a politician can appease an ethnic identity group without risking the wrath of his or her other constituents.

In the realm of public opinion, some groups benefit from their tragic past: the genocide against Armenians during World War I and the Jews during World War II provide them with a reserve of public sympathy and moral legitimacy that translates into significant political influence in the foreign policy process. For example, throughout the conflict of Nagorno-Karabagh, the Armenian-American lobby consistently portrayed the conflict against the Turkic-speaking, Muslim Azeris as a continuation of the Armenian Genocide in order to elicit congressional support for anti-Azerbaijan policies.[50] During the conflict in Kosovo, members of the Kosovo Liberation Army were quick to label Serb atrocities "genocide."[51] Although all mass killings and genocides are unmistakably tragedies, they are also a political resource that ethnic lobbies seek to utilize effectively.

An Open Door

In the previous section, the end of the Cold War was identified as a significant cause for the increased power of ethnic identity groups in the U.S. foreign policy process. Throughout much of the 1990s, U.S. foreign policy was in relative disarray, with policies hampered by the lack of a coherent grand strategy or an identifiable threat to U.S. national interests. This created a policy vacuum, which ethnic identity groups sought to fill to the advantage of their ethnic kin or national homeland. Rather than the door being open, one could argue that in many cases the door barely exists. In other cases where U.S. policy was able to survive changes in the international system (most notably in Israel and Northern Ireland), the congruence between established U.S. national interests and the interests of certain ethnic lobbies helped to boost the latter's strength.

Opposition

It would appear obvious that an interest group's strength is inversely related to the strength of its opposition. Although recent changes in the U.S. foreign policy process have created opportunities for ethnic lobbies, this very fact also permits opposing groups to counter the influence of established organizations. Moreover, areas of concern for ethnic identity groups are also of concern for a myriad of special interests. The Azeri-Armenian conflict over Nagorno-Karabagh did not involve solely these two ethnic groups. Instead, the potential economic boom derived from oil reserves in the Caspian Sea, the geopolitical importance of the Caucasus region, Israel's developing alliance with Turkey, and Turkey's affinity for Azerbaijan coalesced in the mid-1990s to create a curious coalition "of oil companies, administration officials, Jewish-Americans and pro-Turkey lawmakers" with the aim of challenging the Armenian-American lobby.[52] Thus, greater opportunities for one's own group may also yield greater opportunities for one's rivals.

Access and Partnership

Congress has also assumed a larger role in the U.S. foreign policy process since the end of the Cold War. Along with this have come the "symbiotic relationships" that often develop between ethnic lobbies and individual members of Congress. As Paul Watanabe has noted, "[Congress's] representativeness and accessibility ... [make it] such an alluring potential partner for ethnic groups. These tendencies establish the essential link between congressional activism and ethnic group activism. Ethnic organizations rely upon the responsiveness and legitimate policymaking authority of Congress to promote specific policy positions. Congress, to a great extent, relies upon the mobilization of nongovernmental opinion, such as that which emanates from informed ethnic activists, in order to perform effectively and to promote its enhanced foreign policymaking role."[53] Moreover, those members of Congress who are interested in foreign policy and sit on the international relations committees are more likely to represent districts that are ethnically diverse.[54] Consequently, ethnic lobbies are well positioned to directly influence Congress's role in the formulation of U.S. foreign policy.

As the United States embarks on the twenty-first century, it finds itself in an enviable position. It is the sole superpower, with no state matching its preponderance of political, economic, and military power.[55] This gives the United States tremendous latitude in formulating and pursuing its foreign policy objectives. Although ethnic identity groups have long influenced U.S. foreign policy, their role has never been greater and is likely to increase in the future.

OVERVIEW OF THE CASE STUDIES

The chapters included in this volume cover a wide array of case studies but are all centered around the role of ethnic identity groups in the formulation and implementation of U.S. foreign policy. Although each chapter stands by itself, four principle themes emerge, with two chapters fitting into each:

- the traditional (white) role of ethnicity in U.S. foreign policy;
- ethnic identity group mobilization;
- newcomers to the foreign policy process;
- the complexities of ethnic identity politics.

In their chapters, Paul McCartney and Catherine Scott both argue that even before the more recent rise of and concern over a "multicultural foreign policy," U.S. foreign policy has long had an ethnic component. Exploring the Spanish-American War and U.S. reactions to South African apartheid, respectively, these authors show how "Anglo-Saxonism" and "whiteness" promoted racially biased perceptions of the outside world and influenced the foreign policy process. In the first case, foreign policy leaders identified the United States with the "Anglo-Saxon race," which was in turn identified with progress, morality, and civilization itself. This notion propelled the United States into war with what was perceived as the moribund and backward Spanish Empire. It later provided a justification for the acquisition of, and patrimony over, the Philippines.

Writers often present U.S.–South African relations during the Cold War as suffering from a tension between geopolitical realities (alliance with South Africa) and American ideas (multiethnic democracy). Although Scott does not fully discount South Africa's strategic value to U.S. policymakers, she shows that shared conceptions of race and race relations merged with a perception of common historical circumstances to establish a foundation for positive U.S.–South African relations that went well beyond geopolitics. In particular, policymakers of both states perceived a bond of "whiteness" between their two countries. Moreover, a sense of being under siege from a black threat undergirded this relationship.

Fran Scott and Abdulah Osman in chapter 4 and Rachel Paul in chapter 5 tackle the problem of ethnic mobilization. It seems obvious that ethnic identity groups cannot be effective if they are not mobilized to play a role in the political arena. Scott and Osman compare and contrast the differing patterns of African-American responses to South African apartheid and the Rwandan genocide. They argue that African-American identity, given its formation in response to racial oppression and its solidification during the civil rights movement, is inherently tied to political and social factors (although they do not fully discount the cultural bases of identity). Consequently, a crucial component of African-American political mobilization is whether a "similarity of circumstance" exists between the African-American experience and current problems in the symbolic homeland, Africa. In the case of South Africa, a shared history of racial oppression served as the basis of anti-apartheid activism. However, the genocidal campaign by black Hutus against black Tutsis in Rwanda found little resonance in African-American political circles because the crucial component of racial oppression was missing.

Paul's chapter, by contrast, examines attempts to mobilize Serb-Americans for political action during the wars of Yugoslav succession. Serbs in America and the former Yugoslavia shared little in the way of common political circumstances—that is, Serb-Americans were not facing the breakup of a state and the separation of Serbs across international borders. Nevertheless, this did not prevent Serb-American organizations from mobilizing their constituents: rather than common political experiences, history and religion were used as the basis of Serb-American activism.

Michael Jones-Correa and Paul Watanabe provide a look at two of the new "ethnic voices" in American politics: Latino-Americans and Asian-Americans, respectively. Jones-Correa shows that ethnic identity groups are not monolithic. Rather than a unified policy agenda, Latino-Americans have differing interests depending on whether certain members of the group are newly arrived immigrants or native born. With the exception of immigration policy, in which both subsets have taken similar stances, the native-born Hispanic elites are far more concerned with domestic policy issues than are Latino immigrants, who maintain substantial informal ties to their respective homelands. Asian-Americans, as Watanabe's chapter illustrates, are still grappling with fundamental questions of identity, which will be largely defined by the processes of globalization and transnationalism. How Asian-Americans define themselves, and are defined by society, will play a crucial role in determining their level of political activism, as well as delineating an Asian-American policy agenda.

The next two chapters illustrate the complexities of ethnic identity group politics within the United States and abroad. Thomas Ambrosio examines the relationship between international alliances and domestic political constellations within the United States. Focusing on the Turkish-Israeli strategic alliance, he shows how Jewish-American lobbies found themselves supporting the Turkish policy agenda. This, in turn, unintentionally pitted Jewish-American groups against their historic allies, the Armenian-Americans, on issues ranging from sanctions against Azerbaijan to oil pipelines to the Armenian Genocide resolution. This tangled web of international and domestic alliances left many members of Congress scratching their heads and caught in the middle of constituencies that, for some time, have supported each other's policy agenda.

Yossi Shain and Tamara Cofman Wittes's chapter also examines a complex web of relationships, but from a different perspective. Instead of overlapping domestic and international alliances, Shain and Wittes are concerned with the relationship between diaspora and homeland in relation to the latter's peace efforts with longtime enemies. The diaspora may play an independent role in supporting or opposing conflict resolution in communal conflicts and must be considered by homeland leaders and the government of host states who are undertaking peacemaking policies. The authors illustrate this point by investigating the impact of the diaspora on attempts to resolve the Nagorno-Karabagh (Armenian-Americans) and Israeli-Palestinian (Jewish-Americans) conflicts.

As the eight case studies illustrate, ethnic identities have long played a role in the formulation and implementation of U.S. foreign policy and will continue to do so for the foreseeable future. It is therefore appropriate and necessary to consider the cost and benefits of ethnic groups' influence on U.S. foreign policy. The final chapter of this volume provides an overview and evaluation of the arguments for and against this influence with the intent of sparking debate, rather than resolving the issue.

NOTES

1. Quoted in Frank Greve, "Ethnic Lobby Powers Up," *The Armenian Reporter* 28, no. 50 (1995): 16.

2. Very often, ethnic identities themselves are based on religious differences (Jewish- or Muslim-Americans) or racial categories (African-Americans). Consequently, it is difficult to separate ethnic, religious, and racial identities because they often overlap. In order to capture the widest possible range of groups, this definition is purposefully broad. Thus, it captures identities such as "whiteness" and "Anglo-Saxon Protestant."

3. Arthur M. Schlesinger, Jr., *The Disuniting of America* (New York: Norton, 1992).

4. Samuel P. Huntington, "The Erosion of American National Interests," *Foreign Affairs* 76, no. 5 (1997): 28–49; James Schlesinger, "Hyphenating Foreign Policy," *National Interest* 62 (Winter 2000–2001): 110–13.

5. James Nathan and James Oliver, *Foreign Policy Making and the American Political System* (Baltimore: Johns Hopkins University Press, 1994), 197–215.

6. Stephen A. Garrett, "Eastern European Ethnic Groups and American Foreign Policy," *Political Science Quarterly* 93, no. 2 (1978): 305.

7. John W. Dietrich, "Interest Groups and Foreign Policy: Clinton and the China MFN Debates," *Presidential Studies Quarterly* 29, no. 2 (1999): 280–96.

8. Nathan Glazer and Daniel Patrick Moynihan, eds., introduction to *Ethnicity: Theory and Practice* (Cambridge, MA: Harvard University Press, 1975), 23.

9. For an overview of the terminological chaos that too often plagues discussions of the relationship between state, nation, and ethnicity, see Walker Connor, "A Nation Is a Nation, Is a State, Is an Ethnic Group, Is a . . . ," in *Ethnonationalism: The Question for Understanding* (Princeton, NJ: Princeton University Press, 1994), 90–117.

10. It is important to note that in some cases, ethnic identity groups can reinforce policies that are deemed in U.S. national interests, independent of any ethnic lobby influence. For example, American support for Israel, its opposition to the Castro regime in Cuba, and American resistance to Soviet control over Eastern Europe, though supported by ethnic lobbies, were by almost any objective standard in line with U.S. national interests. The role of ethnic lobbies was to augment the legitimacy of these policies and strengthen U.S. commitments abroad. The close correspondence between ethnic lobby support and U.S. interests could be a potential problem if changes in America's international environment call for new policies and a particular ethnic lobby prevents these changes. For example, the end of the Cold War and the collapse of worldwide communism has not resulted in the removal of U.S. trade sanctions against Cuba, largely because of the strength of the Cuban-American lobby.

11. Louis L. Gerson, *The Hyphenate in Recent American Politics and Diplomacy* (Lawrence: University of Kansas Press, 1964). Some writers have dropped the hyphen when designating American ethnic groups such as African American, Asian American, or Serb American. However, in the context of this book, the hyphen has been kept, not to designate disloyalty to the United States (at no time is that implied by the contributors of this volume) but rather to recognize the importance of ethnic identities when formulating foreign policy. If ethnicity were irrelevant to one's "American" identity, the entire notion of a multicultural foreign policy would be moot.

12. Even after the terrorist attacks of 11 September 2001, U.S. officials and civic leaders went out of their way not to link Muslim-Americans with Osama Bin Laden and the al-Qaeda terrorist network.

13. See the Selected Bibliography at the end of this volume.

14. The most notable exception is Tony Smith's *Foreign Attachments: The Power of Ethnic Groups in the Making of American Foreign Policy* (Cambridge, MA: Harvard University Press, 2000).

15. Abdul Aziz Said, ed., *Ethnicity and U.S. Foreign Policy,* revised ed. (Westport, CT: Praeger, 1981); Mohammed E. Ahrari, ed., *Ethnic Groups and U.S. Foreign Policy* (Westport, CT: Greenwood Press, 1987).

16. Alexander DeConde, *Ethnicity, Race, and American Foreign Policy* (Boston: Northeastern University Press, 1992), chap. 2.

17. Smith, *Foreign Attachments,* 51.

18. DeConde, *Ethnicity, Race, and American Foreign Policy,* 82.

19. Garrett, "Eastern European Ethnic Groups and American Foreign Policy," 305–6.

20. Ibid., passim.

21. Michael Clough, "Grass-Roots Policymaking: Say Good-bye to the 'Wise Men,'" *Foreign Affairs* 73, no. 1 (1994): 2–7.

22. This is not to say that ethnic politicking has no role in presidential elections. Rather, ethnic groups have substantially more influence in congressional elections because they tend to be highly concentrated in certain congressional districts (mostly urban areas). In presidential elections, the strength of individual ethnic groups becomes more diffuse, although there are exceptions (the Irish in the northeast United States, for example). Nevertheless, because the formulation of U.S. foreign policy has been traditionally centered in the executive branch, ethnic identity group influence in Congress did not translate into significant influence on foreign policy.

23. Charles McCurdy Mathias, Jr., "Ethnic Groups and Foreign Policy," *Foreign Affairs* 59 (1981): 975–98.

24. "New Ethnic Voices," *Foreign Policy* 60 (1985): 3–39.

25. The only exception is international terrorism. See the section on 11 September 2001 in chapter 10.

26. Quoted in Dick Kirschten, "Ethnics Resurging," *National Journal* 27, no. 8 (1995): 484.

27. U.S. Bureau of the Census, "Population Projections of the United States by Age, Sex, Race, and Hispanic Origin: 1995–2050," *Current Population Reports* P25-1130, February 1996.

28. Yossi Shain, "Multicultural Foreign Policy," *Foreign Policy* 100 (1995): 69–87.

29. Dick Kirschten, "Sarajevo's Saviors," *National Journal* 26, no. 12 (1994): 655.

30. Richard Whitt, "Serbs in Atlanta See Bombing as Unjust," *Atlanta Journal and Constitution,* 13 May 1999, 8A.

31. Tom Tugend, "US Jewish-Muslim Relations Grow Dim," *Jerusalem Post,* 30 September 2001, 7.

32. Mahir Ibrahimov and Erjan Kurbanov, "The Armenian-Azerbaijani Dispute as Seen from the U.S.: An Experienced Armenian Lobby Opposes Azerbaijan," *Washington Report on Middle East Affairs* 13, no. 4 (1995): 28.

33. Art Pine, "Rice Plays Part in Haiti Policy, U.S. Aide Says," *Los Angeles Times,* 11 July 1994, A1.

34. Clough, "Grass-Roots Policymaking," 2–7; I. M. Destler, Leslie H. Gelb, and Anthony Lake, "Breakdown: The Impact of Domestic Politics on American Foreign Policy," in *The Domestic Sources of American Foreign Policy: Insights and Evidence,* ed. Charles W. Kegley, Jr., and Eugene R. Wittkopf (New York: St. Martin's Press, 1988), 17–29.

35. Dietrich, "Interest Groups and Foreign Policy."

36. Anthony Eksterowicz and Glenn Hastedt, "Congress, the Presidency, and World Order: The Interplay of International and Domestic Politics," *Journal of Social, Political, and Economic Studies* 19, no. 3 (1994): 359–80; James M. Lindsay, *Congress and the Politics of U.S. Foreign Policy* (Baltimore: Johns Hopkins University Press, 1994).

37. Quoted in Steven Mufson, "Local Politics Is Global as Hill Turns to Armenia," *Washington Post,* 9 October 2000, A1.

38. Glenn P. Hastedt and Anthony J. Eksterowicz, "Presidential Leadership in the Post Cold War Era," *Presidential Studies Quarterly* 23 (1993): 445–59.

39. Greve, "Ethnic Lobby Powers Up," 16.

40. James M. Lindsay, "Looking for Leadership," *Brookings Review* 18, no. 1 (2000): 43.

41. The possible exception is fighting terrorism. However, President Bush has made it clear that the "war against terrorism" will be like no other war before it. Thus, although the mission may be clear, the path that the United States will follow is not.

42. Patrick J. Haney and Walt Vanderbush, "The Role of Ethnic Interest Groups in U.S. Foreign Policy: The Case of the Cuban American National Foundation," *International Studies Quarterly* 43 (1999): 344–45.

43. Allan J. Cigler and Burdett A. Loomis, *Interest Group Politics,* 5th ed. (Washington DC: Congressional Quarterly Press, 1998). Specifically on ethnic identity groups and U.S. foreign policy, see Eric M. Uslaner's contribution, "All Politics Are Global: Interest Groups and the Making of Foreign Policy," 369–89.

44. For example, the editors of *Congressional Quarterly* have published a guide for those interested in becoming part of the lobbying game. See Bruce C. Wolpe and Bertram J. Levine, *Lobbying Congress: How the System Works,* 2d ed. (Washington DC: Congressional Quarterly, 1996).

45. *Fortune* magazine's report of the most powerful lobbies in Washington ranked the American Israel Public Affairs Committee second, above the National Federation of Independent Business, the National Rifle Association, and the AFL-CIO. Only the American Association of Retired Persons was more powerful than the Israelis. "The Influence Merchants," *Fortune* 138, no. 11 (1998): 134.

46. John Auerbach, "Scattered, a Community Bonds," *Boston Globe,* 23 April 1995, 1.

47. Smith, *Foreign Attachments,* 108.

48. James M. Goldgeier, *Not Whether but When: The U.S. Decision to Enlarge NATO* (Washington DC: Brookings Institution Press, 1999), 61–62; Dick Kirschten, "Ethnics Resurging;" R. C. Longworth, "One Nation, Many Voices," *Chicago Tribune,* 13 April 1998, 1.

49. Greve, "Ethnic Lobby Powers Up," 16.

50. Thomas Ambrosio, "Congressional Perceptions of Ethnic Cleansing: Reactions to the Nagorno-Karabagh War and the Influence of Ethnic Interest Groups," *The Review of International Affairs* (forthcoming).

51. John Pilger, "US and British Officials Told Us That at Least 100,000 Were Murdered in Kosovo," *New Statesman* 129, no. 4502 (2000): 13.

52. "Petro-Politics Greases the Way for a Different US Approach to Nagorno-Karabakh Dispute," *Congressional Quarterly Weekly Report,* 27 June 1998, 1783.

53. Paul Y. Watanabe, *Ethnic Groups, Congress, and American Foreign Policy: The Politics of the Turkish Arms Embargo* (Westport, CT: Greenwood Press, 1984), 40–41.

54. Andrew Napoli (legislative director for Congressman Chris Smith), telephone interview by author, 17 July 2000.

55. William C. Wohlforth, "The Stability of a Unipolar World," *International Security* 24, no. 1 (1999): 7.

Chapter 2

Anglo-Saxonism and U.S. Foreign Policy during the Spanish-American War

Paul McCartney

Although the founders of the United States premised its political order explicitly upon principles of liberty and equality, both they and succeeding generations tragically failed to realize in practice the promise of those ideals. Instead, racial constructs positing Anglo-Saxon supremacy and nonwhite primitivism patterned white Americans' thinking so that they could institute a system of chattel slavery within the world's first flourishing democratic republic. The sheer magnitude of that hypocrisy may seem stunning today, but it demonstrates how Americans, like all people, have been willing to distort ideals to make them conform to baser interests.

It is comforting to imagine that interests and values naturally coincide, but that is a facile and dangerous illusion to entertain. A striking example of this capacity for self-delusion came at the turn of the twentieth century, when Americans believed that they had discovered an intellectually satisfying solution to the contradiction between liberal democratic equality and racism when they used social Darwinism as an overarching rubric explaining the nature of social and moral progress. In this chapter, I show how American leaders relied on a conception of American national identity as being both *Anglo-Saxon* and *democratic* to formulate the normative basis of U.S. foreign policy before and after the Spanish-American War. American leaders mixed racist assumptions with liberal-democratic values in a way that amazingly led them to define their nation as a paragon of virtuous progress worthy of global leadership. By reviewing the actual policy debates surrounding the war and placing them within their broader cultural context, I show how this paradoxical admixture of civic and racial national identities demonstrably influenced U.S. foreign policy during this crucial episode.

This analysis is divided into three main sections. First, I explain the dominant cultural constructs and norms that shaped Americans' perceptions of the circumstances surrounding the Spanish-American War. Second, I demonstrate how Americans justified to themselves the necessity of fighting Spain as resulting from the superior moral character of the United States. Finally, I summarize how racial constructions of American national identity structured the postwar debate over annexing the Philippine Islands.

NORMS, CULTURE, AND AMERICAN NATIONAL IDENTITY IN 1898

Americans in the late 1890s consistently maintained that their nation had a crucial responsibility in leading the progressive advance of human history. They believed that humanity had a collective teleological purpose, with the United States fated to play a key role in the achievement of that purpose. The human race was seen as progressing as "enlightened" civilizations replaced their more "primitive" precursors either from within, through natural evolutionary development, or from without, through conquest. This belief was built on four ideological foundations: evolutionary theory (usually Darwin's theory of natural selection), white racism, a nationalist construction of liberal democracy, and liberal Protestantism. Each of these ideological constructs contributed to Americans' conviction that their nation was morally and politically superior to all others and fitted for world leadership. For the sake of analytic clarity, I will confine my analysis to the first three dimensions of America's turn-of-the-(last)-century cultural identity, leaving aside the religious sources of American nationalism. Although each of these cultural sources was on some level logically contradictory to the others, they were all made mutually amenable (often by conceptual elision) in a way that structured the nation's approach to international relations.

Contemporary interpretation of Charles Darwin's theory of evolution, for example, which posited violent competition within and between groups as the source of progress, coexisted uneasily in the American mind with liberalism's depiction of man gradually educating himself toward perfection. The explanatory power and moral flexibility of Darwin's thesis, however, made it a useful addition to the American worldview. Darwin's theory of natural selection, which was commonly invoked by reference to Herbert Spencer's popular phrase "survival of the fittest," held that the "weak" members of a species are weeded out by the incompatibility between their inherited characteristics and the environment into which they are born, so that only a species' strongest representatives survive and propagate. Its tacit normative message was that "good" qualities abet survival, which was often misinterpreted to mean that those qualities that have survived are therefore "good." In his second book, *The Descent of Man*, Charles Darwin expanded his theory of natural selection to encompass not just biological evolution but evolution within and between human societies.[1] In it,

Darwin argued that the United States, as the world's strongest civilization, was at the forefront of the social-evolutionary process. "There is apparently much truth in the belief that the wonderful progress of the United States, as well as the character of the people, are the results of natural selection," he wrote, "for the more energetic, restless, and courageous men from all parts of Europe have emigrated during the last ten or twelve generations to that great country, and have there succeeded best." This interpretation of American success fit into Darwin's broader theory of civilizational evolution wherein favorable biological characteristics among the population yield greater national power: "Obscure as is the problem of the advance of civilisation, we can at least see that a nation which produced during a lengthened period the greatest number of highly intellectual, energetic, brave, patriotic, and benevolent men, would generally prevail over less favoured nations."[2]

Naturally, America's social and political elite embraced this line of argument because it provided racist paradigms with scientific legitimacy and reinforced the preexisting notion that the United States was in some objective and grandly historical way better than any other nation-state. In particular, Darwinian evolutionism came to shape directly the way Americans understood both international relations and their nation's mission to the world.[3] Nation-states, according to this paradigm, engaged in a bitter competition with each other for survival, and theorists such as naval historian Alfred T. Mahan urged as a result strategic expansionism as a necessary survival tactic. Because the United States had always presumed itself to be in the vanguard of history's flow, moreover, during the 1890s the country took it for granted that it had a particular responsibility to bring other races and nations[4] up to the standards of modern (American) civilization. In addition to structuring the American worldview on a general level in 1898, therefore, social Darwinism also directly shaped some of the country's attitudes regarding foreign affairs.

Darwin's theories also structured American racism at the end of the nineteenth century, although racism obviously rested on much older and more durable assumptions.[5] Darwinism's new methodology for understanding social differences, however, undergirded the rise of the new social sciences, which quickly spelled out the "scientific" basis of racial and civilizational differences. According to the dominant evolutionary/civilizational paradigm, races were arrayed along a hierarchy in which they were not only "ranked" but also assigned distinguishing characteristics. For example, Anglo-Saxons were considered the "best" race—say, a ten on a scale of one to ten, followed by the next most developed race (usually the Germans, or "Teutons"), who would rate a nine, and so on down the scale—but were also believed to embody specific characteristics, such as the capacity for enlightened self-rule, that the "lower" races were inherently unable to emulate.[6] The hierarchical and epistemic nature of racial differences was thus given scientific reinforcement, as the higher races inevitably possessed characteristics that were nobler and more "moral" than those of lesser races, and these attributes fitted them to occupy a paternalistic role over inferior races. These justifications, which were used to defend racial discrimination, one should remember, derived from the research of the social-scientific establishment, not the propaganda of marginal reactionaries.[7]

The Era of the Militant WASP

Social Darwinist research was important for confirming and thereby sustaining the continued viability of what Rogers Smith has termed "inegalitarian ascriptive Americanism," a feature of America's political ideology that defined the United States as a white, Anglo-Saxon nation.[8] Smith calls the last three decades of the nineteenth century "the era of the militant WASP," when the Democrats (still the party of the South) "trumpeted their belief in America as a white Christian nation" and Republicans, though more divided, "insisted that whoever might be included as Americans, the Protestant and Anglo-Saxon character of the national culture had to be not just preserved but enhanced."[9] During this period, notes Smith, numerous immigration laws were passed to prevent "inferior races" from becoming U.S. citizens.[10]

In particular, these years were marked by three significant developments in domestic race relations in the United States: the disenfranchisement of black voters, the establishment of legal segregation, and a sharp increase in the number of lynchings. Blacks were stripped of the vote during these years at an alarming rate—between 1896 and 1904, for example, the number of registered African-American voters in Louisiana fell from 130,334 to 1,342.[11] This decline was not an accident or an incidental byproduct of other social forces. As Congressman John Williams, a Mississippi Democrat, boasted:

We have succeeded in disenfranchising the worst portion of the colored population of the State of Mississippi by subjecting them, as well as white people, to an educational qualification, and as nearly all of the white men can read and write, and as very few negroes can, notwithstanding the fact that the schools are now and have been open to them for thirty years, we manage to secure for the electorate a majority safe for white supremacy and civilization....And if I am the only Democrat in this House, I shall stand for white supremacy in Hawaii, when that question comes up, as I have stood for it in Mississippi....I shall vote for those provisions of the scheme which make for a white man's supremacy.[12]

Other schemes than literacy tests were also used to take the vote away from blacks in the 1890s, including white primaries and poll taxes. Grandfather clauses were usually enacted to allow whites who failed to meet these requirements to continue to vote.[13]

The Supreme Court also provided a proactive defense of the proposition that the United States was a white nation in its prosegregation ruling in *Plessy v. Ferguson*[14] in 1896. Government-sanctioned segregation had only begun in

1887, when Florida mandated separation of the races on trains. Prior to the passage of Florida's law, segregation, at least in the Old Confederacy, was uncommon. C. Vann Woodward discussed in his classic study of segregation, *The Strange Career of Jim Crow*, for example, the case of a Northern black man who rode in integrated railroad cars throughout the South in 1885 and encountered no discrimination.[15] *Plessy*, however, established a precedent that was used to justify segregation laws that were passed with ever-increasing frequency during the era of the Spanish-American War. Segregation attained full legitimacy, legally and socially, during the 1890s.

Not only were blacks disenfranchised and segregated during the 1890s; they also became subject to unprecedented mob violence. No longer protected, invidiously, by their value as property as they were before the Civil War, or by Northern troops as they were immediately after it, African-Americans found themselves suddenly vulnerable to informal but widespread violence that the government countenanced by remaining silent. The Ku Klux Klan rose to prominence just before the 1890s, and lynching became a common practice. In one high-profile episode in 1898, ten blacks were lynched in Wilmington, North Carolina, after "'the best elements' of the local white population organized an armed mob" in response to the efforts of some local blacks to run for government office.[16] Edward A. Johnson, a contemporary black historian, observed with exasperation, that "often there seems no effort even to put the Negro in any particular place save the grave, as many of the lynchings and murders appear to be done either for the fun of shooting some one, or else with extermination in view. There is no attempt at reason or right. The mob spirit is growing—prejudice is more intense. Formerly it was confined to the rabble, now it has taken hold of those of education, and standing."[17]

Anglo-Saxon Foreign Policy

From the twin beliefs that Anglo-Saxons were superior to other races and that the United States was a white nation emerged two kinds of conclusions for the nation's foreign policy. The first, racial essentialism, was that racial differences were permanent and that the status of the races within global civilization was therefore fixed. Regions inhabited by nonwhites were permanently unable to become democratic and were doomed to exist either in a state of anarchy or under colonial paternalism. They could never join the Union, therefore, as states under the Constitution, which required a republican form of government. The second view, racial paternalism, held that the members of different races were essentially equal but that (social) evolutionary development put some races far ahead of others. Proponents of the second view considered "lesser" races to be at least theoretically capable of self-rule but deemed this capacity to be only latent and generations of development away from realization. Those adhering to this view believed that the United States could "educate" the populations of the overseas territories so that they could practice self-government; theirs was a position that reflected the racist norms of the times but not the unreconstructible racism of the racial essentialists. Often, this view also incorporated a sense of moral responsibility to "uplift" nonwhites by sharing with them the inherent blessings of American civilization. Both conclusions could support, at least for the short term, white racial paternalism over "backward" civilizations. As one of the founders of the discipline of political science, John W. Burgess, explained:

[B]y far the larger part of the surface of the globe is inhabited by populations which have not succeeded in establishing civilized states; which have, in fact, no capacity to accomplish such a work; and which must, therefore, remain in a state of barbarism or semi-barbarism, unless the political nations undertake the work of state organization for them. This condition of things authorizes the political nations not only to answer the call of the unpolitical populations for aid and direction, but also to force organization upon them by any means necessary, in their honest judgment, to accomplish this result. There is no human right to the status of barbarism.[18]

The corollary of there being no human right to barbarism, of course, was that there *was* such a right for civilized people to rule over barbarians.

Another axiom of American thought in 1898 held that America's political principles were of universal value (even if they had to be administered to dependent inferior races from above). Americans generally agreed that there had been some apparent inconsistencies between their principles as expressed in the Declaration of Independence and their actual practice, but they still believed that those principles could only attain the universal application that they deserved through the agency of the United States. While the ideal of individual liberty that lay at the heart of American culture was presumed to rest on a universal human nature, its realization in the world relied on implementation by the United States. The political exercise of human freedom and equality had hitherto only been truly manifested in the United States, and so the United States was perceived in a literal way as embodying those values. This logic transmuted the country's universalist philosophy into a nationalist one.[19]

The most obvious conceptual difficulty with the argument that democratic liberty had to be enforced by the United States was that it seemed to deny self-government to others. One dubious way of squaring that circle was to reject the notion that the Declaration of Independence's promise of government "by the consent of the governed" actually meant self-determination. One pamphleteer made that case as follows: "The unalienable right which [the founders] proclaimed was not the right of every *community* of men to national independence, but the right of every individual *man* to life, liberty, and the pursuit of happiness, that personal right which our government is trying to secure ... and which [others] cannot be sure of except under the American flag."[20] If England had reformed itself in a suitable manner prior to the Revolutionary War, this argument implied, then the Americans would have been unjustified in revolting. Despite its title, then, the Declaration of Independence did not demand independence, only individual freedom under a just regime. Because the United States embodied freedom more purely than any other society, therefore, it simply could not violate anyone else's liberty. Like Midas, whatever the United States touched became free.

A more common method of reconciling American theory and practice was to insist that the Declaration of Independence guaranteed liberty only to those who were properly prepared to exercise it. This position did not quite contradict the premise that "all men are *created* equal," but it did limit the nature of that shared equality in such a way that allowed individuals to enjoy different levels of political freedom. Just as children were their parents' equals in the eyes of God without having equivalent political stature, so "child" races and nations could have less political freedom without undermining the Declaration of Independence's fundamental premise.[21] The ideals of the declaration and of the American regime thus could accommodate facial violation if the requisite political capacity was absent. Human equality did not mean political equality. This logic was clear to Americans in the 1890s; persistent discrepancies between the political treatment of racial, religious, and gender minorities on the one hand and their white, Anglo-Saxon Protestant male counterparts on the other had long since acculturated Americans to the notion that political inequality could coexist with fundamental human "equality."

The effect was that the meaning of the term *equality* as expressed in the nation's founding political documents was rigidly bracketed so that it could conform with the culture's other ideological norms. As one writer put it, "among the inalienable rights of man which the Declaration sets up, the right to political equality is not enumerated."[22] If it had been, then Americans would have "persistently departed from it in establishing various property and educational limitations on the suffrage, in denying political rights to the Indians, in governing the territories when first acquired (and some of them still) by Federal agents, in withholding the right of self-government from the inhabitants of the District of Columbia, in refusing to let the people of the Southern States set up an independent government of their own, and in many other particulars."[23] Among those "other particulars," of course, were the myriad ways that whites had deprived blacks of any semblance of liberty or equality.

The argument that the guarantees of the Declaration of Independence were of limited applicability converted that document essentially into a nationalist tract. By building from the two premises—first, that the Declaration of Independence was intended for a white citizenry, and second, that the United States was an Anglo-Saxon nation—Americans found themselves able to reconcile their political principles, racism, and imperialist impulses. Furthermore, the competitive and developmental logic of social Darwinism entrenched this worldview in 1898 and provided it with scientific legitimacy. This intoxicating blend of racism, Darwinism, and nationalistic liberal democracy yielded a jingoistic self-confidence and moral smugness. Americans' belief in their nation's unimpeachable moral supremacy, moreover, spurred them to seek to improve the world by spreading its values to other parts of the world.

THE PREWAR DEBATE

America's cultural matrix was clearly responsible for the deteriorating relations with Spain in 1898. In particular, the United States fought against Spain because it objected to the cruel manner in which Spain had been suppressing a nationalist revolution in Cuba that began in 1895, and it regarded itself as having a special responsibility to do something about it. Although the full range of motives for American intervention into this colonial revolution was complex (and included, most famously, a desire for revenge after the sinking of the battleship *Maine*), humanitarianism was by far the most important one. Americans convinced themselves that the kingdom of Spain was congenitally and irredeemably flawed and that only the United States, with its superior racial and political characteristics, could produce a system of lasting justice on the island—which, significantly, lay immediately off America's coast.

Spanish "Barbarism"

Above all, Americans were incensed by Spanish general Valeriano Weyler's brutal policy of "reconcentration," which entailed moving the entire rural population into small, fenced-in compounds. Inadequate provisions for the "reconcentrados" led to mass starvation, diseases ran rampant, and anyone attempting to leave was shot on sight. Americans were indignant that such a policy could be perpetrated at their nation's doorstep, and descriptions of Cuban suffering such as the following pervaded newspapers and pamphlets:

In Cuba ... by General Weyler's order, 500,000 miserable old men, women, children and babies had their homes burned to the ground, cattle, flour, everything eatable stolen, and they themselves were driven at the point of the bayonet into trochas or fortified fences put around the towns or villages, with sentinels posted with orders to shoot on the spot everyone who dared to try to creep through the fence to get a root to gnaw at, and so save himself from dying. These wretched people had no muskets, and were too weak to use them if they had. So, in cold blood, General Weyler and his men saw them die of starvation before their eyes. I doubt if all history can tell us of another horror as vast, which was as cold blooded as this.[24]

Weyler acquired the nickname "the butcher" as a result of his reconcentration policy, and he confirmed Americans' worst preconceptions about Spanish civilization as cruel and morally primitive. Calling the country "decadent," for example, the text of a contemporary slide-show presentation designed for distribution to American schools had the following to say about Spain: "In her present condition, Spain is utterly unfit to govern either herself or any dependency whatever."[25] In another popular narrative history of the country, the author announced: "The virulent, obstinate, even brutal ignorance of the masses cannot be penetrated by any sentiment of sympathy with high aspiration or disinterested devotion to principle.... The war with Cuba was but an episode; yet it was also the legitimate outgrowth of Spain's policies, which ... have been consistently cruel and unjust toward her colonists, from her earliest occupation of American territory."[26]

Spain became a symbol of the past—an earlier, less-enlightened age when darkness and superstition clouded men's minds. As one writer put it, "In the great march of civilization of Europe and America, Spain has sullenly and uniformly remained in the rear guard, advancing only under compulsion, and retarding, rather than helping, that onward march toward the goal of perfection which Christianity and civilization have ever before them, and which, though still in the far-off distance, is year by year less distant from those who strive honestly to reach it."[27] The eminent Charles Francis Adams, grandson of John Quincy and brother of Henry and Brooks, complained:

I want some one to point out a single good thing in law, or science, or art, or literature—material, moral, or intellectual—which has resulted to the race of man upon earth from Spanish domination in America. I have tried to think of one in vain. It certainly has not yielded an immortality, an idea, or a discovery; it has, in fact, been one long record of reaction and retrogression, than which few pages in the record of mankind have been more discouraging or less fruitful of good.... From the year 1492 down, the history of Spain and Spanish domination has undeniably been one long series of crimes and violations of natural law.[28]

With increasing certitude and virulence, Americans described the Cuban crisis as a natural and inevitable outgrowth of the character of the Spanish regime.

A "Civilized" Intervention

The "yellow press," led by William Randolph Hearst's New York *Journal* and Joseph Pulitzer's *World*, stoked the American public's indignation over the Spanish-Cuban War and contributed to the perception of Spanish decadence. Engaged in a fierce circulation war with each other, these two publishing giants each rushed to be the first to print the most sensational stories, under the most colorful headlines, to attract the largest number of undiscerning readers.[29] The following excerpt from an article published in the *World* is typical of the "news" from Cuba that the yellow press fed Americans beginning in 1895: "The horrors of a barbarous struggle for the extermination of the native population are witnessed in all parts of the country. Blood on the roadsides, blood in the fields, blood on the doorsteps, blood, blood, blood! The old, the young, the weak, the crippled—all are butchered without mercy. ... Is there any barbarism known to the mind of man that will justify the intervention of a civilized power?"[30]

This hysteria found immediate reflection in Congress. Legislators in both houses became eager for war, and their arguments urging intervention neatly encapsulated prevalent notions of American national identity. By far the majority of these speeches held the United States to be a just, humane civilization that was duty bound to aid an oppressed people and to punish their wicked persecutors. The United States had a mission, senators and representatives urged, to share the virtues and blessings of its civilization with the less fortunate, in this case the Cubans. In the upper chamber, for instance, Senator William V. Allen (Pop-Neb.) argued that an American victory would help to spread the nation's universalist ideals beyond its borders:

Our ancestors declared to the world that all men are by nature free and equal and entitled to certain inalienable rights, among which are life, liberty, and the pursuit of happiness. They did not confine themselves to the inhabitants of the colonies; they did not limit the declaration to the people of the Western Hemisphere; but they held that all men, under whatever sun they might be born or whatever soil they might live, were created free and equal and entitled to life, liberty, and the pursuit of happiness. Sir, I hold human freedom and the right to self-government is God-given and inalienable, and whoever violates it flies in the face of Providence and wrests from the individual the most precious gift of all.[31]

Because Spain, obviously, refused to respect these rights, Allen led his listeners to the preordained conclusion that Cuba should shrug off its rule and adopt American values.

In the House, Representative Jerry Simpson (Pop-Kans.) insisted that the United States must become powerful in order to improve the world. He declared that "because of the operation of natural laws, the progress of human society must be evolutionary," and many nations remained in a state of barbarity.[32] Thus, under the prevailing circumstances of international society, the use of military power continued to be a necessary evil, which meant that a large navy was necessary if the United States were to accomplish anything good in the world. The use of military force would allow the United States to extend its civilization and replace morally retrograde throwbacks like Spain. Darwinian competition was the means by which moral progress was to be accomplished, and this required the emergence of the United States as a major power whose geopolitical stature would be commensurate with its moral supremacy. Such visions of American greatness, inspired by the anticipated invasion of Cuba, swept across party lines.

Accompanying the war resolution that would begin this process was a report that detailed America's motives in proposing war. The report repeated the familiar formula justifying American intervention in Cuba as the noble action of a moral superior punishing an endemically wicked people. It characterized the destruction of the *Maine*, for instance, as being emblematic of the "unity of events" in Cuba and the product of either Spanish intent or negligence. The "unity of events" stemmed from "the duplicity, perfidy, and cruelty of the Spanish character," which was ultimately responsible for all the evils that were then visiting the island.[33] The solution to the Cuban crisis outlined in the report was to deny that Spain in fact exercised sovereignty over the island, since sovereignty implies a moral fitness to rule. This Spain manifestly lacked, which meant that it had forfeited its right to continue ruling Cuba:

When publicists and jurists speak of the right of sovereignty of a parent state over a people or a colony they mean that divinely delegated supremacy in the exercise of which man should show "likest God." They never mean that a usurpation of diabolism shall be sanctified upon the plea that it is sovereignty none the less than that of a well-ordered and humane government. Against such reasoning the "Moral laws of nature and of nations speak aloud" and declare that the State which thus perverts and abuses its power thereby forfeits its sovereignty.[34]

This construction of the basis of sovereignty was meant to legitimate American intervention in Cuba on moral grounds. In other words, it allowed the United States to define its moral outrage as being a sufficient cause, under international law, to justify replacing Spanish sovereignty with the United States' more morally acceptable rule.

Divisions in Congress

Battle lines soon appeared in the Congress, however, around the question of who should create the sovereign government that would replace Spain's in Cuba (assuming Spain was ousted from Cuba, an outcome that was never questioned): the people of Cuba or the United States? Embedded in this question were issues relating to the nature of self-government, which in turn implicated the nature of America's mission in the world. If, as the majority held, the United States needed to guarantee for Cuba a just form of government, that implied as a general rule that the United States was a necessary agent by which other countries were to achieve self-government. If, on the other hand, the minority was correct, then no country could in principle serve as an intermediary for the act of achieving true independence. America's mission in the world, in the minority's analysis, was to serve only as an exemplar to the Cubans. Recognition of the Cuban Republic was a backdoor means of addressing this fundamental issue.

There were other, related reasons for the lack of complete unanimity. The Democrats' and Populists' deep mistrust of Republican president William McKinley's economic motives in Cuba was central to their opposition to the majority's position that the United States must drive Spain out of Cuba and replace it with an American-style democracy. If the goal of the Republicans was simply to conquer a foreign land (or market), then the idea of American mission would not be served and in fact would be undermined by the proposed intervention. Furthermore, some members doubted that the Cubans were racially fit to govern themselves, which rendered suspect the wisdom of the United States committing itself to the goal of Cuban democracy. It might be best, they suggested, simply to remove Spain from Cuba and then leave the island's population to its own devices. McKinley's supporters argued, on the other hand, that the United States was intervening in Cuba in order to fix a broken system and that removing Spain from the situation would not go far enough to achieve the goal of justice.

The appointed spokesman for President McKinley's position was Senator Henry Cabot Lodge, a man of broad vision, massive learning, and profoundly racist views. Lodge saw the coming war as an overdue opportunity for the United States to assume its proper role of global leadership. As he intoned during his most important speech leading up to the war:

Mr. President, we are not in this crisis by an accident.... We are face to face with Spain today in fulfillment of a great movement which has run through the centuries.... In our veins runs the blood of Holland and the blood of England. If after all the centuries it comes to us, much as we pray to avert it, to meet Spain face to face in war, it is because we are there in obedience to a greater movement than any man can hope to control. We are there because we represent the spirit of liberty and the spirit of the new time, and Spain is over against us because she is medieval, cruel, dying.[35]

The venerable Senator George F. Hoar (R-Mass.) also emphasized the larger ramifications of the war, noting with approval that America's cause was supported by England, "that nation on earth which is alike the freest, the most powerful, and the most nearly allied to us by language, history, and blood." By contrast, Spain was "a fifth-rate, weak power, a relic of the Dark Ages."[36] Senator Wilson (R-Wash.) expressed a similar sentiment when he declared: "Mr. President, Spain reached the height of her glory during a past age. Unwise and wasteful in her day of power and prosperity, when her splendor dazzled the world, she stands today, without art, without literature, without science, and without hope, a bankrupt and ruined nation. There can be no glory in war over such a carcass."[37]

America's humanitarian mission, therefore, included a duty to eliminate a morally unfit regime. As Senator George Gray (D-Del.) insisted, "We cannot forever keep our place and say we are not our brother's keeper. God Himself will hold us to responsibility if we continue to plead thus."[38] Senator Charles W. Fairbanks (R-Ind.) argued that "we are morally bound to put an end to the wrongs, the outrages, the evils which flow from Spanish rule," because the Cubans, although "not of our race, it is true, [are] fellow-beings created in the image of our Maker," and Spain "has not fairly emerged from the night of the Middle Ages." The intervention in Fairbanks's view was reflective of American national identity: "It is instinctive with us to desire to see people who are oppressed freed from the oppressor and secured in the God-given, inalienable privileges of life, liberty, and the pursuit of happiness.... To the high and holy cause of humanity and the vindication of our national honor we dedicate the lives and fortune of the Republic."[39]

Senator Henry Teller (D-Col.) celebrated in his speech "American pluck" and "Anglo-Saxon vigor" and said that if any European power disagreed with American supremacy on the Western Hemisphere, that was no matter, because the United States was too powerful to be swayed.[40] He nevertheless persuaded his Senate counterparts to amend the original war resolution to include a provision expressly disavowing any intention to annex Cuba. This compromise clause enabled the Senate debate to resolve itself.

The House, meanwhile, had no floor debate about the war resolutions for some time. Speaker Thomas Reed (R-Maine), called the "Czar" by his colleagues for his heavy-handed administration of the House, forbade it. All formal debate was to take place instead in conference, and the results there were not promising. The House and Senate committees haggled and argued with each other over the issue of Cuban independence, and tempers flared as the legislators acknowledged that they were tired and aggravated with each other. At last, after many negative votes on various versions of the resolution, the House approved the Senate's resolution by a vote of 311 to 6.[41] The president signed it, and Spain declared war. On 25 April 1898, the United States declared war in return, and the Spanish-American War was officially underway.

THE POSTWAR EXPANSION

Victory in the war of 1898 was swift and spectacular. No one had expected it to come as quickly or as easily as it did. Less than five hours after the shooting began in Manila Bay in the Philippines on 1 May, Spain's Pacific fleet was shattered. During that first day of fighting, the United States suffered only eight wounded soldiers and lost no ships. Spain, meanwhile, suffered 380 casualties and lost seven ships—its entire Asian fleet.[42] This auspicious inauguration of hostilities proved to Americans that they had been correct to believe that their race and culture were superior to those of Spain—indeed that they were the "best" in the world—and this conviction would only grow firmer after the war ended and the United States basked in victory.

The peace protocol ending hostilities was signed in Washington on 12 August, less than four months after the two states had declared war against each other. With the shooting over, the United States stepped back and measured its situation. Its military was in command of Cuba, Puerto Rico, Guam, and with an uneasy alliance with nationalist insurgents, the Philippine Islands. The question remained: What to do with all of these islands? The Teller Amendment settled the Cuban issue by rejecting annexation, but the other islands had no such restrictions attached. The only certainty was that the islands were not to be returned to Spain, especially after it came to light that Spanish misrule and cruelty had, if anything, been worse in the Philippines than in Cuba.

After a long period of deliberation and of molding and interpreting public opinion, President McKinley ultimately resolved to annex the Philippine archipelago. He therefore directed his negotiators to incorporate into the peace treaty a provision wherein Spain would cede sovereignty of the territory to the United

States, explaining that "this course will entail less trouble than any other and besides will best subserve the interests of the people involved, for whose welfare we cannot escape responsibility."[43] The Senate had to ratify the treaty, however, which required the support of two-thirds of its members, and it was far from clear that such a majority favored annexing territory so far from the mainland, particularly because it was populated with non–Anglo-Saxons. Acquiring colonial territory, moreover, touched on fundamental issues of democratic self-governance whose underlying assumptions dovetailed with racialist conceptions of political capability. As in the prewar debate, therefore, but to an even greater degree, the United States was confronted with a stark choice about how to define itself through its foreign policy, and racial arguments figured especially prominently in the ensuing debate.

Debating Annexation

The treaty debate was historic. In order to make the debate public (treaty debates take place behind closed doors), Senator George G. Vest (D-Mo.) introduced a resolution (S.R. 191) on 6 December 1898 that declared that the United States could not acquire colonies consistent with the Constitution in the same manner of European countries. In his speech explaining the resolution's purpose, Senator Vest held that "the colonial system ... is an appendage of the monarchy. It can exist in no free country, because it uproots and eliminates the basis of all republican institutions, that governments derive their just powers from the consent of the governed."[44]

One week after Senator Vest made his speech about the treaty (in the guise of introducing S.R. 191), Senator Orville H. Platt (R-Conn.) provided the administration's response.[45] "It is time to be heroic in our faith and to assert all the power that belongs to the nation as a nation," he declared. Platt argued that the Constitution may regulate the manner by which the United States government might reach its decisions—that it structured the *procedures* of governance—but that the document was irrelevant to determining the *purposes* to which the government should address itself. Thus he held that Congress could govern colonies as it saw fit, without constitutional restraint. Suffrage, he observed, the mechanism by which individuals give the "consent" celebrated in the Declaration of Independence, was neither a constitutional right nor regulated by the federal government. As he put it: "Citizenship confers no right of voting."

Platt did admit that where the Congress possessed primary jurisdiction, it *should* govern justly and in keeping with "American" norms, but he steadfastly insisted that while the Congress may be "under moral obligations and constraints," those constraints were neither legally nor constitutionally defined. Thus, when he argued that "we must provide for the people of any territory that we may acquire the most liberal, just, and beneficent government which they may be capable of enjoying, always with reference to their development and welfare and in the hope that they may be finally fitted for independent self-government," he was not declaring that colonial populations had any *right* to such a government but that Congress should nevertheless assume a paternalistic role over them. His confidence that the government of the United States would, in fact, govern its colonial territories in an enlightened manner reflected his staunch belief in the destiny of the United States:

I believe the same force was behind our army at Santiago and our ships in Manila Bay that was behind the landing of the Pilgrims on Plymouth Rock. I believe that we have been chosen to carry on and to carry forward this great work of uplifting humanity on earth. From the time of the landing on Plymouth Rock in the spirit of the Declaration of Independence, in the spirit of the Constitution, believing that all men are equal and endowed by their Creator with inalienable rights, believing that governments derive their just powers from the consent of the governed, we have spread that civilization across the continent until it stood at the Pacific Ocean looking ever westward.

The English-speaking people, the agents of civilization, the agency through which humanity is to be uplifted, through which despotism is to go down, through which the rights of man are to prevail, is charged with this great mission. Providence has put it upon us. We propose to execute it. We propose to proclaim liberty in the Philippine Islands, if they are ours. We propose to proclaim liberty and justice and the protection of life and human rights wherever the flag of the United States is planted. Who denies that? Who will haul down those principles?[46]

The Racial Basis for Anti-Imperialism

Many anti-imperialists, on the other hand, argued that the political system of the United States presupposed a homogeneous culture defined by Anglo-Saxonism and Protestantism. Other races and religious cultures would be unable to conform to the rigors of America's political culture, and they would only corrupt American government and society if admitted. Such racist arguments against expansionism came in four varieties. The first was that non–Anglo-Saxons were incapable of maintaining American institutions. The second held that the United States was never intended to incorporate broad racial diversity, especially because nonwhites could only degrade the excellence of Anglo-Saxon institutions and culture. Third, the Filipinos, like all racial minorities, were believed capable of subsisting on such meager sustenance that they would pose an overwhelming threat to American laborers. Finally, anti-imperialists feared the morally degrading effect that a large new minority population would have on white Americans, who had not yet shown themselves capable of treating justly the nonwhites over whom they enjoyed essentially absolute power. These arguments were interconnected and revealed an American worldview that was still far from confronting the massive contradiction of its ascriptive bases of national identification with the color-blind universalism of the nation's regime principles.

The speeches of Senator Donnelson Caffery of Louisiana were particularly effective in demonstrating how it was possible in 1899 for a subtle mind to hold simultaneously a commitment to freedom and self-government and a steadfast belief that some people deserved neither. He argued that it would be impossible for the United States to establish a constitutional, democratic government in the Philippines due to the race of its inhabitants. "Our power can go there; our flag can float there; but the genius of American liberty will remain upon our shores. It can not be implanted there. The material is not there for it to flourish and grow."[47] He added: "The proposition now before us is whether it is constitutional to incorporate [into the United States] 10,000,000 people no whit superior to the Africans in many respects, people who have been used to despotism all their lives, utterly unacquainted with republican institutions, and who never will be acquainted or familiarized with republican institutions. It is not their nature; they can not understand them; they have not that requisite degree of enlightenment and self-restraint that are absolutely requisite for a people to govern themselves."[48] It therefore was simply impossible for the United States to incorporate the Philippines unless it did so as a despotic overlord. Senator Caffery also cited Benjamin Kidd as an authority proving that whites could not thrive in the tropics. According to Kidd, different climates yielded different races of people with different qualities, characters, and capacities. For Anglo-Saxons, who were bred in northern Europe, to attempt to conjoin with tropical races was therefore too absurd even to contemplate. Because the races of the Philippines were incompetent to govern themselves, the United States could only extend the reach of its civilization to encompass that archipelago if it populated those islands with Anglo-Saxons. "You can extend your power, but if you want to extend your nationality, extend your institutions, extend your liberty, you must do it with people of your own kind."[49] But as Kidd and other scholars had demonstrated, Anglo-Saxons could not succeed in the Philippines. It was a catch-22 that Americans could only avoid by dropping their imperial ambitions.

Senator John L. McLaurin (D-S.C.) explained the underlying premise of the first argument, that the United States must rule the Philippines not democratically but in a way contrary to and debasing of American principles of governance, as resting in "the divine right of the Caucasian to govern the inferior races."[50] Following this principle, Senator Stephen White of California thus declared, "Mr. President, especially in the Tropics, there is no occasion for civilization or capacity as we understand it, and there control is always by the sword."[51] University of Chicago professor Hermann Von Holst provided academic support for this position when he held that Anglo-Saxons had developed democratic government because they had the "racial faculties, instincts, and tendencies" to do so. The Filipino population that the United States hoped to annex, by contrast, was "a variety of hues and utterly destitute of the qualities without which the privilege cannot be intelligently exercised."[52] Senator H. De Soto Money (D-Miss.) elaborated:

Others have the form of a republic, but not the genius and spirit. They are good enough republics on paper, but in practice they fall short of the principles which they declare. The Asiatic mind, in my opinion, never will conceive the idea of self-government as we understand and as we practice it. ... Whatever form of government any people have is exactly the government which they need. It is the result, and has been everywhere, of an outgrowth and development; it is the evolution of the moral, spiritual, and intellectual nature of man, and it can not be anything else. If he wanted or needed anything to make him better or happier, he would have it by the very law which gave him that which he has; and it is useless for you to attempt to fit this Government upon them.[53]

Because the Filipinos were by nature unable to absorb Anglo-Saxon government, therefore, they must either devise some other form of governance by and for themselves or they must be ruled from above by Americans following a colonial system fitted to their capacities. The simple transfer of American institutions to the Philippines was impossible, which meant that Americans would have to govern the islands in a way contrary to their own principles.

Other senators forwarded theories of race that presumed the second point, that the United States was designed by and for Anglo-Saxons alone. Senator White, for instance, described the Filipinos as "a very peculiar mass, a heterogeneous compound of inefficient oriental humanity." In his opinion, "the vast mass of the inhabitants are, and will for many years remain, in a condition far below that which every well-informed American believes to be essential to citizenship within our borders."[54] Senator John W. Daniel (D-Va.), a proponent of racial essentialism, spoke most alarmingly about the race of the Filipinos: "Mr. President, there is one thing that neither time nor education can change. You may change the leopard's spots, but you will never change the different qualities of the races which God has created in order that they may fulfill separate and distinct missions in the cultivation and civilization of the world."[55] From this premise, he contrasted in startling language the race of the Filipinos and the presumed racial identity of the United States:

We are asked to annex to the United States a witch's cauldron—"Black spirits and white, red spirits and gray, Mingle, mingle, mingle, you that mingle may." We are not only asked to annex the cauldron and make it a part of our great, broad, Christian, Anglo-Saxon, American land, but we are asked to annex the contents of this brew—mixed races, Chinese, Japanese, Malay Negritos—anybody who has come along in three hundred years, in all of their concatenations and colors; and the travelers who have been there tell us and have written in books that they are not only of all hues and colors, but there are spotted people there, and, what I have never heard of in any other country, there are striped people there with zebra signs upon them.[56]

To modern ears, Senator Daniel's weird rant about striped and spotted people might suggest an unrefined, backwoodsy intellect, but the Virginia senator's speech was, like Senator Caffery's, replete with copious, refined references to history, literature, and America's political tradition, with citations from the Federalist Papers, Abraham Lincoln, and other venerated figures. His were the fears of a "sophisticated" gentleman in 1899.

The most serious consequence of admitting the Filipinos into the Union on an equal footing as whites was that doing so would absolutely destroy the United States as it was then defined. Clearly, many senators regarded American national identity to rest on an ethnically and culturally defined construction of America's political principles. Senator Turner (Fusion-Wash.), for instance, railed against annexation because he thought it would yield "a universal miscegenation of blood, of religion, and of government with the yellow Buddhists, Mohammedans, and Confucians." While that policy would be consistent with "the principle of liberty on which our Government is founded," he continued, "it would do such violence to our blood, to the history and traditions of our race, and would leave such frightful results in mongrelizing our citizenship, that the advocates of the new movement in favor of a greater America prefer the alternative risk of debauching our institutions rather than do that."[57] In the event the Filipinos were admitted to the Union, according to Senator Turner, the choice for Americans was clear: either keep pure the nation's character or its institutions—one or the other, but not both. As David Starr Jordan, the president of Stanford University, explained, "Democracy demands likeness of aims and purposes among its inhabitants. . . . The Anglo-Saxon will not mix with the lower races."[58] These arguments presupposed that the United States was an Anglo-Saxon nation and that the challenge of expansion was to force the new populations into the Anglo-Saxon mold. No one ever considered accommodating cultural diversity as a worthwhile, possible goal, and certainly no one believed it to be required under "American" norms.

The third type of race-based argument was calculated more basically to appeal to the self-interest of American workers. Senator Chilton of Texas stated the issue most plainly: "There are two distinct dangers which it is hardly possible to avert. Those dangers are, first, the competition of the pauper laborers of the Philippine Islands who may come to our shores. The second is the danger of the competition of the pauper-made products sent out from the Philippine Islands to flood and disparage American markets."[59] Opposition of this variety reflected the influence of the Populist wing of the anti-imperialist movement but nonetheless reinforced the other kinds of racial arguments. "In annexing these islands we annex labor which, thank God, is yet unknown in America," warned one pamphleteer. "We annex labor trained for centuries to subsist on nothing. It is an acknowledged fact that the Filipinos can live and become fat on what would starve the average American."[60] Imperialism might therefore aid the captains of industry in increasing their profit margins, went this line of argument, but it would devastate the labor market and harm American workers. "The annexation of those islands to the United States, in whatever form it may come, whether as States or as colonies, means free and full competition by the American laborer, of every trade and condition, with the underpaid and half-clad workers of the tropics."[61]

South Carolina's Senator McLaurin merged the labor-theory argument with the fourth race-based position, which held that mixing the races would tend to corrupt the white population: "To permit cheap Asiatic labor to come into competition with our intelligent, well-paid labor will be to degrade and lower our civilization. Already in Illinois Negroes from Alabama have been shot and driven from the State, and such actions defended by the governor."[62] Senator McLaurin's observation that black workers had been "shot and driven from the State" was not meant to serve as a warning that whites might treat the incoming Filipinos unjustly but to inform his colleagues of the righteous, understandable, and defensible indignation that white Americans would feel when challenged by nonwhite competitors in the labor market. As Senator White reminded his fellow senators, a similar problem to that which would be created by an influx of Filipinos had only recently been settled on the West Coast, that of the Chinese. "We excluded Chinese laborers from our shores," he noted proudly. "We kept them out, although they sought to come in occasional shiploads only. Here it is proposed to bring in an entire population, possessing to a large degree the same competitive character, containing millions and millions of people."[63] Where, he wondered, was the logic in that policy?

Those who opposed expansionism on the streets rather than in the Senate chamber were most likely to argue the fourth position, that contact with "lower" races tended morally to corrupt whites. "The relation of our people to the lower races of men of whatever kind has been one which degrades and exasperates," David Starr Jordan complained.[64] Thus, it was unwise to annex more racial minorities because the white majority would almost certainly debase itself by acting with unfettered and capricious cruelty toward its new charges. As Carl Schurz wrote, "[A] good many of our people have very little regard for the rights and interests of so-called inferior races, and consider cheating and robbing such races a privilege of the superior being.... The idea that our colonial service will become a seminary of political virtue is, therefore, a highly grotesque one."[65] Another anti-imperialist added, "We have a race problem here at home in our 'parochial politics' so vast that we should not be greedy of another in the Philippines. The latter will inevitably distract us from the former, which demands all the intellectual and moral energy we can command."[66] Far from seeing the annexation of the Philippines as providing Anglo-Saxons with an opportunity to "uplift" other races, the anti-imperialists were convinced of precisely the opposite: that it would bring whites down.

Annexation of the Philippines

Despite these arguments, the imperialist position prevailed. The racial logic of the anti-imperialists was effectively countered by claims that the noble path lay in "lifting up and assisting to better conditions and larger liberty these distant people who have through the issue of battle become our wards."[67] The expansionists did not win the day by denouncing the racist arguments of their opponents but by convincingly demonstrating that an imperial policy would render consistent the racial and political norms of American society in a humane way that would reinforce America's national moral supremacy. Annexing the Philippines from Spain would not be inconsistent with American national identity, as the anti-imperialists claimed, but would actually fulfill the Anglo-Saxon yearnings of its people. Such a claim, of course, presupposed the ethnic basis of American national identity. As Senator Edward O. Wolcott (R-Colo.) argued:

This Republic represents the first and only experiment in absolute self-government by the Anglo-Saxon race, intermingled and reinforced by the industrious of all the countries of the Old World.... Who is to say that in the evolution of such a Republic as this the time has not come when the immense development of our internal resources and the marvelous growth of our domestic and foreign commerce and a realization of our virile strength have not stimulated that Anglo-Saxon restlessness which beats in the blood of the race into an activity which will not be quenched until we have finally planted our standard in that far-off archipelago which inevitable destiny has intrusted to our hands?[68]

Imperialism would be the apotheosis of Anglo-Saxonism and thus the realization of Americanism.

Under the circumstances, imperialism would also strengthen the moral supremacy of the nation. The United States would selflessly and benevolently assume the responsibility, the burden, of assisting a backwards race and helping them to achieve a society more like America's. Senator Wolcott's colleague from Colorado, Senator Teller, explicitly linked the racial incapacities of the Filipinos with the nature of America's virtuous self-sacrifice: "The people who live in the Tropics are not qualified, and, I fear, never will be qualified to maintain such a government as is maintained by Anglo-Saxon people. A torrid climate does not develop high mental or moral qualities....The Asiatic people will never maintain such a government as the Anglo-Saxon. He is incapable of it." Thus, the United States would need to remain in the islands "for a time, with kindness and justice." It could enjoy "no greater glory" than to "take eight or ten million men, bound down by the power of a wicked government [Spain], and lift them up and put them on the plane of citizenship in a great republic."[69] In his 1899 State of the Union address, McKinley drove this point home: "We shall continue ... in every way in our power to make these people whom Providence has brought within our jurisdiction feel that it is their liberty and not our gain we are seeking to enhance. Our flag has never waved over any community but in blessing. I believe the Filipinos will soon recognize the fact that it has not lost its gift of benediction in its worldwide journey to their shores."[70] In short, by sharing the virtues of its Anglo-Saxon republic with the nonwhite Filipinos, the United States would demonstrate its superior virtue and take one more step toward achieving the universalization of its civilization.

Emphatically, neither side in the debate over annexation began from the premise that the United States was anything but an Anglo-Saxon democracy. Whatever other motives may have also helped lead the United States to its annexationist position in 1898–1899, and there is not space here to address them, America's leadership at a minimum felt obligated to frame its actions in a way buttressing this national identity. The primary arguments advanced on either side of the issue presumed that the United States was an Anglo-Saxon liberal democracy and disagreed only on what this fact meant for U.S. foreign policy under the unprecedented circumstances. As it turns out, the racial essentialists lost the debate and the racial paternalists were able successfully to defend their position by appealing to the same spirit of humanitarianism that had spurred the initial war effort. The most noble dimensions of American national identity, rooted in a sincere commitment to the ideals of liberty and equality, thus fused with the most discreditable and contradictory ones, and racism, liberal democracy, and imperialism combined to structure a new commitment to internationalism that had strong roots in America's diverse cultural norms.

CONCLUSION

I have argued in this chapter that it is necessary to interpret the pivotal events of 1898 through the prism of the nation's norms, culture, and identity. Both intervening in Cuba and retaining Spain's island possessions afterward were motivated above all by the commitment of America's leaders in 1898 to the idea of American mission, a construction of American national identity that posits that the United States embodies virtues of universal merit and that mankind can only benefit by their diffusion. When Americans very self-consciously embarked upon their new, internationalist course in 1898, they did so under a full apprehension that their actions needed to be squared with their nation's deepest values and most fundamental traditions.

I have also argued here that the values and traditions of the United States upon which Americans drew in 1898 included not just those grounded in liberal-democratic norms but also those assuming the United States to be an Anglo-Saxon nation. American elites—those who formulated U.S. foreign policy before and after the Spanish-American War—believed that their racism and their commitment to America's universal ideals were not only consistent but reinforcing. Furthermore, they imagined that the intersection of the ethnic and civic bases of American national identity, where Anglo-Saxons benevolently shared *their* government with *others*, demonstrated the moral superiority of the United States. This self-definition, when overlaid with the compelling logic of Darwinism (and the religious benediction of liberal Protestantism, which this chapter has left aside), enabled the United States in the final analysis to believe that it had a special duty to uplift the world through its foreign policy. Unmistakably, cultural norms relating to race and to civic nationalism strongly influenced the course of U.S. foreign policy during the pivotal period in 1898–1899 when the United States announced its arrival on the world stage, and the legacy of that episode remains powerful today.

NOTES

1. Charles Darwin, *The Descent of Man and Selection in Relation to Sex* (New York: D. Appleton and Company, 1871). The main purpose of the book was to demonstrate how humans evolved from "lower" animals, primarily by describing similarities between human and animal behavior. A clear rebuke to what is now called the "creationist" paradigm of human origins, *The Descent of Man* was (and still is, for some) a controversial text.

2. Darwin, *Descent of Man*, 179–81.

3. Richard Hofstadter, *Social Darwinism in American Thought, 1860–1915* (Philadelphia: University of Pennsylvania Press, 1944), 175.

4. The distinction between races and nations was not clearly drawn at the time. See Mike Hawkins, *Social Darwinism in European and American Thought 1860–1945* (New York: Cambridge University Press, 1997), 184.

5. Michael H. Hunt, *Ideology and U.S. Foreign Policy* (New Haven, CT: Yale University Press, 1987), 51.

6. See George Cotkin, *Reluctant Modernism: American Thought and Culture, 1880–1900* (New York: Maxwell Macmillan, 1992), 57.

7. Ibid., 52.

8. Smith writes, "Adherents of what I term inegalitarian ascriptive Americanist traditions believe that 'true' Americans are 'chosen' by God, history, or nature to possess superior moral and intellectual traits associated with their race, ethnicity, religion, gender, and sexual orientation. Hence many ascriptive Americanists have believed that nonwhites, women, and various others should be governed as subjects or second-class citizens, not as equals, denied full individual rights, including property rights, and sometimes excluded from the nation altogether." Rogers Smith, *Civic Ideals: Conflicting Visions of Citizenship in U.S. History* (New Haven, CT: Yale University Press, 1997), 508n5.

9. Ibid., 348, 350.

10. Racial justifications for immigration laws were openly provided by legislators, citizens, and presidents. Smith, *Civic Ideals*, 357–71.

11. Cotkin, *Reluctant Modernism*, 67.

12. *Congressional Record*, 55th Cong., 3d sess., 342.

13. C. Vann Woodward notes that between 1895 and 1910, all of the states of the former Confederacy (plus Oklahoma and Kentucky) amended their constitutions using these and other strategies in an effort to prevent blacks from voting. C. Vann Woodward, *The Strange Career of Jim Crow*, 2d ed. (New York: Oxford University Press, 1957), 67–68.

14. 163 U.S. 537 (1896).

15. Woodward, *Strange Career of Jim Crow*, 19–22.

16. Daniel B. Schirmer, *Republic or Empire: American Resistance to the Philippine War* (Cambridge, MA: Schenkman, 1972), 101.

17. Edward A. Johnson, *History of Negro Soldiers in the Spanish-American War* (1899; reprint, New York: Johnson , 1970), 141.

18. John W. Burgess, *Political Science and Comparative Constitutional Law,* Vol. I, 45–46, quoted in Julius Pratt, *Expansionists of 1898: The Acquisition of Hawaii and the Spanish Islands* (Baltimore: Johns Hopkins University Press, 1936), 9.

19. Theodore W. Noyes, *Oriental America and Its Problems* (Washington, DC, 1903), 110.

20. George E. Adams, *McKinley and Bryan; Principles and Men; Issues of the Campaign* (pamphlet of speech, Quincy, IL: 3 October 1900), 16. (Emphasis added.)

21. No less a defender of freedom than John Stuart Mill advanced this position when he qualified his defense of near-absolute individual liberty by declaring, "It is, perhaps, hardly necessary to say that this doctrine is meant to apply only to human beings in the maturity of their faculties. We are not speaking of children.... For the same reason we may leave out of consideration those backward states of society in which the race itself may be considered as in its nonage.... Despotism is a legitimate mode of government in dealing with barbarians." John Stuart Mill, *On Liberty,* ed. Gertrude Himmelfarb (New York: Penguin Books, 1974), 69.

22. Nathan Matthews, Jr., *Oration before the City Authorities of Boston on the Fourth of July, 1899* (Boston, 1899), 11.

23. Matthews, "Oration before Boston," 11–12.

24. S. R. Calthrop, *The Wars of 1898* (pamphlet, 1898), 6–7.

25. W. Edwin Priest, *Spain and Her Lost Colonies* (Washington, D.C.: Judd & Detweiler, 1898), microfiche.

26. B. Essex Winthrop, *Spain and the Spaniards* (New York: Street and Smith, 1899), 244–45.

27. Charles Henry Butler, *The Voice of the Nation, the President Is Right: A Series of Papers on Our Past and Present Relations with Spain* (New York: George Munro's Sons, 1898), 54.

28. Charles Francis Adams, *"Imperialism" and "The Tracks of Our Forefathers"* (Boston: Dana Estes, 1899), 6–7.

29. See John Tebbel, *America's Great Patriotic War with Spain: Mixed Motives, Lies, and Racism in Cuba and the Philippines, 1895–1915* (Manchester Center, VT: Marshall Jones, 1996), 1–43; and Marcus M. Wilkerson, *Public Opinion and the Spanish-American War: A Study in War Propaganda* (Baton Rouge: Louisiana State University Press, 1932).

30. *New York World,* 17 May 1896, 1, quoted in Wilkerson, *Public Opinion and the Spanish-American War,* 32.

31. *Congressional Record,* 55th Cong., 2d sess., 3412.

32. Ibid., 3465–66.

33. "Report of the Committee on Foreign Relations regarding S.R. 149," *Congressional Record,* 55th Cong., 2d sess., 3773–74.

34. Ibid., 3774. (Some punctuation changed from the original text.)

35. *Congressional Record,* 55th Cong., 2d sess., 3782–83.

36. Ibid., 3830–35.

37. Ibid., 3972.

38. Ibid., 3842.

39. Ibid., 3844–46.

40. Ibid., 3898–99.

41. The debates are contained in the *Congressional Record*, 55th Cong., 2d sess., 3988–4064. The Senate vote is on page 3993, the House vote on pages 4063–64. The dialogue that surrounded these votes contained little that substantively contributed to the resolution or to a clear understanding of its purpose, but it is interesting for revealing the dynamics of an angry legislative debate about an important issue. Speaker Reed, for instance, was ruthless (and successful) in squelching opposition to any Republican initiative, and senators started to call each other out by name, in violation of parliamentary procedure.

42. David Traxel, *1898: The Birth of the American Century* (New York: Knopf, 1998), 137.

43. Senate, *Papers Relating to the Treaty with Spain*, 56th Cong., 2d sess., S. Doc. 148, 35.

44. *Congressional Record*, 55th Cong., 3d sess., 93–96.

45. Ibid., 295–96.

46. Ibid., 502–3.

47. Ibid., 438.

48. Ibid., 437.

49. Ibid., 438.

50. Ibid., 639. McLaurin also stated that "[u]niversal suffrage in the South long since degenerated into a race question, and as such led to the practical elimination of the Negro from politics; a policy that is today wisely advocated by the great leaders of the race like Professor Miller and Booker Washington, and which in time, without outside interference, under the guidance of the best thought of both races, will lead to a just and mutually satisfactory settlement of the gravest problem that has ever confronted any people of modern times. Conscious of the rectitude of purpose and feeling that the Negro was not responsible for the position into which he was thrust, the South, not defiantly, but by protestation, has patiently appealed to the nation to judge her righteously."

51. Ibid., 927.

52. Herman E. Von Holst, *The Annexation of Our Spanish Conquests: An Address Delivered before "The Sustaining Members of the National Association of Merchants and Travelers"* (Chicago, June 1898), 21, 23.

53. *Congressional Record*, 55th Cong., 3d sess., 1419.

54. Ibid., 922.

55. Ibid., 1424.

56. Ibid., 1430.

57. Ibid., 785.

58. David Starr Jordan, *The Question of the Philippines: An Address before the Graduate Club of Leland Stanford University* (pamphlet, Palo Alto, CA: 1899), 62.

59. *Congressional Record*, 55th Cong., 3d sess., 1446.

60. James Vernon Martin, *Expansion: Our Flag Unstained* (pamphlet, St. Louis: self-published, 1900), 21.

61. George S. Boutwell, *In the Name of Liberty* (pamphlet, Boston: Anti-Imperialist League, 1899), 2.

62. *Congressional Record*, 55th Cong., 3d sess., 641.

63. Ibid., 924.

64. Jordan, *Question of the Philippines*, 62.

65. Carl Schurz, *For American Principles and American Honor* (pamphlet, New York: Anti-Imperialist League, 1900), 11–12.

66. John White Chadwick, *The Present Distress: A Sermon upon Our Oriental War* (pamphlet, New York: 1899), 20–21.

67. "Speech at the Banquet of the Ohio Society, New York, 3 March 1899," *Papers of William McKinley,* microfilm.

68. *Congressional Record,* 55th Cong., 3d sess., 1451.

69. Ibid., 330.

70. "President's Message to Congress, 5 December 1899," *Papers of William McKinley,* microfilm.

Chapter 3

White Mischief: U.S. Support for Apartheid, 1948–1961

Catherine V. Scott

Historians have written numerous works that compare and contrast South Africa and the United States in terms of slavery, segregation, and capitalist development.[1] The comparisons, however, have not tended to extend beyond domestic society to explore the way in which *whiteness* itself operates in foreign policy and international relations.[2] When we think of race, we usually think of domestic politics; we also tend to think of people of color. The cost of domesticating the study of race means that we risk ignoring "how race has worked in the past in constructing various aspects of global politics, the various transformations it has undergone, and if and how it continues to work today."[3] Conceptualizing race only in terms of nonwhite peoples also tends to treat white as an unmarked category, "unreproduced and essentialized instead of unpacked and debunked."[4] My contention is that U.S. support for apartheid can be explained by examining the interactions and intersections of narratives of whiteness in each country. Using the numerous secondary sources on South African–U.S. relations, South African parliamentary debates, and print media in both countries, I explore parallel narratives of whiteness for the National Party (NP) victory in 1948 until the early 1960s, when grand apartheid had been fully entrenched in South Africa. My argument is that U.S. and South African policymakers observed each other through an often-distorted and unstable lens of whiteness, which helps to explain U.S. support for, and acquiescence in, the apartheid regime. This exploration contributes to our understanding of the role of race in constructing foreign policy in a specific case and suggests other ways in which race and foreign policy could be examined in contemporary foreign policy analysis.

The first section of this chapter offers a critique of common explanations for U.S. support for South Africa, most of which ignore or pay only passing attention to the role of jointly shared meanings, intersubjective understandings, and collective constructions of parallel white experience in the two countries. I suggest that white narratives based on notions of "natural kinship" between European descendants in the two countries, working alongside strategic imperatives or class interest, are crucial for understanding U.S. foreign policy toward South Africa from 1948 to 1961. In addition, I explore the way the construction of the "South African problem" took place through a long-standing American tendency to project its own (often mythical) experience upon that of South Africa. This tendency, often in the face of recalcitrant and annoyed South African whites, helps explain continued U.S. tolerance for the NP.

STRATEGIC AND CLASS "INTERESTS" VERSUS RACIST "IDEAS"

Extant explanations for the United States' support for South Africa from 1948 to 1994 lie largely with either geopolitical realpolitik or imperial interests. Despite the many criticisms of realism's focus on pregiven state interest and immutable structures (i.e., the assumptions of both self-interest and anarchy), analysts of foreign policy framed U.S. foreign policy toward South Africa as caught between "hardcore" geopolitical realities and other interests such as racial equality or social justice. As Grundy put it, "Despite denials to the contrary, U.S. relations with Pretoria in the post–World War II era, from the formation of the United Nations until around 1989, were predicated on Washington's perceived need to enlist South African assistance on the overall global policy of containment of the Soviet Union and its communist allies and ideologies."[5] Grundy's stress on the apartheid government's staunch anticommunist credentials thus explains U.S. tolerance for apartheid. U.S. priorities were to fight Soviet communism, and the greater the number of allies recruited against the Soviets, the more likely the U.S. would be to win the Cold War.

Some analysts also use the "naturals laws" of geopolitics to explain U.S. support for South Africa. As O'Tauthail and Agnew note, treating the geopolitical world as one of "hard truths, materials realities and irrepressible natural facts" has a long pedigree.[6] South Africa's chrome, uranium, manganese, and other precious metals were vital to the U.S. industrial economy; shifting support to the communist-backed African National Congress (ANC) would have risked having strategic metals fall into the wrong hands. Under attack for his resistance to the imposition of sanctions against South Africa in the mid-1980s, President Reagan expressed years of implicit U.S. sentiment: "Can we abandon a country that has stood by us in every war we've ever fought, a country that strategically is essential to the Free World in its production of metals we have and so forth?"[7] Realist commentators were often quick to point out that national security interests posed a painful choice for policymakers. Noer, for example, commented on the dilemma confronting the Truman administration in the aftermath of the

NP victory in 1948: "The U.S. would have to weigh the advantages of South African gold and anti-communism against the liability of American identity with institutional racism."[8] Legum professed that it "is a dilemma faced by all trading and investor countries faced with a contract between economic and political interests: where does the balance lie?"[9]

Emphasis on the primacy of imperialism often replicated the logic of framing strategic interests in tension with racial justice. Chakaodza defined Reagan's foreign policy of constructive engagement as "an imperialist policy designed to appease the white minority in South Africa," and contended that American concerns in the region lay largely with "protecting American business interests."[10] Lerumo defined U.S. and British policy in southern Africa in the early 1970s as aimed at creating a bloc of white minority governments to "speed up the rapacious exploitation and looting of African human and material resources."[11] While often characterizing Western imperialist maneuvers as those of capitalist racists—emphasizing more than the realist the inhumanity of racist injustices and stressing the compatibility between capitalism and racism in the world system—the "class interest" explanation of U.S. support for apartheid tends to take an instrumental view of race. The chief focus was on the "well orchestrated global strategy aimed at safeguarding American and other capitalist interests in the region, if not throughout Africa."[12] In addition to crucial minerals, imperialists were also interested in cheap labor; rather than being confronted with dilemmas between support for apartheid and geostrategic security, the struggle for class analysts was between "empire management" and the threat of national revolution.[13]

This tendency to juxtapose interests against ideas (in the case of South Africa, anticommunism or class interests with ideas about racial equality) has been challenged by international relations theorists of various persuasions, including constructivists, structuralists, and feminists. Wendt contends that it is "collective meanings that constitute the structures which organize [state actions]" rather than objectively constituted interests.[14] A state's interests are forged through interactions with other states, and this necessarily has an ideational or psychological component. States do not have pregiven interests; rather, interests emerge in their interactions with other states. Laffey and Weldes criticize international relations scholars who tend to define ideas as "causal beliefs" that produce action.[15] Maintaining the distinction between ideas and interests "assumes that interests are given" and ideas are "merely tools."[16] Revisionist scholarship on U.S. foreign policy has stressed the importance of exploring the role that ideas play in the very constitution of interests. Dean, for example, has argued that John F. Kennedy's New Frontier rested on powerful "internalized symbols of manliness"; hence, gender "should be considered as part of the very fabric of reasoning employed by officeholders."[17] Laffey and Weldes suggest that we should view both ideas and interests as "shared forms of practice, sets of capacities with which people can construct meaning about themselves, their world and their activities."[18]

The problems attendant with countering interests with ideas are especially acute in explanations of U.S. foreign policy toward South Africa. Positing either an a priori overwhelming interest in thwarting "any resulting destabilization and progress toward majority rule [as] profitable to the Soviet Union" or explaining apartheid's existence as part of the West's substantial economic and other interests in the area begs the question as to how U.S. interests were constituted through the interaction of material interests and ideas.[19] In other words, in positing a pregiven national interest either in geopolitical or imperialist terms, analysts have tended to neglect the ways in which such interests emerge through shared meanings across borders and interpretations of interstate relationships by state leaders.[20]

Furthermore, assuming the primacy of geopolitical or class interests denies that states have multiple interests that are often mutually reinforcing or at least compatible. When Legum pointed to U.S. foreign policy failures in South Africa as a "tragedy of missed opportunities," he implied that Western interests were in conflict with Western ideals.[21] Instead, a constructivist reading suggests that apartheid did not disrupt interrelationships between strategic dictates, class interests, and racial supremacy. There is ample evidence to suggest that state leaders in the United States created representations of South Africa that served to construct an imagined white community that extended across the territorial boundary of each country. These interests were constructed in ways that made whiteness, geopolitics, and class interests interrelated—at times mutually compatible and at times opposed. As Rogin puts it, "race is a cultural field inseparable from the economic and political forces that help[ed] constitute it."[22] A constructivist approach supports an interpretation of U.S. support for apartheid not in terms of dilemmas but as a bundle of interrelated interests and ideas.

NARRATING WHITENESS

> So you have been living among the Afrikaners. They must be a fine people. General Smuts and I started the United Nations together.
> —Harry S. Truman[23]

The construction of the problem of apartheid by U.S. officials did not occur in a vacuum. The white Afrikaner-dominated NP victory of 1948 took place within a local context of white fears of the "black threat" and a global context hostile toward formal colonialism but permissive toward many other expressions of white supremacy. American policymakers in the late 1940s grew up in a "segregated world in which blacks occupied subordinate roles and where Europeanist concerns circumscribed their worldviews."[24] George Kennan's Orientalist worldview lumped Asians, Arabs, Latin Americans, and Africans together as impulsive, fanatical, ignorant, and lazy, and Americans viewed the NP-led government of 1948 "almost exclusively through the eyes of whites."[25]

Nevertheless, U.S. reactions to the 1948 NP victory in South Africa also contained contradictory and negative responses. Noer notes that American policy-makers were dismayed and surprised by the 1948 victory, "thinking that Nationalists were impractical extremists and could never defeat Smuts," hero of the Boer War and prime minister of South Africa during the 1920s and from 1939 to 1948.[26] The U.S. minister in South Africa in May 1948 called the Nationalists "narrow racialists and parochial in outlook."[27] Borstelmann cites a State Department Office of Intelligence Research report that warned of the "Nazi-minded, anti-democratic elements whose influence will permeate the government" in the coming years.[28]

Although individual opinions and commentary supplied by observers provide valuable evidence of U.S. views on apartheid, comparing individual-level assessments fails to capture the broader frames of reference within which U.S. foreign policy was formulated. As collective knowledge, memories, and narratives, articulations of whiteness have an existence apart from the individuals who present them at various discrete moments and under a variety of circumstances. In other words, whiteness itself should be examined as a set of interests, practices, and ideas that are reproduced, challenged, and reformulated in the unfolding context of U.S.–South African relations in the forty-five years after the NP victory. Furthermore, apartheid was at least partially mediated through the varying self-representations of the United States. That is, for American policymakers and (increasingly) the public, apartheid was viewed through self-understandings of the American identity.

Layoun's discussion of nationalism as narrative is useful for exploring the intersections, tensions, and divergences in U.S. and South African relations through narratives of whiteness. Requiring acts of imagination and storytelling, nationalism "lays claim to a privileged narrative perspective on the nation ('the people')."[29] If nationalism is thought of as a scripted performance of the nation's story, the ways in which state discourses construct meanings become key sources for understanding other states, including South Africa. Thus far, analysts have only alluded to the role that narratives of whiteness have played in these discourses, and interestingly enough, African writers or writers of African descent have made the most insightful statements. Nolutshungu explained one facet of U.S. foreign policy toward South Africa as a "rich and predominately white country" that "naturally backed those who were rich and white in a world created by imperialism in which race and class were not only the instruments of Western dominance but also the deepest sources of Western anxieties for the future."[30] Okhamafe argued that the debate about the ANC's Marxism obscured "the fundamental cause of this historic conflict: the institutionalization of a religiously and governmentally sanctioned white supremacy."[31]

Treating race consciousness as at least equal to strategic and class interests, and perhaps at times preceding those interests, means treating white narratives as neither residual nor minor aspects of U.S.–South African relations. Whiteness, in fact, can be viewed as a critical component of American narratives of nationalism, both about itself and about South Africa. In order to do this, one can supplement Anderson's "modular" notion of nationalism with an analysis of how publics imagine their own communities (as well as others) through a continuous, yet unstable, process.[32] Ullock's notion of imagined communities as acts of creation or becoming, as opposed to already-settled identities, is useful.[33] Just as nationalism required the circulation of nationalist ideas, constituting nations in both the United States and South Africa entailed domestic and international imaginative acts. In the "family" of nations, there is ample evidence to suggest that South African and U.S. opinion leaders have historically considered themselves to be "related."[34] Whiteness, then, can be viewed as an invented international kinship, much like some religious or cross-border ethnic identities.[35]

Placing race consciousness at the center of analysis also allows a reevaluation of 1948, the year of the NP victory. Whereas many scholars paint a picture of divergent paths and sharp contrasts between South Africa's embarkation on apartheid policies and the U.S. civil rights movement, some observers in both South Africa and the United States hold that the late 1940s in both countries mark the emergence of new forms of white dominance rather than marked departures.[36] In the United States, Katznelson[37] and others[38] contend that the 1940s marked the search for new arrangements to reconcile liberalism and racism. In the case of South Africa, Butler challenges the usual view of 1948 as pivotal year, arguing that other "governments of the 1950s moreover, do not appear bizarre in comparative terms."[39] O'Meara also characterizes apartheid as more of a "generalized impulse for radical racial separation" rather than a carefully planned departure from prevailing global racial practices.[40] Rather than insisting on a sharp break within South Africa or between South Africa and the United States after 1948, the NP victory may best be viewed as an important development in the unfolding contradictory yet interdependent relationship between the two countries. While U.S. officials in 1948 were dismayed by D. F. Malan's victory, these individual-level perceptions and motivations did not disrupt the overall impulse on the part of the United States to continue to identify with white interests in South Africa.

WHOSE STORY IS IT? NARRATING SOUTH AFRICA THROUGH THE "AMERICAN EXPERIENCE"

Ample evidence exists suggesting that U.S. policymakers and the U.S. media often viewed the South African experience as a mirror or an extension of the American experience, in both positive and negative terms. Teddy Roosevelt, for example, viewed the Afrikaner Great Trek of the 1830s as an American-style odyssey, and in 1900 another American commentator called South Africa the "New England of Africa."[41] In 1942 the American minister to South Africa wrote to President Franklin D. Roosevelt that he believed it was the "manifest destiny of this country to grow, as a white man's country, into a powerful and industrial state."[42]

Nixon has explored, through film, music, art, and television, how "South Africans and Americans have imagined each other in ways that reflect a vexed sense of half-shared histories."[43] Political scientists have commented on the similarities as well. Sisk begins his examination of the U.S. reception of the 1994 South African elections by noting that "images of South Africa in the American psyche conjure up a mirror image of its own dilemmas, albeit a somewhat inverted reflection."[44] Grundy catalogs the various reasons for U.S. interest in South Africa, asserting that "there must be more to the issue" than strategic interests, economics, or extensive media coverage: "Indeed, the curiosity of Americans about South Africa grows out of the distinctive features that these two societies hold in common. Americans want to know about and influence South Africa's future because its social problems vaguely resemble our own—a fact that intrigues some and troubles others."[45] Mildly annoyed South African historians and politicians have also noted the tendency on the part of the United States to "judge South Africa in terms of America's own internal problems and experiences."[46] In a parliamentary debate on John Vorster's[47] controversial meeting with Vice President Walter Mondale in May 1977 in Lusaka, Zambia, Vorster reported on the discussions about (then) Rhodesia and Southwest Africa and remarked: "If you were to ask me what the basic difference is between the outlook of the United States and that of South Africa, ... it stems from the fact that the United States government wants to equate the situation and the position of the American Negro with the South African Black."[48]

Foreign policymakers and the media have tended to project the structure of American national narration onto the stories of other nations, including South Africa.[49] Through metaphor and analogy, attribution, and quasi-causal statements, South African problems have been "domesticated" by purveyors of American common sense. A number of writers have remarked on this tendency to "reconstruct foreign places in an American image."[50] *Reader's Digest's* 1930s rewriting of the Soviet Union's economic system as striving for capitalism,[51] Reagan's invocation of the Contras as "Freedom Fighters," and the extension of the "War on Drugs" to Panama[52] are all pertinent examples of the permeability of boundaries between America and other national communities. While in 1948 *Newsweek* reported that "South Africa is like the America of half a century ago, when men with money to invest wedded virgin land to virile capital,"[53] Culverson characterizes Carter's South African foreign policy initiatives as a "repackaging of the sixties as lessons to export to the world."[54] Klotz argues that "the political salience of the arguments of sanctions proponents [in the mid-1980s] rested upon their ability to draw an explicit connection between U.S. domestic racial issues and the institutionalized racism of South Africa."[55]

One of the most important factors that shape the contours of these narrations is their instability and contradictions. In other words, imagining South Africa through white narratives must recognize the variety of forces that are central to the process of imagining the bonds of whiteness. One of the key influences, of course, is changing assertions and forms of black identity. White narratives of identity and interests interacted dynamically with local narratives of opposition, which in turn are transnational. In fact, transnational "kinships" between whites helped provide frames of reference that made sense of white identity and interests vis-à-vis the dynamics of black opposition. This can be seen during the time from 1948 to 1961, between the period of the NP victory, implementation of apartheid laws, and the declaration of Republic status.

CONVERGENT WHITE MYTHOLOGIES: THE UNITED STATES AND SOUTH AFRICA ON THE EVE OF THE NATIONAL PARTY VICTORY

U.S.–South African relations on the eve of the May 1948 NP victory were already racially imagined in important ways. Domestic similarities in the construction of white supremacy made it easier for U.S. policymakers to make sense of NP policies, and NP politicians and media spoke a language of white identity that resonated with white racial identity in the United States. In other words, the Truman administration made sense of 1948 South Africa "through terms and ideas already extant within the culture" of white supremacy in the United States.[56] Many of these understandings were based on empirically discredited myths about white experiences in the two countries, but as Dubow emphasizes in his study of apartheid's origins, the symbols and myths surrounding white experience provided "a sense of continuity and purpose, which was achieved by seamlessly linking the present to a mythological past."[57]

By 1948, both countries shared remarkably similar "sacred histories" that told nationalist stories of white bravery against the forces of barbarism in the forging of national identity.[58] In societies where slavery was the "basis of the whole social order," a set of parallel mythologies had emerged by the 1940s that papered over the important historical differences between the two countries' development.[59] Slotkin calls myth the "language of historical memory," and with repetitive telling mythologies became a key component in narratives of white nationhood in the United States and South Africa.[60] A number of key myths enabled U.S. policymakers to frame and "colonize" South Africa's racial order, thus making it possible for seemingly divergent domestic political systems to cooperate throughout the 1940s and 1950s.

Both South African and American mythologies have depended on what Hofmeyer calls "brazen inversions," which depicted white settlers as victims of uncivilized barbarism and Native Americans and Africans as the instigators of wars of extermination.[61] The *Yearbook of South Africa* explained that in the "pioneering days, the Afrikaner farmers had to be constantly on their guard against wild animals or marauding Bantu tribes."[62] Gustav Preller, an important interlocutor of *voortrekker*[63] mythology, portrayed Africans as murderous enemies "who tore small helpless children from their mother's arms and smashed their heads to bits,"[64] just as Buffalo Bill's wild west shows presented

American identity through fables of a race war that pitted brave whites against vicious Indians.[65]

White victimology was also an important catalyst for unity in both societies. Just as the fear of an ambush has been an integral part of the white American imagination,[66] the "failure-anxiety-laager" pattern found in white minority culture in South Africa has had a long-standing existence.[67] The mythical renderings of a succession of sneak attacks upon whites in both societies have been reproduced in countless popular explanations of white identity. There are parallels between the slaughter of "innocent" Piet Rietief in 1838 and "Custer's Last Stand" in 1876 in the United States. Leaders have continuously invoked these mythologies, as simultaneous declarations of victimhood and unity, in order to further white collective understandings of purpose. For example, on 16 December 1983, Andries Treumicht, leader of the Conservative Party in South Africa, declared, "Today our people are again a surrounded people,"[68] while a senior army officer declared that U.S. troops, attacked in Somalia in the fall of 1993, were "flat playing Custer's Last Stand."[69] These analogies are more than mere conveniences; they reflect years of collective mythological and symbolic work in the construction of white identity.

The white male heroics of the likes of Daniel Boone and Andries Pretorius are another parallel component of white collective knowledge in both societies. Feats of virile masculinity entailed in taming a wilderness, being a pioneer, and maintaining an (imagined) egalitarian political order all constitute a mélange of symbols associated with manhood and the mythical frontier. Rogin's commentary on war fighting in America applies to South Africa as well: "In the American myth we remember, men alone risk their lives in equal combat. In the one we forget, white men show how tough they are by resubordinating and sacrificing the race and gender of others."[70] In important ways potential victimhood and feats of military prowess are two sides of the same coin of virile, self-assured nationalism. The military heroics of the soldier also allow for the rescue of innocent victims.

Furthermore, in the twentieth century, the ideology behind "white men's country" often collapsed the black and communist threat in both countries. In South Africa, the *swart gevaar* and *rooi gevaar* (black danger and red danger) were often paired, and in the U.S. blackness and communist subversion were long-standing components of the demonizing of opponents to the government. Such ideology made it possible to conceive of blacks as inferior at organizing and thus needing outside support, whereas the role of outside forces in destabilization made the black threat that much more sinister. Both countries passed draconian legislation designed to fight communism while also thwarting black opposition, creating post–World War II systems fundamentally organized around an imagined black-communist threat and making it easier for observers in both countries to conflate the two.

In white U.S. Southern and Afrikaner constructions of memory, Southern secession and the Anglo-Boer South African War represent courageous resistance on the part of segments of the white population to the larger forces of urbanization and industrialization that undermined romantically constructed rural ways of life, whereas the outcomes of the wars represent capitulation to a stronger power. Northern U.S. elite and British elite depictions of Southerners and Afrikaners as "tribal, idiotic, the captive of irrational fears, and savage" helped reinforce notions of distinctive "Boer" and "Southern" ways of life.[71] Just as in some respects the 1948 NP victory represented a reversal of the Anglo-Boer War, Southern defiance of Reconstruction and of federal desegregation statutes represented an attempted Southern reversal of Reconstruction.[72]

Such shared experiences, myths, and imaginings made available a set of categories through which American and South African policymakers could make sense of each other. American power and the impulse and ability to absorb the experience of other countries have been recognized by South African historian Kapp: "[T]he establishment in the American north often compared the Afrikaner to southern planters whom they viewed as reactionary and a barrier to economic development."[73] Whereas pre-1948 relations made possible empathy, solidarity, and an imagined community of whiteness, 1948 signaled a reaction on the part of the United States comparable to that of the federal government toward the South: empathy, tinged with condescension, producing accommodation to the emerging NP project.

APARTHEID IN A GLOBAL CONTEXT

The emergence of South Africa as a faithful ally of the United States in the struggle against Soviet communism unfolded in a context whereby the ideology of apartheid interacted with segregationist discourses in both South Africa and the United States. In fact, imperialism and segregation were much more entrenched than the concept of apartheid, a slippery phrase used by the NP in the 1948 election to tap into white anxiety about perceived threatening changes that had taken place in South Africa during the war, including urbanization and the relaxation of segregation. This context of white collective understandings enabled Truman to work with Smuts in the forging of the United Nations. Smuts, himself a staunch advocate of segregation, shared a mutually constituted world with Truman in which they were aware of the problems of decolonization but not of racism in world politics. Including Smuts and not the ANC in the deliberations at the United Nations conferred legitimacy upon one way of understanding the world while simultaneously excluding another.

The compatibility of apartheid with other versions of white supremacy can be seen in the parliamentary questions for the opposition as well as in foreign commentary on the emerging NP platform of apartheid. After the May 1948 electoral victory, the United Party opposition frequently quizzed Minister D. F. Malan and the minister of native affairs about the intentions of the NP. One United Party member of parliament (MP) praised the concept of Native Reserves and claimed, "We would like to see some apartheid. We would like to see residential separation," and yet he did not want to "see apartheid taken to ridiculous extremes."[74] The minister of native affairs laid the ground rules for the 20 August 1948 discussion of apartheid by noting: "I take it we are all agreed that the Europeans in South Africa stand to the non-Europeans in the relationship of guardians toward a ward."[75] An observer for *The Roundtable* reported in June 1949 that the differences between the United Party and the NP on some of the issues "do not seem to be very great," with the Nationalists aiming "to harden practice into law, and general custom into a rigid caste system."[76] What Nixon has called a "transnational vision of advancement in which whites remain cast as the 'race' of progress" characterized the debates in parliament during this period as well as U.S. commentary on the Nationalists.[77]

There is ample evidence of similar everyday frameworks of white solidarity operating in American and South African society in the early 1940s. One commonly shared assumption was that blacks and whites were inherently different. *Deep South*, an anthropological study of Southern U.S. segregation, noted that whites attributed "Negro" inferiority to inherent differences between whites and blacks.[78] Like South African whites, many Southern whites considered "race mixing" to be unclean and contaminating.[79] MacCrone's landmark South African study of white attitudes toward blacks pointed to long-standing (and contradictory) images of black savagery and criminality alongside images of blacks as children.[80] Similarly, U.S. anthropologists studying Southern attitudes four years later found whites perceiving blacks as "unsocialized beings" who displayed "child like behavior."[81] The centrality of biological theories of race and myths about blacks in segregationist and apartheid discourses meant that they "shared a good deal of similarity in ideology and spirit"; these ideas undoubtedly helped shape American calculations about South Africa's economic and strategic importance.[82]

Evidence also indicates that whites in the United States and South Africa recognized their commonality of racial interests in the 1940s and 1950s. In the *New Era*, a short-lived English-language newspaper devoted to the NP cause, an anonymous author noted with surprise that the U.S. media criticized South Africa's policy in Southwest Africa: "[T]here is in fact colour discrimination in the United States of America in the treatment of the Negro population, and at the back of the minds of those Americans who are in favor of such discrimination there are the same considerations as those operating in the minds of most South Africans with regard to the colour question."[83] The *South African Observer* regularly published articles from Southern U.S. newspapers that decried integration (e.g., "Integration Will Destroy the U.S.A.") as well as anti-integration articles by American authors.[84] For example, in January 1959, Michael Wilson wrote a critical article on a recently formed U.S.–South African Leader Exchange Programme. He hoped for an exchange program that would further understanding between "beleaguered Whites in South Africa and in the Southern States who have become the main targets of so-called world opinion and the world's integrationist press."[85]

Despite the obvious demographic differences, whites in both countries expressed repeated fears of being "submerged" by the black population through race mixing and miscegenation. In the American South, the animus of the "one drop rule" was to prohibit intermarriage between whites and blacks,[86] while in South Africa the architects of apartheid often posed white choices as absorption or survival through the maintenance of separate communities.[87] Although there are numerous contrasts between Jim Crow and apartheid, the worldviews that supported them were remarkably similar.[88]

These shared interests thus call into question the so-called gap between rhetoric and action noted by most observers of U.S.–South African relations during this period. Kline's framing of U.S. foreign policy in terms of a dilemma between racial equality and strategic interests leads him to quote without comment from a South African Institute of Race Relations spokesperson in the early 1970s: "It seems that United States businessmen—and they are not alone in this attitude—adapt very easily to the South African situation and that they become conditioned to South African norms with facility."[89] A different framing of the issue, one that begins from transnational collective knowledge and institutionalized practice, examines the way in which ideas and interests constitute a unitary process that in turn creates a social reality in which U.S. foreign policy is articulated.[90] The very norms of white supremacy in fact produced the picture of the United States with its "hands tied" in South Africa. These everyday frameworks of practice ensured that bureaucratic lobbying for closer ties between the United States and South Africa would be successful in the aftermath of the NP victory.

FROM THE 1948 ELECTION TO THE AFTERMATH OF SHARPEVILLE

Parliamentary debates after the NP victory in May 1948 demonstrate that whites were acutely aware of international, particularly Western, opinion of the apartheid slogan and the defeat of the "paternalistic racism" represented by the United Party. Prime Minister D. F. Malan chided the opposition for "continually bringing South Africa in discredit [sic] abroad."[91] Put on the defensive, parliamentary debates unfolded in ways that portrayed South African race problems as echoes of American race problems, just as a number of Afrikaner intellectuals sought to present South African race problems as European, "with showy affirmations of racial, ethnic, and cultural Europeanness."[92]

One rhetorical technique used in parliament was to maintain that apartheid indeed was not a significant departure from segregation. MP Oost pointed out, "The fact is that every intelligent person knows that the principle of segregation ... is exactly the same as what in the current political idiom we call apartheid."[93] NP MPs described conditions in South Africa in ways that many whites everywhere would likewise find disturbing: engulfment by the black population, the dangers of committing white racial suicide, and the prospects of whites working under the supervision of blacks.[94] Furthermore, after being in power for two years, the NP stressed the links between race and "communistic intellectual poison" that thrived in sites such as mixed racial residential areas.[95] In mid-1953, an NP MP approvingly quoted John Foster Dulles on the threat of communism in Africa: "Throughout Africa the communists are trying to arouse the Native peoples into revolt against the Western Europeans who still have political control of most of Africa. If there should be trouble there, that would break the contact between Europe and Africa—Africa being a large [supplier] of raw materials for Europe."[96] As Horne puts it, "The tagging of anticolonialists as 'red' slowed down the movement against colonialism" and, perhaps not coincidentally, gave "white supremacy a new lease on life."[97]

NP politicians also trumpeted biological affinities between European, North American, and South African whites. MP Mitchell recommended "greater contacts ... with those who are common stock with the peoples of the Union of South Africa."[98] Speaking in support of the Group Areas Act of 1950, Prime Minister Strydom opined that "it is becoming more and more difficult ... for the white man to maintain himself as a white man."[99] Even the opposition used white identity as a rallying cry. During the 1957 debates on whether to make "Die Stern" ("The Voice") the sole national anthem of South Africa, a United Party MP pointed out that "we are just as capable of maintaining what is here called white civilization as any of the gentlemen opposite."[100] In 1959 debates about instituting complete segregation at universities, a United Party MP speaking against the bill argued that whites should "carry the light of Western civilization amongst the peoples on the continent of Africa ... so that they too can enjoy the benefits of civilization."[101]

Simultaneous constructions of white identity and strategic interests were taking place in the United States during the same period. After 1948, U.S. policymakers and the media continued to produce significant race commentary on U.S.–South African relations. Secretary of State Dean Acheson and George Kennan, who devised the Cold War containment policy, were ardent supporters of white minority rule in southern Africa long after the wave of decolonization swept sub-Saharan Africa.[102] Culverson summarizes the rather extensive documentation on policy thinking between the end of World War II and the Korean War, remarking, "Truman administration officials remained captive to orientations that encouraged identification with white supremacist states in Southern Africa."[103]

Culverson's view is congruent with Katznelson's argument that the very contours of the American "Janus-like liberal state" have been framed by the racial accommodations of national and Southern elites.[104] He notes that Southern opposition to "hands on economic steering, development, planning, and corporatism" thwarted the use of such active government instruments in the United States. Thus, Southern fears that a state active in the domestic sphere could intervene in regional race relations blocked the establishment of corporatist institutions, practices, and politics typical of most social democratic states. Things were otherwise in the sphere of foreign policy, however, where the South led the nation in favoring militant internationalism. As Katznelson observes, in the arena of national security, by contrast, the South promoted the "world's largest planning instrument, ... the military, and it advanced a process of representation which privileged big business and their unions in a quasi-corporatist fashion."[105] Thus, instead of competing with racial interests, America's geostrategic security needs should be recognized as being defined by a national security state that is itself the product of a racial accord among white political elites.

Like questions surrounding geostrategic realities and economic investments, whiteness itself was naturalized in both South Africa and the United States. Constructing a shared experience, congruent frontier histories, and similar memories of victimhood and triumph over adversity, white policymakers and opinion leaders in the United States and South Africa developed mirror-image rhetorical strategies and patterns of communication to help make sense of their interstate relations. Although the language used in South African parliamentary debates has a certain formality, it should also be read as a reflection of everyday discourses that constituted the social landscape, one that extended beyond the borders of South Africa to the familiar territory of the United States. Moreover, although the 21 March 1960 Sharpeville massacre in South Africa would seem to portend a change in interstate relations, evidence suggests that white identity continued to frame U.S. and South African calculations of the stakes involved in their continued interaction, albeit in a more attenuated and contradictory fashion.

The nonviolent protest at Sharpeville provoked police shootings, the death of sixty-seven unarmed African protesters, and the wounding of over two hundred other Africans. The incident made the front page of all major U.S. newspapers. The *San Francisco Chronicle* reported that "[h]owling native mobs ran wild through the towns, fighting pitched battles with police," commentary that evoked images of "primitives" rising up against imperial power.[106] The language in the story shifted from describing the protesters as natives to Africans to Negroes—the latter term bringing greater familiarity to the analysis and even suggesting similarities between the situation of blacks in South Africa and blacks in the United States (particularly the Southern United States). The *Atlanta Constitution* juxtaposed stories about closing Southern schools rather than integrating with a story about "twelve thousand Negroes" who converged on the Sharpeville police station, "besieging 25 policemen inside."[107] Assuming a concerned white readership, the subheading of the 23 March 1960 story in the *Atlanta Constitution* proclaimed, "whites spared," even though "resentful Africans hid in the bush around their villages."[108] The parallels between the two nations' stories was furthered by a reporter who questioned Secretary of State Christian Herter about whether U.S. racial problems also should be brought before consideration of the United Nations Security Council.[109]

Noer has chronicled the bureaucratic infighting that ensued after State Department press officer Lincoln White issued an unauthorized statement that deplored the violence against Africans and called African grievances legitimate.[110] Higher-level officials, including Herter, denounced the statement. Schraeder characterizes the outcome of the debate as one in which the "bureaucratic missions associated with the Cold War ensured continued cooperation" between South Africa and the United States.[111] Schraeder, Noer, and Borstelmann stress the U.S. fear that South Africa would stop selling strategic minerals to the United States or close down the Cape Town fleet, but a different consideration seemed to be operating in Assistant Secretary of State Francis Wilcox's speech given a few weeks after the Sharpeville killings. Wilcox cautioned against "the premature withdrawal of white men from positions of authority" in South Africa.[112] Racial privilege and strategic advantage worked in tandem to protect U.S. interests.

In South Africa, the opposition read Lincoln White's statement into the parliamentary record, with MP Russell emphasizing the gravity of the rebuke: "The two countries from which the White races in this country draw their origins, have told us very sadly and regretfully that they cannot approve of our policies. ... And now we have the USA turning against us. ... They have looked upon us almost as brothers."[113] Verwoerd, however, correctly noted that "there was no such thing as a 'U.S. protest.'"[114] He portrayed the meeting between the U.S. ambassador to South Africa, Philip Crowe, and Foreign Minister Eric Louw as one in which the American was told by Louw that White released the press statement without first acquainting himself with the "full facts." Nevertheless, a shift in tone ensued among some NP MPs the following month, with some warning against reliance upon U.S. friendship. MP Schoonbee complained, "[W]hat the outside world wants and what members before me want is that the White man should capitulate before the Black man."[115] He warned that the United States had not stood beside the Hungarians in 1956, or the French, English, and Israelis in the Suez Crisis; by implication, they would not stand beside whites in South Africa. "Mr. Chairman, we must save ourselves or go under."[116] Two years later, another MP proclaimed that U.S. racial policy "left much to be desired, and [that] it offers many openings where we can attack them if we wanted to."[117]

The opposition continued to point to U.S. criticisms of apartheid, but NP ministers maintained that the "relationship of South Africa vis-à-vis other countries is just as good and even better than it was before."[118] On one occasion, Foreign Minister Louw explained that he had met with U.S. Secretary of State Dean Rusk and had a cordial discussion, assured that comments by lower-level officials did not reflect a change in U.S. policy.[119] Indeed, in a memorandum dated 15 June 1963, Rusk pointed out that it was "worth reminding ourselves that there are other states where obnoxious practices of one sort or another exist.... I will admit that apartheid presents a case of unusual difficulty but I would not put it ahead of the violations of human rights within the communist bloc or in certain countries governed on an authoritarian basis with which we have correct and sometimes even friendly relations."[120] Rusk's sketch of de facto collaboration with South Africa was a portent of U.S. foreign policy throughout the 1960s and 1970s.

Arguments that collaboration was a distasteful by-product of strategic concerns dictated by the Cold War fail to explain why American diplomats and media continued to construct a South Africa and United States with similar worldviews and accomplishments. Such gestures of goodwill and empathy were detected in South Africa. *South Africa International,* for example, reprinted George Kennan's *Foreign Affairs* essay in which he called Afrikaner identity "remarkable," as it was "forged and affirmed over the course of centuries, at times in struggle and adversity, and against a background of circumstances in some respects different from that which any other people has ever had to face."[121] *South African Digest* cited a *Fortune* magazine editorial lauding South Africa's development of Southwest Africa.[122] Despite growing international pressure, the ties of "natural kinship" made an identity of interests possible. In a biting exposé of U.S. economic interests in South Africa, *Africa Today* asserted that the "United States is responsible for making apartheid prosperous," even though "it is impossible to operate a business in South Africa without violating U.S. ideals."[123] On the contrary, it was both possible to do so and could be viewed as analogous to federal government officials "doing business" with Dixiecrats. White identity helped make possible the struggle against communism. Neither white identity nor anticommunism should be viewed as being more urgent. They worked in tandem to produce a foreign policy that perpetuated new permutations of white supremacy.

CONCLUSION

In an interesting irony, a writer for the *New Republic* has recommended that the United States follow South Africa's post-1994 strategy in dealing with its paramilitary white right. After noting the connections between the white right in the United States and South Africa, Stengel points out, "If you step back a moment, South Africa and America look curiously similar, like twins separated at birth and evolving under different circumstances."[124] After World War II, the U.S. government came to resemble more the stern parent, with the American South and South Africa playing the roles of recalcitrant children whose behavior was more often than not tolerated by a power that wrote the book on permissive parenting. During the apartheid era, many white South Africans complained that other countries looked at it in terms of their own experiences,[125] but it was the United States that did so most often.

As the 1960s and 1970s progressed, the U.S. government became more annoyed with South Africa, but Reagan's policy of constructive engagement was in many ways an echo of Truman's equation of black aspirations with communism, as well as cozy identification with whites. Once again, expressions of white identity and interests coalesced with definitions of geostrategic interests. Like

George Kennan, Chester Crocker (Reagan's assistant secretary of state for African affairs) "urged Americans to consider the needs and insecurities of whites before endorsing demands for majority rule."[126] Rather than view Reagan's policy as a marked departure, including white identity in an explanation of U.S. foreign policy toward apartheid, South Africa allows for the significance of prior meanings and prior representations to take their rightful place alongside strategic and economic motives. Together, all three constituted an important context of meaning and a complex of ideas and institutions that explain the reasons for the official and unofficial, formal and customary, public and private relationship that unfolded after 1948. In this context, white identity and geostrategic calculations cannot be separated. There is a long-standing relationship in both South Africa and the United States between race and security. In his classic treatise on Southern politics published in 1949, V. O. Key, Jr., identified the black belts—those counties with majority black populations—as the core of the political South. Key compared the black belts of the American South with colonial rule in the Third World. For whites in these areas, Key noted, "the problem of governance is similarly one of control by a small, white minority of a huge, retarded colored population. And as in the case of the colonials, that white minority can maintain its position only with the support, and by the tolerance, of those outside—in the home country or in the rest of the United States."[127] Thus Key observed that for the Jim Crow, Solid South, as for South Africa, the maintenance of white supremacy required the abrogation of democracy internally and collusion of sympathetic white elites externally. A perceived black threat to whites' innate superiority and right to rule was the key to both legs of the structure. The politics of fear—fear of the "primitive" other, fear of "engulfment," fear of "mixing"—has long produced a search for white security. And geopolitics and economic interest both rest on worldviews about the cultural superiority of white rule. A Mandela government in the 1960s in South Africa was no more preferable than a Lumumba government in the Congo; both were racially coded conflicts in which black people threatened white security interests. Borstelmann's interesting analysis of the Kennedy administration's navigation between the opposing forces of racial justice and strategic interests replicates the long-standing tendency to pose the question in either/or terms, as one of dilemmas and "rhetorical support for racial equality, combined with calls for restraint on all sides and deep sensitivity to the political power of white authorities in the region."[128] His framework, however, produces a misleading analysis of the "gaps" between rhetoric and action, as well as outrage about the supposed distance between ideals and action in U.S. foreign policy. Analyzing foreign policy through a constructivist lens enables us to see white identity and security as two sides of the same coin rather than two different options.[129]

Why is this analysis important? First, it contributes to the broad effort underway in international relations theory to understand the very meaning of the concept of the national interest, which, according to new theorizing, "emerges out of the representations of identities and relationships constructed by state officials."[130] The shared imagined histories, identities, and interests between the United States and South Africa rested on robust foundations of white identity that made each community intelligible to the other. Of course, although the shared meanings produced familiarity, they did not automatically produce a harmony of interests. Nevertheless, the imagined shared worlds did help produce a commonsense understanding of the other. Understandings of U.S. race relations, for example, helped to make South African race relations comprehensible.

This analysis also underscores the continuing importance of white identity in explaining U.S. foreign policy. Although this connection has been commented on by a number of observers of the U.S. "humanitarian" mission in Somalia and in a recently released United Nations report on U.S. inaction during the genocide in Rwanda,[131] why is white identity so regularly ignored by political scientists who study U.S. foreign policy? The debt of foreign policy analysts to extant theories in international relations begs the question: Why assume that politics becomes nonracial when we move to the international realm?[132]

Finally, the contemporary state of U.S.–South African relations should be understood in light of these powerful narratives of whiteness. Characterized by one South African political scientist as evincing a "lack of trust," the Mandela and Mbeki governments have sought to forge an independent foreign policy based on solidarity with the South instead of the North or the West.[133] What Vale calls the "cadences and discourses" of South Africa's foreign policy during the apartheid era was challenged by Mandela's maintenance of friendships with Iraq and Libya, the protests against pharmaceutical companies, and most recently, Mbeki's refusal to concede that "Western" science has the solution to the AIDS crisis in Africa.[134] In many respects, these disagreements are racially coded and racially charged. If "race talk" is ultimately about power and exclusion, South Africa's postapartheid foreign policy in some respects represents an important criticism of the maintenance of international white hegemony. That it has been, practically speaking, relatively ineffective is testimony to the continuing resilience of white power rather than to its demise.

NOTES

1. John Cell, *The Highest Stage of White Supremacy: The Origins of Segregation in South Africa and the United States* (Cambridge, England: Cambridge University Press, 1982); Stanley Greenberg, *Race and State in Capitalist Development: Comparative Perspectives* (New Haven, CT: Yale University Press, 1981); Howard Lamar and Leonard Thompson, *The Frontier in History: North America and Southern Africa Compared* (New Haven, CT: Yale University Press, 1981); Anthony Marx, *Making Race and Nation: A Comparison of the United States, South Africa, and Brazil* (New York: Cambridge University Press, 1998).

2. An exception is Thomas Borstelmann in "'Hedging Our Bets and Buying Time': John Kennedy and Racial Revolutions in the American South and Southern Africa," *Diplomatic History* 24 (2000): 435–61.

3. Roxanne Lyn Doty, "The Bounds of Race in International Relations," *Millennium* 22 (1993): 445.

4. Kathryn A. Manzo, *Creating Boundaries: The Politics of Race and Nation* (Boulder, CO: Lynne Rienner, 1996), 30.

5. Kenneth Grundy, "Stasis in Transition: United States–South African Relations," in *Change and South Africa's External Relations,* ed. Walter Carlsnaes and Marie Muller (Johannesburg: Thomson International Publishing, 1994), 132.

6. Geroid O'Tauthail and John Agnew, "Geopolitics and Discourse: Practical Geopolitical Reasoning in American Foreign Policy," *Political Geography* 11 (1992): 192.

7. Peter J. Schraeder, *United States Foreign Policy toward Africa: Incrementalism, Crisis, and Change* (Cambridge, England: Cambridge University Press, 1994), 220.

8. Thomas J. Noer, *Black Liberation: The United States and Black Rule in Africa, 1948–68* (Columbia: University of Missouri Press, 1985), 24.

9. Colin Legum, "International Rivalries in Southern Africa," in *Southern Africa: The Continuing Crisis,* ed. Gwendolyn Carter and Patrick O'Meara (Bloomington: Indiana University Press, 1979), 6.

10. Austin M. Chakaodza, *International Diplomacy in Southern Africa: From Reagan to Mandela* (London: Third World Press, 1990), 112.

11. Anton Lerumo, "Imperialist Strategy and African Resistance," *World Marxist Review* 15 (1977): 97.

12. Rukudzo Murapa, "A Global Perspective on the Political Economy of the U.S. Policy toward Southern Africa," *Journal of Southern African Affairs* 2 (1977): 93.

13. Werner Biermann, "U.S. Policy towards Southern Africa in the Framework of Global Empire," *Review of African Political Economy* 17 (1980): 28.

14. Alexander Wendt, "Anarchy Is What States Make of It: The Social Construction of Power Politics," *International Organization* 46 (1992): 397.

15. Mark Laffey and Jutta Weldes, "Beyond Belief: Ideas and Symbolic Technologies in the Study of International Relations," *European Journal of International Relations* 3 (1997): 198.

16. Ibid., 200.

17. Robert Dean, "Masculinity and Ideology: John F. Kennedy and the Domestic Politics of Foreign Policy," *Diplomatic History* 22 (1998): 30.

18. Laffey and Weldes, "Beyond Belief," 210.

19. Robert I. Rotberg, "Confronting the Common Danger: South Africa and the United States in the Reagan Era," in *The American People and South Africa: Publics, Elites, and Policy Making Processes,* ed. Alfred Hero and John Barratt (Lexington, MA: D. C. Heath, 1981), 201.

20. Jutta Weldes, "Constructing National Interests," *European Journal of International Affairs* 2 (1996): 277.

21. Colin Legum, *The Battlefront of Southern Africa* (New York: Africana Publishing, 1988), xix.

22. Michael Rogin, "'Make My Day!': Spectacle as Amnesia in American Politics," *Representations* 29 (1990): 109.

23. Edwin S. Munger, "The Afrikaner as Seen Abroad," in *Looking at the Afrikaner Today,* ed. Hendrick W. Van der Merwe (Cape Town: Tafelberg, 1974), 91.

24. Donald R. Culverson, "Rumors of Apartheid: Myth and Stereotype in U.S. Foreign Policy toward South Africa," in *Tales of the State: Narrative in Contemporary U.S. Politics and Public Policy,* ed. Sanford F. Schram and Philip T. Neisser (Lanham: Rowman and Littlefield, 1999), 205.

25. Thomas Borstelmann, *Apartheid's Reluctant Uncle: The United States and Southern Africa in the Early Cold War* (New York: Oxford University Press, 1993), 51.

26. Noer, *Black Liberation*, 19.

27. Ibid., 21.

28. Borstelmann, *Apartheid's Reluctant Uncle*, 90.

29. Mary Layoun, "Telling Spaces: Palestinian Women and the Engendering of National Narratives," in *Nationalisms and Sexualities*, ed. Andrew Parker (New York: Routledge, 1992), 411.

30. Sam C. Nolutshungu, "South African Policy and United States Options in Southern Africa," in *African Crisis Areas and U.S. Foreign Policy*, ed. Gerald R. Bender, James S. Coleman, and Richard L. Sklar (Berkeley: University of California Press, 1985), 57.

31. E. Imafedia Okhamafe, "South Africa: A Story in Black and White," in *The Anti-Apartheid Reader: South Africa and the Struggle against White Racist Rule*, ed. David Mermelstein (New York: Grove Press, 1987), 375.

32. Benedict Anderson, *Imagined Communities: Reflections on the Origins and Spread of Nationalism*, 2d. ed. (London and New York: Verso, 1991), 81.

33. Christopher Ullock, "Imagining Community: A Metaphysics of Being or Becoming?" *Millennium* 25 (1996): 431–32.

34. Borstelmann's *Apartheid's Reluctant Uncle* suggests just such a familial relationship between the United States and South Africa.

35. Rob Nixon, *Homelands, Harlem, and Hollywood: South African Culture and the World Beyond* (New York: Routledge, 1994), 48.

36. Leonard Thompson, *The Political Mythology of Apartheid* (New Haven, CT: Yale University Press, 1985), 71; Timothy Sisk, "A U.S. Perspective of South Africa's 1994 Election," in *Election '94 South Africa*, ed. Andrew Reynolds (London: James Curry, 1994), 145; Borstelmann, *Apartheid's Reluctant Uncle*, 48.

37. Ira Katznelson, "Southern Origins of Our Time," Research Seminar Paper no. 58 (Wilmington, DE: The Center for the History of Business, Technology, and Society, 10 December 1998).

38. Robert Huckfeldt and Carol W. Kohfield, *Race and the Decline of Class in American Politics* (Urbana: University of Illinois Press, 1989), 10.

39. Anthony Butler, *Democracy and Apartheid: Political Theory, Comparative Politics, and the Modern South African State* (New York: St. Martin's Press, 1998), 17, 22.

40. Dan O'Meara, *Forty Lost Years: The Apartheid State and the Politics of the National Party, 1948–1994* (Athens: Ohio University Press, 1996), 66.

41. Borstelmann, *Apartheid's Reluctant Uncle*, 47–48.

42. Ibid., 50.

43. Nixon, *Homelands, Harlem, and Hollywood*, 3.

44. Sisk, "A U.S. Perspective of South Africa's 1994 Election," 145.

45. Kenneth, Grundy, *South Africa: Domestic Crisis and Global Challenge* (Boulder, CO: Westview Press, 1991), 22.

46. P. H. Kapp, "The Historical Experience," in *United States/South African Relations: Past Present and Future*, ed. P. H. Kapp and G. C. Olivier (Cape Town: Tafelberg, 1987), 23.

47. John Vorster was the NP prime minister of South Africa from 1966 until 1978.

48. *Hansard* (South Africa), 27 May 1977, col. 8716.

49. Joanne P. Sharp, "Reel Geographies of the New World Order: Patriotism, Masculinity, and Geopolitics in Post–Cold War American Movies," in *Rethinking Geopolitics*, ed. Geroid O'Tauthail, and Simon Dalby (London: Routledge, 1998), 155.

50. O'Tauthail and Agnew, "Geopolitics and Discourse," 196.

51. Joanne P. Sharp, "Hegemony, Popular Culture, and Geopolitics: The Reader's Digest and the Construction of Danger," *Political Geography* 15 (1996): 565.

52. Cynthia Weber, *Simulating Sovereignty: Intervention, the State, and Symbolic Exchange* (New York: Cambridge University Press, 1995).

53. Quoted in Borstelmann, *Apartheid's Reluctant Uncle*, 96.

54. Culverson, "Rumors of Apartheid," 206.

55. Audie Klotz, *Norms in International Relations: The Struggle against Apartheid* (Ithaca, NY: Cornell University Press, 1995), 100.

56. Weldes, "Constructing National Interests," 284.

57. Saul Dubow, *Racial Segregation and the Origins of Apartheid* (Basingstoke: MacMillan, 1989), 225.

58. Hermann Giliomee, "The Development of the Afrikaner's Self Concept," in *Looking at the Afrikaner Today*, ed. Hendrik W. Van der Merwe (Cape Town: Tafelberg, 1974), 23–24.

59. Andre Du Toit and Hermann Giliomee, eds., *Afrikaner Political Thought: Analysis of Documents. Volume One, 1780–1850* (Cape Town: David Philip, 1983), 7.

60. Richard Slotkin, *The Fatal Environment: The Myth of the Frontier in the Age of Industrialization, 1800–1890* (Norman: University of Oklahoma Press, 1985), 21.

61. Isabel Hofmeyer, "Popularizing History: The Case of Gustav Preller," in *Regions and Repertoires: Topics in South African Politics and Culture*, ed. Stephen Clingman (Johannesburg: Ravan Press, 1991), 80.

62. "State of the Union," *Yearbook for South Africa* (Cape Town: Culemborg Publishers, 1957), 41.

63. The *voortrekkers* were one of the original Dutch emigrants into the Transvaal region of South Africa.

64. Hofmeyer, "Popularizing History," 80.

65. Richard Slotkin, *Gunfighter Nation: The Myth of the Frontier in Twentieth Century America* (New York: HarperCollins, 1992).

66. Tom Englehardt, *The End of Victory Culture: Cold War America and the Disillusioning of a Generation* (New York: Basic Books, 1995).

67. Willem Van Vuuren, "Symbolic Politics and the Electoral Success of Policy Failure in South Africa," *Politikon* 14 (1987): 21.

68. Quoted in Thompson, *Political Mythology of Apartheid*, 145.

69. Louise Leif and Bruce B. Auster, "What Went Wrong in Somalia?" *U.S. News and World Report*, 18 October 1993, 34.

70. Rogin, "'Make My Day!'" 104.

71. Manzo, *Creating Boundaries*, 73.

72. Borstelmann, *Apartheid's Reluctant Uncle*, 88.

73. Kapp, "The Historical Experience," 18.

74. *Hansard* (South Africa), 16 August 1948, col. 234.

75. *Hansard* (South Africa), 20 August 1948, col. 604.

76. "The Doctrine of Apartheid," *Roundtable* no. 155 (1949): 214.

77. Nixon, *Homelands, Harlem, and Hollywood*, 67.

78. Allison Davis, Burleigh B. Gardner, and Mary R. Gardner, *Deep South: A Social Anthropological Study of Caste and Class* (Chicago: University of Chicago Press, 1941), 15.

79. Ibid.

80. I. D. MacCrone, *Race Attitudes in South Africa* (Johannesburg: Witswatersrand University Press, 1937) 260–63.

81. Davis, Gardner, and Gardner, *Deep South*, 17–18.

82. George M. Frederickson, *White Supremacy: The Origins of Segregation in South Africa and the American South* (New York and Oxford: Oxford University Press, 1981), 241.

83. "Americans Want Segregation," *New Era*, 27 June 1946, 7.

84. John U. Barr, "Integration Will Destroy the U.S.A.," *South African Observer*, June 1958, 9.

85. Michael J. Wilson, "United States–South Africa Leader Exchange Programmme," *South African Observer*, January 1959, 4.

86. Frederickson, *White Supremacy*, 271.

87. W. W. M. Eiselen, *Harmonious Multi-Community Development* (n.p.: Optima, 1956), 3.

88. Frederickson, *White Supremacy*, 241–50.

89. Benjamin Kline, *Profit, Principle, and Apartheid, 1948–94: The Conflict of Economic and Moral Issues in United States–South African Relations* (Lewiston: Edwin Mellen Press, 1997), 79.

90. Emanuel Adler, "Seizing the Middle Ground: Constructivism in World Politics," *European Journal of International Relations* 3 (1997): 322.

91. *Hansard* (South Africa), 16 August 1948, col. 220.

92. Mark Sanders, "'Problems of Europe': N.P. van Wyk Louw, the Intellectual and Apartheid," *Journal of Southern African Studies* 25 (1999): 609.

93. *Hansard* (South Africa), 16 August 1948, col. 248.

94. *Hansard* (South Africa), 20 August 1948, col. 606; 31 August 1948, col. 1291; 2 September 1948, col. 1482.

95. *Hansard* (South Africa), 31 May 1950, col. 7709.

96. *Hansard* (South Africa), 10 August 1953, col. 1283.

97. Gerald Horne, "Race from Power: U.S. Foreign Policy and the General Crisis of 'White Supremacy,'" *Diplomatic History* 23 (1999): 454.

98. *Hansard* (South Africa), 31 August 1948, col. 1293.

99. *Hansard* (South Africa), 31 May 1950, col. 7726.

100. *Hansard* (South Africa), 3 May 1957, col. 5309.

101. *Hansard* (South Africa), 10–11 April 1959, col. 3672.

102. Borstelmann, *Apartheid's Reluctant Uncle*, 40.

103. Culverson, "Rumors of Apartheid," 202.

104. Katznelson, "Southern Origins of Our Time," 39.

105. Ibid., 39–40.

106. "Police Machinegun Africans—67 Dead," *San Francisco Chronicle*, 22 March 1960, 1.

107. "Police Kill 50 Africans in Crowd," *Atlanta Constitution*, 22 March 1960, 1.

108. "Africans Set Fires, Stone Firemen," *Atlanta Constitution*, 23 March 1960, 2.

109. "U.N. to Meet Tuesday on South Africa Issue," *Washington Post*, 26 March 1960, 5.

110. Thomas J. Noer, "Truman, Eisenhower, and South Africa: The 'Middle Road' and Apartheid," *Journal of Ethnic Studies* 11 (1983): 95.

111. Schraeder, *United States Foreign Policy toward Africa*, 199.

112. Francis O. Wilcox, "The Challenge of Africa," *Vital Speeches of the Day* 26 (1960): 476–80.

113. *Hansard* (South Africa), 23 March 1960, col. 3924.

114. Ibid., col. 3987.

115. *Hansard* (South Africa), 19 April 1960, col. 5572.

116. Ibid., col. 5573.

117. *Hansard* (South Africa), 18 April 1962 April 1962, col. 4184.

118. *Hansard* (South Africa), 11 April 1962, col. 3698.

119. *Hansard* (South Africa), 18 April 1962, col. 4158.

120. Dean Rusk, "Secretary Dean Rusk, Memorandum for Averell Harriman et al., June 15, 1963: 1–3," in *South Africa and the United States: The Declassified History*, ed. Kenneth Mokoena (New York: New Press, 1993), 56–57.

121. George Kennan, "Hazardous Courses in Southern Africa," *South Africa International* 1 (1971): 178. Reprint from *Foreign Affairs* 49 (1947).

122. "South Africa Has Done 'Quite a Lot' for South West Africa," *South African Digest* 6 (December 1966): 3.

123. Frances Wilcox, "Partners in Apartheid: United States Policy on South Africa," *Africa Today* 11 (1964): 3, 7.

124. Richard Stengel, "White Right," *The New Republic*, 29 May 1995, 14–16.

125. See, for example, Roy McNab, "Can South Africa Make Sense to the World?" *South Africa International* 3 (1973): 160.

126. Culverson, "Rumors of Apartheid," 208.

127. V. O. Key, *Southern Politics in State and Nation* (New York: Knopf, 1949), 5.

128. Borstelmann, "'Hedging Our Bets and Buying Time," 452.

129. Vale uses this metaphor to analyze South Africa's regional policy in the apartheid and postapartheid eras. Peter Vale, "Dominion and Discourse in the Making of South Africa's Security" (paper presented at the International Studies Association Annual Meeting, Washington, DC, February 1999).

130. Weldes, "Constructing National Interests," 282.

131. See, for example, Catherine Besteman, "Representing Violence and 'Othering' Somalia," *Cultural Anthropology* 11 (1996): 120–33.

132. Doty, "Bounds of Race in International Relations," 443.

133. Roland Henwood, "South African Foreign Policy and International Practice—1998—An Analysis," *South African Yearbook of International Law* 23 (1998): 304.

134. Peter Vale, "Explaining South Africa's Foreign Policy," *South Africa Political and Economic Monthly* (December 1998): 14.

Chapter 4

Identity, African-Americans, and U.S. Foreign Policy: Differing Reactions to South African Apartheid and the Rwandan Genocide

Fran Scott and Abdulah Osman

The literature on the influence of ethnic/racial groups[1] on U.S. foreign policy identifies a number of factors that help determine an ethnic identity group's effectiveness. These factors include the state of American race relations and ethnic diversity, relations between the United States and the group's homeland, and the homeland's policies toward its overseas diaspora. In addition, organizational resources and ethnic/racial group characteristics influence a particular group's success or failure. The organizational resources available to a group allow it to mobilize its constituency, enter into political coalitions with other groups, and obtain economic resources and an institutional infrastructure. Ethnic/racial group characteristics include the level of group consciousness, whether the group has established a consensus on a particular issue, whether the members actively participate in the political process, demographic features (such as size and location), and the economic resources of the group.[2]

Group consciousness—"the collection of beliefs through which ethnic groups view their collective identity and status in American society"[3]—is possibly the most important factor because it is necessary for political action. Without a sense of collective identity, individuals will be unable to mobilize on issues that affect them and on foreign policy issues concerning their ethnic kin and historic homeland. The forces affecting group consciousness are of critical concern for ethnic group elites seeking to mobilize their potential constituents, which, in turn, is needed to maximize the group's impact on the foreign policy decision-making process.

This chapter focuses on the mobilization of African-Americans to influence U.S. foreign policy toward problems in Africa, the African-American historic

homeland. Given that African-American identity is closely tied to political struggles in the United States, our approach introduces a new factor affecting group
consciousness: the similarities and differences between the problems in the
United States and the problems in the homeland. We argue that *commonality
of circumstance* helps establish a salient identification with Africa among
African-Americans, leading to a heightened level of group consciousness and
mobilization on the problems facing that continent. Without such commonality of circumstance, consensus and mobilization become difficult. In order to test
this hypothesis, we examine two cases: apartheid South Africa and the Rwandan genocide.

HISTORICAL BACKGROUND

African-Americans have historically felt a sense of kinship with the land of
their ancestors. In fact, many slaves attempted to return to Africa. One such
attempt was support by several religious and philanthropic organizations,
which played a key role in the back-to-Africa movement in the early nineteenth century. For example, the American Colonization Society was formed
in 1817 to send free African-Americans to Africa as an alternative to eman-
cipation in the United States. In 1822, the society established a colony on the
west coast of Africa (which became the independent nation of Liberia in 1847)
and repatriated over thirteen thousand African slaves. Although repatriation
remains controversial, it was a good example of the strong identification with
Africa among blacks in America. Some blacks supported the move because
they felt that they would never reach equality and justice in the United States.
Others, however, believed that blacks should remain in the United States, fight
against injustices, and integrate into the society as full and legal American
citizens. Still others believed that repatriated African colonists would bring
"civilization" and Christianity to the Africans. Thus Joseph Jenkins Roberts
emigrated from Petersburg, Virginia, in 1829 and became the first black governor of the colony in 1841. Roberts was later elected as the first president
of the Republic of Liberia and served from 1848 to 1856 and again between
1872 and 1876.

In the United States, many black American "liberation movements" remained
focused on the continent because it was believed that a strong free black Africa
could contribute to the political liberation of blacks in America.[4] To this end,
Africans in North America and the Caribbean sought to organize for the eman-
cipation of the entire black race. W.E.B. Du Bois helped organize an international
Pan-African movement against white colonial rule and imperialism, which he
defined as "organized protection of the Negro world, led by American Negroes."[5]
In 1900 thirty-seven men of African descent met in London for the first Pan-
African conference. The issues discussed included uneven social development
and the widening gap between the races. At the conference, Du Bois predicted:

"The problem of the twentieth century would be the problem of color line, a white effort to limit black progress and development."[6]

During the 1920s and 1930s, the activities of the Pan-African movement increased. Black leaders such as Marcus Garvey, who saw little hope of justice and equality for blacks in America, envisioned "a black grandeur rooted in Africa."[7] Paul Robeson and Max Yergan, in cooperation with the London African Community (particularly revolutionaries such as Kwame Nkrumah and Jomo Kenyatta), created the Council of African Affairs (CAA). This organization was designed to educate and appeal to the African-American community through its journal, *New Africa*. The motto of the journal, "Africa's problems are your problem," always reminded its readers, mostly black Americans, of the connection between the struggles of the African-American and Africa.[8]

World War II gave a boost to anticolonial movements in the United States and Africa as the conscription of thousands of black soldiers fighting side-by-side with white soliders helped to dispel the myth of white superiority.[9] The war had similar effects in Africa, which also exposed the myth of white invincibility and energized anticolonial movements: "Africans in the colonial armies had become empowered by their association with white soldiers during the world war. As one historian put it, 'Africans had fought alongside white men, seen brave Africans and white cowards, slept with white women, met whites who treated them as equals, or who were like themselves, hardly educated.'"[10]

As a result, many activities intended to influence U.S. foreign policy, domestically through the formation of interest groups and internationally through the newly created United Nations, arose during the 1940s. Thus, the National Association for the Advancement of Colored People (NAACP) selected W.E.B. Du Bois and others to attend the United Nations founding conference in San Francisco, where Du Bois argued for ending colonialism. The Cold War, however, altered America's anticolonial rhetoric as the Truman administration sought to protect former and remaining colonies from communism.

Anti-Soviet policies also affected black American freedom movements and Pan-Africanism. For example, Paul Robeson and the CAA allied themselves with the Soviet Union because they believed that it had emerged as the leading force for decolonization.[11] Consequently, many prominent African-Americans and others became a target for the House Un-American Activities Committee headed by Senator Joseph McCarthy, where an effort to silence the anticolonial movement among African-Americans was led. While testifying before the committee, Robeson addressed the appropriateness of African-Americans fighting for the U.S. government and instead suggested "that this U.S. government should go down to Mississippi and protect my people."[12] Du Bois, as a spokesman for the NAACP, also addressed the United States' Cold War policy: "It is not Russia that threatens the U.S. so much as Mississippi; not Stalin and Molotov but ... internal injustice done to one's brother is far more dangerous than aggression of strangers from abroad."[13] Nevertheless, as a result of these congressional activities, many black leaders changed the tone of their movements in order to prove their loyalty to America as well as to prove that the civil rights movement was not communist in nature.

During the 1950s and 1960s, African-American support for the freedom movement was strong but sporadic. As racial tensions in the United States subsided during the 1970s, many doors were opened for African-Americans. For example, the number of black representatives increased from four in 1960 to thirteen in 1971 (the year that the Congressional Black Caucus was created).[14] Many black members of Congress focused on the struggles on the African continent, especially against the apartheid regime of South Africa. The release of Nelson Mandela in 1991 marked the completion of the liberation movement in Africa. However, the suffering of the African people did not end there.

In the 1990s, Africans suffered from civil wars, genocide, starvation, destruction, and the looting of its natural resources (e.g., diamonds).[15] The suffering has been the same, if not worse, than under colonialism. However, this time it was fundamentally different: the suffering is now perpetrated by Africans themselves. The causes of the most recent chaos include both internal (bad leadership, weak states, and tribalism and ethnic conflicts) and external (neocolonialism, the legacies of the Cold War, intra-African border disputes) factors. Throughout the 1990s, in fact, the situation in Africa deteriorated.[16]

Despite worsening conditions, support among African-Americans for solving problems in Africa subsided. Ironically, many prominent African-Americans embraced brutal dictators such as the late Sanni Abacha of Nigeria and Al-Turabi of Sudan. This situation raises an interesting question: Why did African-American involvement in resolving African problems, previously a significant part of African-American identity and political activism, decline with the conclusion of the racial liberation movement in Africa? The next section outlines the commonality of circumstance as the critical factor linking ethnic and racial identity to political mobilization among African-Americans.

IDENTITY FORMATION AND MOBILIZATION

Identification with a group can lead to consensus and mobilization on issues affecting that group. Categories divide people by race, sex, ethnicity, religion, class, and so on, and these categories often reflect power and status relationships in society.[17] It is the categorization of people into groups that causes them to identify with a particular group and compare their group to others.[18] "[T]he extent to which ethnicity can be freely constructed by individuals or groups is quite narrow when compulsory ethnic categories are imposed by others. Such limits on ethnic identification can be official or unofficial. In either case, externally enforced ethnic boundaries can be powerful determinants of both the content and meaning of particular ethnicities."[19]

Group comparison can produce either negative or positive feelings toward the group to which an individual belongs. If this is a disparaged or subordinate group, individuals may either deny or embrace the group. For example, they can try to become a member of the dominant group by assimilating and rejecting their own group. If allowed to assimilate into the dominant group, they may pursue individual social mobility to gain entry into the dominant society. If, however, they cannot, will not, or are not allowed to assimilate, one of two types of group behavior may occur. If members of the group do not recognize an alternative to the status quo, they can opt for the politics of recognition and reform. This may mean that the group will try to redefine its image in the eyes of the dominant group and/or try to establish reforms that will help the group. On the other hand, if the group sees the society and its hierarchy as illegitimate, the group may opt for more radical political strategies in order to affect real change in the system.[20]

For group behavior to occur, however, a number of things must take place. First, there must be an understanding that the social structure, rather than the individual or the group, is the cause for group inequalities and disparities. This brings about discontent with inequalities and allows a strong group identity to emerge.[21] Second, there must be a sense of common fate—that is, the realization that one's conditions are linked to those of the group—and of power imbalances between groups. This is important for group formation because discrimination affects the entire group despite individual accomplishments.[22] Finally, the relative coherence of the group and its subsequent actions depend on the social context of the time.[23]

Although all groups have multiple identities,[24] the choice of identity is limited for African-Americans because of the dominance of race in African-American history. Consequently, racial oppression and injustice have been the rallying point for black political mobilization. From the 1950s to the 1970s, African-Americans fought for inclusion into the American political system. Blacks demanded and struggled for real social change. The racially charged atmosphere of the time may have been responsible for linking black group consciousness to political participation.[25] Today, however, African-Americans are no longer fighting for inclusion but instead are involved in more conventional political activities. This has had a dampening effect on the prevalence and impact of group identity and the salience of a shared identity with Africa; the latter being crucial for mobilizing the group to deal with problems relating to Africa. For example, the Congressional Black Caucus (CBC) tends to be more focused on the domestic, and sometimes parochial, concerns of their constituents, whereas foreign policy and defense concerns are usually considered less important.[26] Foreign policy ultimately competes with the unresolved domestic racial and economic problems of African-Americans at home.[27] Emerson, for example, argued that blacks are more likely to vote for candidates and on issues that directly affect them and their communities and are neither knowledgeable nor too concerned about African affairs.[28]

At times, however, African-Americans have linked together domestic and foreign problems. In the past, the basis of this link was the racial oppression of blacks in the diaspora, with the ultimate goal being global racial liberation. The advocacy of black diaspora kinship by Du Bois, Garvey's back-to-Africa movement, and the civil rights and black power movements all attempted to connect the plight of all of those of African descent, whether they be in North America, Africa, the Caribbean, or elsewhere. Moreover, this association has been seen as an effective way to help organize and mobilize African-Americans on domestic policy issues.[29] For example, African-Americans have expressed concern over racial disparities in foreign policy, have identified their struggle with that of black South Africans and the plight of Haiti and Haitian refugees, and also condemned the U.S. invasion of Grenada, the majority of whose population was black.[30]

Political inclusion and the adoption of American ideals may have reduced the feeling of identification with Africa, however, and the link between problems at home and those in Africa may now be less evident to African-Americans. Cox, for example, argued that African-Americans, like other ethnic groups in American society, want to assimilate and achieve social mobility in a way accepted by the dominant group.[31] As society loosened its restrictions and eased discrimination against blacks, African-Americans would no longer act as a group but rather as individuals in American society. Moreover, as the effects of civil rights legislation alter the relationship between blacks and the dominant society, the political salience of the group identity, as well as an identification with Africa, may subside in time. This, in turn, would have the effect of reducing the willingness of blacks to mobilize on issues concerning Africa.

According to this line of reasoning, African-Americans were forced to work as a group because of racial disparities and oppression, not out of cultural or blood ties like other immigrant groups who have come to the United States. Instead, the common experience of discrimination and exploitation is ultimately the foundation of group consciousness. It is partially the historic rejection of African-American equality in the United States that causes African-Americans to identify symbolically with Africa, because any objective identification with Africa was lost during slavery. Thus, African-American identification with Africa is inherently fluid and based on political conditions. With full inclusion, African-American identity would become merely "American," and Africa would be of vastly less concern to African-Americans.

Alternatively, others have argued that African-Americans do have a more objective basis for collective action on domestic and international issues. Du Bois, for example, documented black culture as coming from its African past,[32] and Robinson argued that black collective identity comes from African culture and philosophy.[33] Even if Du Bois and Robinson are correct, that a Pan-African collective identity is pervasive, it is clear that this identity ebbs and flows with changing circumstances. Although African-Americans have used their African culture and history to create the common meanings and language necessary to act as a group, it is the shared culture, history, and symbolic vocabulary of racial oppression that has united blacks on issues at home and abroad.[34] African-American activists use this to mobilize their constituency for political action.[35]

African-Americans identify with Africa generally, but it is clear that some parts of Africa have attracted greater attention from African-Americans than others. Given that African-American identity is so closely tied to its history of racial oppression, consensus and mobilization on a particular issue will be more likely if there are similarities between the struggles in the United States and Africa—which we have called the commonality of circumstance. In particular, if African-Americans perceive racial oppression in Africa or racial differences in foreign policy, they will be more likely to mobilize to alter U.S. foreign policy. Without a salient identification with the situation in Africa, consensus and mobilization will be less likely. Thus, we hypothesize that similarity of circumstances, concerns, and problems between the African-American community and those in the symbolic homeland (Africa) create a salient identification between the diaspora and the homeland, which leads to both consensus in and mobilization of the diaspora community toward resolving the problem in the homeland.

The following two sections explore two cases that have attracted variable attention from African-Americans: South African apartheid and the Rwandan genocide. In the same year that Nelson Mandela became the first black president of South Africa, upwards of one million Africans became the victims of genocide in Rwanda. Opposition to institutionalized racial stratification in South Africa served as the basis of African-American political action to pressure the United States to impose sanctions on South Africa. However, the absence of obvious racial oppression in Rwanda and the lack of a shared vocabulary regarding black-on-black genocide hampered efforts to mobilize African-Americans to put pressure on the United States to intervene in order to prevent or stop the genocide. These two cases appear to illustrate how the commonality of circumstance affects group activism and influence on U.S. foreign policy.

SOUTH AFRICAN APARTHEID

On 11 February 1990, Nelson Mandela walked hand-in-hand with his wife Winnie from the Robben Island Prison, where he had been jailed for twenty-seven years. Four years later, he was sworn in as South Africa's first black president. This success story has been shaped, at least partially, by the international pressures mounted against the apartheid regime of the white minority rulers in South Africa, including economic sanctions imposed by the United States. These

sanctions were the result of one the most successful efforts by any ethnic identity group to alter U.S. foreign policy. Through group mobilization, demonstrations, and boycotts, the African-American community effectively mobilized for
substantive policy change. At the forefront of this struggle was TransAfrica,
which helped to get the 1986 Comprehensive Anti-Apartheid Act passed through
Congress over President Reagan's veto.

Historical Context

In historical development, political rhetoric, national identity, and race relations, American and South African societies are similar in many ways.[36] The
year 1948 was a watershed for race relations in both countries. In South
Africa, the electoral victory of the Afrikaner-dominated National Party led to
the imposition of apartheid (racial separation) and legitimized white minority rule. In the United States during that same year, President Truman de-
segregated the U.S. military, and southern Democrats walked out of the Democratic National Convention when a civil rights plank was added to the party's
platform.

As the Cold War and containment policies gained permanency in the American political landscape, America's anticolonialism, self-determination, and democratic rhetoric was overshadowed by U.S. economic and strategic interests. This,
coupled with the influence of a strong and well-financed pro-Pretoria lobby,
meant that U.S. policy toward South Africa would not support these rhetorical
principles when it came to black Africa. A report by the State Department cited
South Africa's economic and strategic importance: "[T]he need for South Africa's
minerals, port facilities, and votes in the UN [United Nations] were sufficient to
seek 'the maintenance and development of friendly relations' regardless of Nationalist's domestic policies."[37] A similar pattern of placing support for anti-
communism above democracy and independence came to characterize U.S. policy toward the whole of Africa.

Although the Eisenhower administration largely maintained the previous
administration's policies toward Africa, the overall attitude toward Africa in
the United States began to change. In his 1957 speech at the ceremony of
Ghana's independence, Vice President Nixon called for Americans to lend
greater support to African decolonization. The next year, the Bureau of African
Affairs was established at the State Department. The 1960 election, which
brought John F. Kennedy to the presidency, gave hope to the racial equality
movement both at home and abroad. Kennedy's policy toward Africa in general, and South Africa in particular, came into conflict with America's Cold
War objectives. Kennedy and his successor, Lyndon B. Johnson, were thus
forced to compromise their rhetorical support for racial equality: both "publicly and privately protested apartheid, integrated U.S. facilities in South
Africa, defended the rights of Black Americans, and embargoed weapons. Nei-

ther, however, had used all possible American power against [South African] nationalists."[38]

As the civil rights movement among black Americans gained strength in the 1960s, U.S. support for South Africa's apartheid system became an issue. International pressure against South Africa began to grow, including scattered boycotts of South African goods and Pretoria's expulsion from several international sports. Inside South Africa, the struggle by South African blacks continued to grow despite the ban against the African National Conference (ANC) in 1960, the arrest of ANC leaders such as Nelson Mandela, and a tightening of the apartheid system. New leaders such as Stephen Biko (who was murdered by South African police) and his organization, the South African Students Association, rose to challenge apartheid.

African-American Opposition to Apartheid

African-Americans came to identify with black South Africans on the basis of similarities between the struggle for racial equality in the United States and South Africa: black self-determination and empowerment were seen as juxtaposed to racially based oppression by a politically and economically dominant white society. Identification with Africa created consensus and thus mobilization on the issue of apartheid, which in turn helped to strengthen the case against racial oppression in the United States. For example, the Reverend Joseph Lowery of the Southern Christian Leadership Conference stated in 1985: "The popular issue today is apartheid.... The reason it is so popular is it reminds us of the apartheid remaining here in our country."[39] As another example, many used Dr. Martin Luther King's birthday not only to celebrate the civil rights movement but also to protest apartheid in South Africa, making a link between the black American struggle and the struggle against apartheid.[40] The perception of the Reagan administration's insensitive attitude toward civil rights at home and apartheid abroad subsequently reinforced the link between the domestic concerns of black Americans and the plight of black South Africans. Consequently, during the time African-Americans were mobilizing against apartheid, they were renewing their black identity.

In the United States, the increasing number of elected black officeholders, especially in the U.S. Congress, helped to facilitate the struggle against apartheid. The CBC, black churches, and other African-American organizations pressured many multinational corporations to divest from South Africa. For example, General Motors, Kodak, and a host of other corporations pulled or reduced their investments in South Africa, moves that caused the South African economy to go into recession. In desperation, the government began creating tribal homelands, which many in the United States saw as modern Indian reservations. By 1974, the successful liberation movements by South Africa's neighbors—Rhodesia, Angola, and Mozambique—further destabilized South African politics and brought new attention to apartheid. The election of Jimmy Carter, and especially his focus on the importance of human rights in U.S. foreign policy, gave a boost to the international struggle against apartheid. Moreover, the American media, especially television, increased their reporting of the brutality of South African police against the black majority.

In an effort to change U.S. foreign policy toward South Africa, the CBC began creating pressure points to influence the policymaking process. Among these was the creation of TransAfrica, established to organize and direct anti-apartheid movements in the United States, under the leadership of Randall Robinson. By 1978, the organization was one of the most powerful forces in the transformation of the American policies towards South Africa. Church groups, nonprofit organizations, the NAACP, unions, political leaders, celebrities, college students, and others lent their voices to protest South African apartheid. As evidence of black church involvement, the Southern Christian Leadership Conference protested outside of business offices with investments in South Africa and threatened boycotts as well. There were even songs educating the public on the issue of apartheid South Africa. For example, a song by the African-American rap group Stetsasonic called for freeing black South Africans and linked the struggle against apartheid with the fate of African-Americans at home. As evidence of the effective mobilization of African-Americans, the South African government was reported to have hired a lobbyist to attempt to convince African-Americans to stop their calls for sanctions.[41] This lobbyist was able to get black reporters to talk to South African politicians, and also talked to black businesspeople about doing business in South Africa, but was largely ineffective.

During the 1985–86 congressional term, the CBC sponsored thirty-eight pieces of legislation opposing apartheid. There were several resolutions that would have given asylum to black South Africans and diplomatic recognition to the ANC, bills prohibiting the sale of certain military equipment to South Africa, and bills and resolutions calling for divestiture and economic sanctions against South Africa. Around the same time, the South African Embassy in Washington, D.C., was occupied by anti-apartheid activists, and members of the CBC marched in Washington to protest the policies of the South African government.[42]

In 1986, the House and the Senate passed the Comprehensive Anti-Apartheid Act (CAAA), despite heavy pressure from the Reagan administration. The CAAA specifically prohibited investment or loans to South Africa and prevented goods controlled by the South African government from coming into the United States. Among other things, it also prohibited U.S. and South African military cooperation and eliminated a tax treaty with South Africa. Most important, it officially expressed U.S. support for dismantling apartheid. Although the legislation did not contain a total economic embargo against South Africa, like many in the movement wanted, the CBC still considered the CAAA a significant victory.[43] Just as significant was the fact that both the House and Senate overrode Reagan's veto, thus signaling the beginning of the end of South Africa's apartheid system, which was dismantled just four years later. Although U.S.

pressure alone did not end the apartheid regime, African-Americans played a decisive role in altering long-standing policy toward South Africa.

RWANDAN GENOCIDE

During a period of approximately one hundred days in 1994, the world witnessed the most efficient mass murder as between eight hundred thousand and one million lives vanished in Rwanda. Philip Gourevitch estimated the killing rate as "three hundred and thirty-three and a third murders an hour—or five and one-half lives terminated every minute," surpassing the rate (but not the number) of Jewish deaths during the Holocaust by three times.[44] Unlike the apartheid system in South Africa, this nearly unprecedented human catastrophe received little attention at the time from the international community in general, and African-Americans in particular.

Rwandans: Hutus and Tutsis

Rwanda is a land-locked country located at the center of the Great Lakes region of east-central Africa. Its population consists of two major and one minor ethnic groups: the Hutu (85 percent), Tutsi (14 percent), and Twa (1 percent). All three ethnic groups would be considered black or African by American standards, but there are significant political differences between them. Hutus have historically been regarded as cultivators and sedentary, Tutsis as pastoralists, and Twa as hunters and gatherers. Over the centuries, the two main groups formed a common language called Kinyarwanda and a set of common religious beliefs and culture. At the heart of their common history, however, was the fundamental divide between cultivators and pastoralists. The pastoralists occupied the ruling apparatus in which the number of cattle one owned determined one's place in the power hierarchy. In fact, the word *Tutsi* means "one rich in cattle," whereas *Hutu* means "the follower of a powerful person." Initially, these two words did not fit the tribal/clan lineage in the traditional African context in which one belongs to a group through blood relations only. Rather, this divide reflected a more sophisticated social structure that reached something approximating the feudal stage, unlike the majority of the African societies.[45]

The establishment of colonialism deeply affected the Rwandan political system. Germany initially occupied the region but was forced to relinquish it with the Treaty of Versailles in 1918. The colony, known as Rwanda-Urundi, was made into a League of Nations mandate administered by Belgium. The Belgians used the Tutsi-Hutu divide to secure their governance of the territory by reinforcing the hierarchical structure and transforming it into a permanent class system (or, one could say, a caste system). The Belgians then began to favor the Tutsi minority over the Hutu majority, providing them with extra political privileges and Western education.

In the 1920s, the Belgians consolidated their control over Rwanda-Urundi by replacing traditional local leaders with Tutsi administrators. Moreover, the Belgians introduced an identification system in 1926 that officially differentiated individuals into either the Tutsi or Hutu ethnic group. This identification system further polarized the Rwandan society into a privileged elite associated with Tutsiness and the underprivileged associated with Hutuness.

After World War II, once independence for Rwanda was becoming a realistic possibility, Belgium's exclusive support for the Tutsi began to change. Appointments of Hutus to some government posts did little to satisfy Hutu demands for greater political power. Hutu uprisings began in 1959 and led to the overthrow of the Tutsi ruling family two years later. Once they achieved political power from the Tutsis and independence from Belgium, Hutus began to kill Tutsis en masse from 1961 to 1962, causing tens of thousands of Tutsis to flee to the neighboring countries of Uganda and Burundi. Exiled Rwandans, mostly Tutsis, formed the Rwandan People's Front (RPF) to reclaim power.

In 1973, the civilian government of Rwanda was overthrown in a coup led by army general Juvenal Habyaramana. Soon thereafter, Habyaramana instituted a one-party state, under the guise of the Revolutionary Movement for Development, which ruled the country until his death in 1994. Despite good economic times during the late 1970s and early 1980s, the collapse of the international coffee market (the largest source of hard currency for Rwanda) in 1988 placed Rwanda into economic turmoil. Western donor countries pressured the Habyaramana government to allow for multiparty democracy. At the same time, RPF incursions into Rwanda led to renewed anti-Tutsi sentiments, and the government began training militia groups known as the *Interhamwe,* "those that stand together."

After many months of negotiations, Habyaramana and representatives of the RPF signed a cease-fire agreement. In response, the UN created the United Nations Assistance Mission in Rwanda (UNAMIR) and deployed twenty-five hundred peacekeepers to the capital, Kigali, to implement the accords. Individuals within the Habyaramana's own ruling circle, however, rejected any peace with the Tutsi-dominated RPF. They continued the training of the Interhamwe and effectively used the airwaves to flame anti-Tutsi sentiments. On 6 April 1994, President Habyaramana and Burundi president Cyprien Ntaryamira were killed when their plane crashed while returning from a peace conference. Immediately afterward, the Interhamwe, along with the Rwandan armed forces, began to round up Tutsis in the capital. The 1994 Rwandan genocide thus began.

A report published by the Human Rights Watch indicates that by the end of 1993 the UN and other Western countries had ample warning about the upcoming genocide.[46] The most significant warning came on 11 January 1994 in the form of a cable sent to the UN headquarters by General Dallaire, the head of UNAMIR forces. The report gave details about the increasing preparation of the Hutus for massacres against Tutsis, in terms of both the number of young men and women joining the Interhamwe and the stockpiling of arms provided by the French government. General Dallaire requested permission to confiscate some of these weapons. The following day, Dallaire's request was denied, citing UNAMIR's limited mandate. Worse still, General Dallaire was ordered to present his findings to President Habyaramana, thus alerting those in the president's inner circle of security leaks.

In April 1994, with the death of Habyaramana, the genocide began. Rather than increasing the UN's presence, the UN Security Council sharply reduced UNAMIR forces from twenty-five hundred to only two hundred fifty following the murder of the Rwandan prime minister Agathe Uwiliyingi and the torture and murder of ten Belgian peacekeepers. As the genocide spread from the capital to the countryside, the international community did nothing; in fact, it took several weeks for the UN and Western countries to call the mass killings "genocide." One of the main reasons for this hesitancy was the fact that the United States had just pulled its forces out of Somalia (following the debacle in Mogadishu in which eighteen American soldiers were killed) when Habyaramana's plane went down. Washington refused to become involved in another military operation in Africa (or allow anyone else to become involved, lest the United States be required to "rescue" any failed operation). In addition, the 1948 Genocide Convention seemingly required the international community to become involved in a situation where genocide was being committed. By refusing to call the mass killings genocide, the international community and the United States could more easily justify their nonintervention.

African-Americans and Rwanda

Although many African-Americans consider Africa their symbolic homeland and the people of Africa their ethnic kin (and therefore believe that African-Americans have an obligation to aid Africans),[47] there was a lack of interest among African-Americans for an active U.S. role in the Rwandan crisis. One reason for this was that average African-Americans have little knowledge about Africa or its problems, as Randall Robinson acknowledged at the time.[48] More important, however, African-American mobilization in support of African issues have historically emerged largely out of a sense of common racial oppression.[49] In the case of Rwanda, the issue was not one of white-on-black oppression but rather black-on-black violence. Although certainly black-on-black violence is a problem for African-Americans at home, the absence of this crucial racial context exposed the lack of symbolic vocabulary and shared meanings between conditions in the United States and the genocide in Rwanda. Without this racial context, mobilization became extremely difficult. Moreover, the problem was presented as a humanitarian crisis (refugees fleeing the genocide), which made it more alien to the African-American condition.[50]

According to Representative Alcee Hastings (D-Fla.), a member of the House Foreign Relations Subcommittee on Africa and the CBC in 1994, ordinary African-Americans did not consider Rwanda a vital interest for African-Americans. Hastings explained that the Haitian crisis was closer to home and therefore considered more important: "Africa seems so far away and there is no vital interest that my constituency sees."[51] Some analysts have also speculated that the overall silence on Rwanda was because African-Americans had many problems in the United States and did not have the resources to help Africa.[52] According to the *Washington Informer*, the CBC still had not issued a statement on Rwanda by August, even though the killings had gone on since April of that year.[53]

The CBC did take some limited steps to prod the Clinton administration toward a more active role, but nothing like its massive effort against apartheid. For example, the CBC wrote President Clinton asking him to take up the request by the UN Secretary Boutros-Ghali and the Organization of African Unity to allow additional peacekeeping forces to be sent to Rwanda. These additional troops would not have come from the United States but neighboring African countries, as well as others. Three letters (4 May, 16 June, 21 July 1994) were sent in all, and only two received even a cursory response from the administration.[54] The CBC also boycotted a conference on Africa sponsored by the White House in order to protest Clinton's Africa policies, although it is unclear how boycotting the conference would have helped the Rwandans.[55]

African-American lawmakers, for their part, were divided on how to approach the Rwandan problem. Representative Edolphus Towns (D-N.Y.) brought the atrocities in Rwanda to the attention of the House of Representatives but did not propose any particular course of action. In the Senate, a resolution sponsored by Carol Moseley-Braun (D-Ill.) and seven other members in April 1994 deplored the atrocities in Rwanda, but it also did not offer a specific solution to the problem. The resolution suggested, however, that the UN should consider possible diplomatic and military options and provide help with any peace agreement, as well as provide humanitarian relief. In a public statement, Moseley-Braun argued that military intervention in Rwanda should only be considered as a last resort; instead, she preferred the U.S. to try sanctions first.[56] Again, it is unclear how economic sanctions, which normally take months to have any effect, would have even slowed the genocide. When asked in April 1994 if he knew what could be done in Rwanda to stop the killings, Representative Hastings thought that negotiations, diplomacy, and political pressure should be used.[57] He also advocated a war crimes tribunal for those committing the atrocities.[58]

Others supported the notion that an international peacekeeping force be sent to Rwanda. For example, Ron Dellums, a black lawmaker instrumental in getting South African sanctions passed in Congress,[59] and Congressman Donald Payne advocated the use of a multinational UN peacekeeping force.[60] Officially, the CBC supported such a force, but only after the genocide was nearing completion. The most outspoken critic of U.S. policy was Randall Robinson of TransAfrica, who complained of U.S. inaction and prodded the administration to exert the necessary political pressure, commitment, and resources to help solve the problem. Although there was some agreement on what should be done, such agreement came late, and no attempt was made to mobilize the African-American masses to pressure the Clinton administration.

Where African-Americans did mobilize was in regard to the post-genocide refugee crisis in Zaire/Congo. After most of the Tutsis in Rwanda were murdered, the RPF launched an invasion of Rwanda and managed to capture the capital, driving out the ruling Hutu government. Many Hutus fled into eastern Zaire, thus precipitating a humanitarian crisis. In fact, many Hutus were forced out of Rwanda by their own "Hutu Power" elites, through the use of force and scare tactics, in order to provide cover for the perpetrators of genocide (the *géno-cidaires*). Gourevitch criticized the international community's relief efforts in Zaire as supporting those who had just committed genocide, rather than acting earlier to prevent the genocide:

This is one of the great mysteries of the war about the genocide: how, time and again, international sympathy placed itself at the ready service of Hutu Power's lies. It was bewildering enough that the UN border camps should be allowed to constitute a rump genocidal state, with an army that was regularly observed to be receiving large shipments of arms and recruiting young men by the thousands for the next extermination campaign. And it was heartbreaking that the vast majority of the million and a half people in the camps were evidently at no risk of being jailed, no less killed, in Rwanda, but that the propaganda and brute force of the Hutu Power apparatus was effectively holding them hostage, as a human shield.[61]

Nevertheless, the crisis of the Hutus in Zaire was presented as a humanitarian crisis somehow connected to the genocide—Western media, relief workers, and world governments made no distinction between the Tutsis slaughtered by the *génocidaires* and the Hutu refugees, thus obfuscating the real cause of the refugee crisis and leading to much public confusion. In fact, many truly believed that the refugees in Zaire were the victims of genocide, rather than its perpetrators.

Despite the moral and ethical problems of supporting the *génocidaires* through humanitarian relief efforts, many African-Americans, ignorant of whom they were supporting, wanted to help the refugees because they felt a duty to all Africans. For example, when Africare, a nonprofit organization founded to assist the African continent in 1971 and provide a way for African-Americans to rediscover their heritage, put out a call for help, many African-Americans responded.[62] Some new organizations were created for the relief effort, such as the Pan-African Relief Fund, and a series of rallies were held to raise funds. Moreover, churches, the NAACP, celebrities, and others were involved in a major effort to obtain funds for relief for the refugees.[63] In addition, there was a call to pressure the U.S. government to give more money to the relief effort

and development assistance to Africa.[64] It should be noted that these efforts occurred after the genocide was already over.

Even though several hundred thousand African lives were lost, the efforts of
African-Americans to influence U.S. foreign policy toward Rwanda had been
sketchy at best. Black officeholders could not reach a consensus on the proper
approach to the Rwandan genocide, and the African-American masses did not
mobilize. In fact, the only significant mobilization took place after the genocide
was already over, and it was (largely unwittingly) designed to help the perpetrators of genocide.

CONCLUSION

Absent circumstances of racial oppression or racial differences in foreign policy,
African-American interest in events overseas and subsequent mobilization to influence U.S. foreign policy are hampered. Despite rhetorical support for the
American ideals of democracy and human rights, the subsequent application of
American ideals to African countries may not be sufficient to facilitate the crucial identification of shared or common struggle. With the inclusion of African-
Americans into the American political process, domestic issues have dominated
the attention of African-Americans and their leaders.[65] Furthermore, researchers
have argued that African-Americans actually want their representatives to focus
primarily on domestic issues, even at the risk of ignoring foreign policy concerns.[66]

There was a significant difference between African-American reactions to
apartheid in South Africa and genocide in Rwanda. Despite the fact that the latter possibly led to more deaths of Africans than the former (certainly more in
a shorter period of time), African-Americans were largely silent throughout the
period leading up to and during the genocide. At first glance, this lack of reaction may be somewhat surprising: African-American influence on the apartheid
issue illustrated the potential political strength of the ethnic group, African-
Americans had unprecedented representation at the national level, and unlike
the 1980s, African-Americans in 1994 had a sympathetic ear in the White House.
However, when one considers the importance of commonality of circumstance
for group interest in and mobilization on a particular issue, the disparate reactions become more comprehensible. Unlike South Africa, where a white minority government was suppressing black political aspirations and had institutionalized racial inequality, Rwandans had already gained their independence
and were ruling themselves. African-Americans identified with black South
Africans because of a shared symbolic language of racial oppression; consequently, they were far more motivated to oppose apartheid. The conflict between
Hutus and Tutsis, both black, did not provide for a similar identification because
issues of racial justice were not relevant.

The ideals of democracy and human rights in Africa are less-salient issues for
African-Americans. Rwanda is a good example of this: the situation there was

discussed in terms of a humanitarian crisis, and therefore mobilization only occurred for that need. Two other recent examples are Nigeria and Sudan. The Nigerian military coup and subsequent human rights violations that began in 1990 failed to attract significant attention from the CBC and the NAACP until the mid-1990s.[67] Slavery in Sudan, however, is a more glaring inconsistency for African-Americans because black Africans are being enslaved by Muslim Arabs. In addition to Louis Farrakhan's controversial 1996 trip to Sudan, where the slavery issue was ignored and Farrakhan praised the oppressive regime, Donald Payne, the chair of the CBC, asserted that slavery in the Sudan had to take a backseat to more pressing domestic issues that African-Americans were facing, such as affirmative action, black male imprisonment, redistricting, housing, and unemployment.[68] The current dissimilarity in circumstances between African-Americans and Africans has meant that many issues facing Africa have not received much attention.

Although democracy and human rights are less salient to African-Americans, economic development may be more so. Economic development is needed in many African-American communities, and it is needed in Africa as well. Therefore, this similarity of circumstance has led African-Americans to actively push for economic development and trade legislation. African-Americans have felt limited economic opportunities at home, and some hope that Africa will be opened to trade and mutual economic opportunities.[69]

Of course, other issues may affect the saliency of ethnic identity and subsequent mobilization. These may include media attention and black leadership. Media attention can have an effect on the public's attention to problems in other countries. With sufficient leadership, the media can be harnessed to focus on African issues of concern, thereby helping to organize and mobilize African-Americans.[70] If African-American leadership organizations such as the CBC and TransAfrica want to mobilize African-Americans on issues of human rights and democracy, they will have to find a way to use the symbolic language of racial oppression and injustice to succeed. The promotion of democracy as human rights, while important goals in and of themselves, will be meaningless unless the problems of Africa are related to the problems African-Americans find at home. Without this, mobilization will be lacking, and there will be few foreign policy successes for African-Americans.

NOTES

1. African-American identity is considered both racial and ethnic and fits under the broad definition of *ethnic identity groups* outlined in chapter 1.

2. For a discussion of these factors, see David A. Dickson, "American Society and the African-American Foreign Policy Lobby," *Journal of Black Studies* 27, no. 2 (1996): 139–51.

3. Ibid.

4. Howard H. Bell, introduction to *Search for a Place: Black Separatism and Africa,* by M. R. Delaney and Robert Campbell (Ann Arbor: University of Michigan Press, 1969), 1–22.

5. James L. Roark, "The Response to Colonialism and the Cold War: 1943–1953," in *The African American Voice in U.S. Foreign Policy Since World War II,* ed. Michael Krenn (New York: Garland), 36.

6. Owen Charles Mathurin, *Henry Sylvester Williams and the Origins of the Pan-African Movement, 1869–1911* (Westport, CT: Greenwood Press, 1976), 49. See also Judith Stein, *The World of Marcus Garvey: Race and Class in Modern Society* (Baton Rouge: Louisiana State University Press, 1986).

7. Mark Solomon, "Black Critics of Colonialism and the Cold War," in *The African American Voice in U.S. Foreign Policy Since World War II,* ed. Michael Krenn (New York: Garland), 54.

8. Edwin P. Hoyt, *Paul Robeson: The American Othello* (Cleveland, OH: World Publishing, 1967).

9. Roark, "The Response to Colonialism and the Cold War," 36.

10. Abdel-Fatau Musah and J. 'Kayode Fayemi, "Africa in Search of Security: Mercenaries and Conflicts—An Overview," in *Mercenaries: An African Security Dilemma,* ed. Abdel-Fatau Musah and J. Kayode Fayemi (London: Pluto Press, 2000), 19.

11. For details, see Solomon, "Black Critics of Colonialism and the Cold War," 53–88.

12. Paul Robeson, *Here I Stand* (Boston: Beacon Press, 1958), 42.

13. Roark, "The Response to Colonialism and the Cold War," 43.

14. Donald R. Culverson, "The Politics of the Anti-Apartheid Movement in the United States, 1969–1986," *Political Science Quarterly* 111, no. 1 (1996): 127–50.

15. For details on the role of resources, especially diamonds, on Africa's current wars see New York Times, "Special Report: Africa's Diamond Wars," <http://www.nytimes.com/library/world/africa/040600africa-diamonds.html> (accessed October 2001).

16. See Adebayo Adedeji, "Comprehending African Conflict," in *Comprehending and Mastering African Conflicts: The Search for Sustainable Peace and Good Governance,* ed. Adebayo Adedeji (London: Zed Books, 1999), 3–21.

17. Michael A. Hogg and Dominic Abrams, *Social Identifications: A Social Psychology of Intergroup Relations and Group Processes* (New York: Routledge, 1988).

18. Henri Tajfel, ed., *Differentiation between Social Groups: Studies in the Social Psychology of Intergroup Relations* (New York: Academic Press, 1978).

19. Joane Nagel, "Constructing Ethnicity: Creating and Recreating Ethnic Identity and Culture," in *New Tribalisms,* ed. M. W. Hughey (New York: New York University Press, 1998), 243.

20. John Turner and Rupert Brown, "'Social Status, Cognitive Alternatives, and Intergroup Relations," in *Differentiation between Social Groups: Studies in the Social Psychology of Intergroup Relations,* ed. Henri Tajfel (New York: Academic Press, 1978), 201–26.

21. Patricia Gurin, Arthur H. Miller, and Gerald Gurin, "Personal and Ideological Aspects of Internal and External Control," *Social Psychology* 41, no. 4 (1978): 275–96; Patricia Gurin, Arthur H. Miller, and Gerald Gurin, "Stratum Identification and Consciousness," *Social Psychology Quarterly* 43, no. 1 (1980): 30–47.

22. Jacob M. Rabbie and Murray Horowitz, "Arousal of Ingroup-Outgroup Bias by a Chance Win or Loss," *Journal of Personality and Social Psychology* 13 (1969): 269–77.

23. Hogg and Abrams, *Social Identifications.*

24. T. K. Oommen, "Race, Ethnicity, and Class: An Analysis of Interrelations," *International Social Science Journal* 46 (1994): 83–93.

25. Sidney Verba and Norman H. Nie, *Participation in America: Political Democracy and Social Equality* (New York: Harper and Row, 1972); Richard D. Shingles, "Black Consciousness and Political Participation: The Missing Link," *American Political Science Review* 75, no. 1 (1981): 76–99; Arthur H. Miller, Patricia Gurin, Gerald Gurin, and Oksana Malanchuk, "Group Consciousness and Political Participation," *American Journal of Political Science* 25, no. 3 (1981), 494–511; Bryan O. Jackson, "The Effects of Racial Group Consciousness on Political Mobilization in American Cities," *Western Political Quarterly* 40 (1987): 631–46.

26. Roxanne L. Gile and Charles E. Jones, "Congressional Racial Solidarity: Exploring Congressional Black Caucus Voting Cohesion, 1971–1990," *Journal of Black Studies* 25, no. 5 (1995): 622–41.

27. Dickson, "American Society and the African-American Foreign Policy Lobby."

28. Rupert Emerson, "Race in Africa: United States Foreign Policy," in *Racial Influences on American Foreign Policy,* ed. George W. Shepherd (New York: Basic Books, 1970), 165–85.

29. O. B. C. Nwolise, "Blacks in the Diaspora: A Case of Neglected Catalysts in the Achievement of Nigeria's Foreign Policy Goals," *Journal of Black Studies* 23, no. 1 (1992): 117–34.

30. Yossi Shain, "Multicultural Foreign Policy," *Foreign Policy* 100 (1995): 80–83. Many African-Americans also identify with the Palestinians vis-à-vis Israelis because the Israelis are often seen as being "white" and the Palestinians "non-white."

31. Oliver Cromwell Cox, *Caste, Class, and Race: A Study in Social Dynamics* (Garden City, NJ: Doubleday, 1948).

32. W.E.B. Du Bois, *The Souls of Black Folk* (New York: New American Library, 1969).

33. Cedric J. Robinson, *Black Marxism: The Making of the Black Radical Tradition* (London: Biblio Distribution Center, 1983).

34. Nagel, "Constructing Ethnicity."

35. Ibid.

36. See Catherine V. Scott's chapter in this volume. Also see Robert Massie, *Loosing the Bonds: The United States and South Africa in the Apartheid Years* (New York: Doubleday, 1997).

37. Thomas J. Noer, *Cold War and Black Liberation: The U.S. and White Rule in Africa, 1948–1968* (Columbia: University of Missouri Press, 1985), 23.

38. Ibid., 183.

39. Quoted in Juan Williams, "Black Caucus Proud of Political Record; Members at Low Boil over Apartheid in South Africa, Attacks on Affirmative Action," *Washington Post,* 29 September 1985, A20.

40. Karlyn Barker, "Effi Barry, 16 Others Arrested," *Washington Post,* 16 January 1985, A8; Karlyn Barker, "D.C. Workers Protest at Embassy," *Washington Post,* 5 April 1985, A4; "U.S. Reflects on Dream of a Battler for Rights," *New York Times,* 16 January 1985, B3.

41. Juan Williams, "South Africa's Newest Lobbyist Is a Black American," *Washington Post,* 21 November 1985, E1.

42. Courtland Milloy, "Politics and Fantasy," *Washington Post,* 19 September 1985, C3.

43. Larry Martz, "A Sanctions Deadlock," *Newsweek,* 6 October 1986, 22.

44. Philip Gourevitch, *We Wish to Inform You That Tomorrow We Will Be Killed with Our Families: Stories from Rwanda* (New York: Farrar, Straus and Giroux, 1998), 133.

45. The majority of the African societies did not make the transition from communalism to feudal stage, with the exception of Ethiopia, where powerful landlords known as *Ras* emerged as politically dominant.

46. Human Rights Watch, "Warnings," <http://www.hrw.org/reports/1999/rwanda /Geno4-7-01.htm#P6_37> (accessed December 2001).

47. Ron Daniels, "The Need to Respond to the Crisis in Africa," *New Pittsburgh Courier,* 7 September 1994, A7.

48. Randall Robinson, "An Understanding of History Is Needed in Rwanda, Haiti Crisis," *Michigan Chronicle,* 9 August 1994, A-6. Also see John-Thor Dahlburg, "African-Americans Aiding Rwandans Find Special Tie," *Los Angeles Times,* 12 September 1994, A1.

49. Williard R. Johnson, "Getting Over by Reaching Out: Lessons from the Divestment and Krugerrand Campaigns," *The Black Scholar* 29, no. 1 (1999): 2–19.

50. The Clinton administration, too, worked to counter interest in Rwanda in an effort to keep it off of the public's radar screen.

51. National Public Radio, "Increased Media Reporting Leads to Interest in Rwanda," *All Things Considered,* 22 July 1994, transcript no. 1551-4.

52. Daniels, "Need to Respond to the Crisis in Africa."

53. Alvin Peabody, "Black Leaders Blasted for Silence on Rwanda Genocide," *Washington Informer* 30, no. 40 (1994): 1.

54. See comments by Representative Payne in the Africa Subcommittee of the House Foreign Affairs Committee, *Situation in Rwanda* (Panel II), 103rd Cong., 2nd sess., 22 July 1994, reproduced by Federal News Service.

55. "Clinton Blasted on Africa," *Houston Chronicle,* 25 June 1994, A25.

56. "Braun Speaks Out on Rwanda, Haiti," *Washington Afro-American* 102, no. 50 (1994): A1.

57. *MacNeil/Lehrer Newshour,* 29 April 1994, transcript no. 4917.

58. Africa Subcommittee of the House Foreign Affairs Committee, *Situation in Rwanda* (Panel I), 103rd Cong., 2nd sess., 22 July 1994, reproduced by Federal News Service.

59. John B. Judis, "The Dellums Dilemma," *The New Republic,* 4 July 1994, 23.

60. *MacNeil/Lehrer Newshour,* 29 April 1994, transcript no. 4917.

61. Gourevitch, *We Wish to Inform You,* 266–67.

62. "Africare Responds to Rwanda," *New York Amsterdam News,* 24 August 1994, 2.

63. "UNICEF Rwanda Efforts Receive Atlantic City Assistance," *New York Voice,* 23 November 1994, 12; Kenneth Coleman, Jr., "NAACP Raises over $550,000 for Refugees," *Michigan Chronicle,* 16 August 1994, B6; Kizer Bryant, "Rwanda Relief Campaign Kicks Off This Week," *(Cleveland) Call and Post,* 25 August 1994, A6.

64. Daniels, "Need to Respond to the Crisis in Africa."

65. Chicago Council on Foreign Relations, *American Public Opinion and U.S. Foreign Policy,* 1994 (computer file), Inter-university Consortium for Political and Social Research version (Princeton, NJ: The Gallup Organization, 1995; distributed by Inter-university Consortium for Political and Social Research, Ann Arbor, MI).

66. Carol M. Swain, *Black Faces, Black Interests: The Representation of African Americans in Congress* (Cambridge, MA: Harvard University Press, 1993), 216.

67. "Causing Black Americans Grief," *Interpress News Service,* 28 August 1995.

68. Golbert A. Lewthwaite, "Black Leaders Speak Up on Slavery," *Baltimore Sun,* 2 July 1996, A1.

69. See Wil Haygood, "African-Americans and Americans: 'We Want to Give the Issue of AIDS and Sexual Behavior the Same Level of Visibility That a Previous Generation Gave Apartheid in South Africa,'" *Boston Globe,* 13 October 1999, A1; Tony Marshall, "Free Trade between U.S. and Africa Faces Snags," *Washington Times,* 7 May 1998, A17.

70. Emmanuel U. Onyedike, "Re-Positioning Africa: The Role of African-American Leaders in Changing Media Treatment of Africa," *Journal of Third World Studies* 13 (Spring 1996): 51–60.

Chapter 5

Serbian-American Mobilization and Lobbying: The Relevance of Jasenovac and Kosovo to Contemporary Grassroots Efforts in the United States

Rachel Paul[1]

While the importance of pressure groups in the policymaking process in the United States has been studied widely and generally accepted as a given, the role that these groups play in foreign policy development is less well known. However, the explosion of ethnic conflicts abroad, the increasingly "global" economic environment, and calls for U.S. intervention in trouble spots abroad have increased the number of pressure groups focusing on foreign policy and brought new attention to the role that these groups may play in influencing U.S. foreign policy. Noting the relative success of the Israeli, Cuban, and Irish lobbying efforts, ethnic and diasporic groups are now frequent voices in today's pluralist universe, and a new literature is emerging that attempts to explain the proliferation of ethnic lobbying.[2] These groups focus predominantly on policies affecting their countries of origin and must rely on grassroots lobbying techniques to legitimize their causes to members of Congress and the executive branch.

Despite the increased attention to ethnic interest groups, scholars know little about the ways in which these groups form, attract membership, and mobilize to influence U.S. policy. Social scientists have not adequately explained why some groups successfully mobilize their communities to produce powerful ethnic lobbies while other groups remain politically dormant, failing to translate ethnic solidarity into political activism. The post–Cold War conflict in the Balkans gave rise to activism by a number of ethnic groups in the United States and offered a unique opportunity to study how ethnic groups develop and implement strategies to mobilize ethnic Americans in an attempt to sway U.S. policymakers. As global attention turned to the bloody conflict in the former Yugoslavia, Serbs, Croats, Muslims, and Kosovars in the United States strove to have their views heard as successive U.S. administrations debated appropriate responses. This study examines the mobilization strategies of the Serbian Unity Congress (SUC), with a particular emphasis on the efforts of SUC leaders to mobilize Serbian-American citizens during the 1998 escalation of tensions between the North Atlantic Treaty Organization (NATO) and the Serbian government. I propose here that Serbian ethnic elites in the United States have relied on the rhetorical use of historical trauma for the purpose of mobilizing Serbian-American masses. I have used in-depth interviews with the SUC leadership and analysis of organizational archives to assess the use of historical references by elites to stimulate grassroots lobbying among Serbian ethnics.

SERBIAN-AMERICAN POLITICAL ORGANIZATIONS AND THE SERBIAN UNITY CONGRESS

A large variety of Serbian cultural and religious institutions thrive in the United States, but only a few Serbian-American political organizations exist. Early organizations that represented anticommunist elements among the Serbian-American community flourished until the collapse of communism in Eastern Europe. Although a number of small political organizations remain, the SUC claims to be the most highly organized and influential Serbian interest group in the United States.

The SUC is a relatively small organization. Blitz describes its offices as "small, one-person outfits, and the SUC therefore remains highly dependent on the activism of its reported six thousand members."[3] The organization was established in 1990 by a group of Serbian-American professionals and the late Prince Andrej Karadjordjevic. According to one SUC president, Dr. Vojin Joksimovich,[4] it was founded "to gather experienced and accomplished individuals who would be willing to help post–communist Serbia make a transition to democracy."[5] Over time, the SUC has evolved to include cultural and humanitarian functions among its activities. At the time of this study, its central offices were located in Napa, California, but the organization is affiliated with the Serbian Orthodox Church of America—an organization headquartered in Washington, D.C. The SUC is registered as a nonprofit organization that serves to unite the Serbian diaspora, and it has chapters throughout the world. Despite the broad nature of the organization's agenda, it has been described as "the most extensive Serb-nationalist organization in North America," and organizational literature clearly demonstrates the political nature of the interest group.[6]

The SUC agenda supports the establishment of democracy and capitalism in the Serbian state, and the organization was critical of both Yugoslav president Slobodan Milosevic and U.S. policies that SUC leadership deemed "supportive" of Milosevic.[7] The organization publishes periodic news bulletins and posts these bulletins, political action notices, press releases, and letters from SUC leadership to policymakers on its Internet site http://www.suc.org. Yearly conventions are held to discuss future goals and the situation of Serbian coethnics around the world.

The organization reports three types of membership—those who fully pay their dues (about fifteen hundred individuals), those who skip dues payments, and "Internet members." There are between five and six thousand members of the SUC, with numbers fluctuating with events abroad.[8]

The SUC and the Wars in Bosnia and Croatia

According to Joksimovich, the SUC "served as the principle spokesmen for the Serbian-Americans in Washington" during the wars in Bosnia and Croatia, meeting with members of Congress, the State Department, the National Security Council, and other members of the Bush and Clinton administrations. The SUC supported implementation of the Dayton Accords and sees one of its roles as campaigning for "evenhandedness and fairness. Where appropriate, the SUC has drawn attention to the use of double standards and prejudice in the international community's approach to the Serbian interests."[9] The organization used the Manatos and Manatos public relations firm for lobbying in the past but now primarily relies on grassroots lobbying. However, the SUC has periodically engaged a public affairs consultant for contact with Congress.

The SUC was not the only organization that mobilized in response to the war in Bosnia. Serbian-American organizations around the country collectivized, forming a coalition organization called the Serbian Information Network or SerbNet.[10] The purpose of SerbNet was to counter claims of Serbian atrocities in the war (highlighting that all sides committed atrocities) and to question media accounts of the conflict. A review of SerbNet literature demonstrated periodic reference to the genocide of Serbs during World War II, and the organization spearheaded an April 1995 vigil commemorating the Serbs, Jews, and Gypsies killed at the Jasenovac concentration camp on the fiftieth anniversary of its liberation.

The SUC's Political Opportunity Structure

Sydney Tarrow defines "opportunity structure" as "dimensions of the political environment which either encourage or discourage people from using collective action."[11] Scholars of ethnic organizations view the dimensions of opportunity structure as critical to determining group success in both the mobilization process and in influencing public policy.[12] Evaluating the opportunity structure for any group involves focusing both on institutional availability to the group and on those practices, environmental benefits, and constraints that contribute to mobilization.

The opportunity structure for the SUC has been mixed. It has not been difficult to mobilize Serbian-Americans and convince them to write letters to policymakers, according to SUC President Milenkovich; the "demonizing of the

Serbs by the media" has made the SUC's job easy as Serbs and Serbian-Americans have an earnest desire to "spread the truth."[13] However, this "demonization," coupled with a lack of interest or knowledge of Serbian history, complicates the effectiveness of Serbian-American grassroots lobbying.

Serbian-American leaders contend that American political elites are generally ignorant of Serbian circumstances, and SUC officials lament of a general lack of education of politicians concerning Serbian history and a weak understanding of the Serbian cause. Joksimovich complained:

For example, Senator Dole's knowledge of history goes back to the day before yesterday. Hence we have all but given up the idea of educating [members of Congress]. Frequently, prior to my speeches I get warned "Vojin, no history please." ... They listen carefully but still in disbelief how a fifty-year-old genocide could be so much present in 1991–1995 conflicts in Croatia and Bosnia. World War II veterans, as well as veterans of other wars such as the Korean one, are very careful listeners. This is not true for the young generation. A responsible person for the European Affairs in the National Security Council told me: "I come from Iowa, how do you expect me to know anything about the Balkans?"[14]

Nevertheless, SUC president Milenkovich contends that access to policymakers has not been a particular problem for two reasons. First, the main mode of contact between the SUC membership and policymakers is via letters and press releases, not direct personal lobbying contact. Second, he maintains that after being deluged by the opposition (presumably Albanian lobbyists), policymakers welcome the few Serbs who make their case in person. Despite the ease of access, Milenkovich noted that a number of members of Congress were openly hostile to the Serbian cause, particularly Representative Tom Lantos (D-Calif.), former Senator Alphonse D'Amato (R-N.Y.), and former Representative Susan Molinari (R-N.Y.). He also noted, however, that a few members of Congress were supportive of SUC causes—including Lee Hamilton (D-Ind.), Dan Burton (R-Ind.), and Duke Cunningham (R-Calif.). At the time of these interviews, the SUC expected newly elected Senator George Voinovich (R-Ohio), who is of Serbian descent, to play a leading role in fighting for the Serbian-American cause.

The Serbian Orthodox Church is an important component of the opportunity structure for Serbian and Serbian-American organizations. Blitz notes that preexisting Serbian-American institutions, particularly the Serbian Orthodox Church, were invaluable in the formation of a coalition lobbying group during the war in Bosnia. He contends that churches "served as meeting points for foreign representatives, political figures, and the diaspora community as a whole."[15] Joksimovich claims that the organization's initial goals involved supporting the unification of the two factions of the Serbian church in North America and establishing relations with Serbs in Serbia. As such, an SUC office was established in Belgrade in 1993. The SUC employs a director who works as a personal liaison to the Serbian Orthodox Church, and Joksimovich notes close cooperation with the church in Kosovo. The SUC does not actively work to recruit members through churches, but churches are used for organizational meetings and fund-raisers.

Overall, the political opportunity structure is not particularly amenable to the Serbian cause because access to policymakers is limited to periodic person-to-person contact between SUC leaders and officials. Most "lobbying" is done via written correspondence and media outlets, including advertisements in major U.S. newspapers. The institutional and environmental constraints on SUC lobbying result in a need to rely heavily on grassroots mobilization to influence policymakers.

POLITICAL MOBILIZATION AND ETHNIC IDENTITY

The Serbian community in the United States is probably relatively small. Although data for the Serbian-American population is not reliable because Serbian-Americans may also identify themselves as "Yugoslav," the number of Americans identifying themselves as "Serbian" in the 1990 census totaled 89,500.[16] Even though the actual total is probably significantly higher than this number, Serbian-Americans do not constitute a large U.S. minority. Their numbers are dwarfed by other groups that have successfully launched influential ethnic interest groups—Irish-Americans, Armenian-Americans, and Cuban-Americans, for example. Given their small numbers, and the general portrayal of Serbs as the aggressors in recent conflicts, their ability to affect American foreign policy is consequently retarded. Thus unifying and activating a "Serbian voice" was imperative to gain access to U.S. policymakers. Attempts at mobilizing Serbian-Americans depended on the sharing of a common historical experience and the ability of SUC leaders to convince Serbian-Americans that contemporary events were similar enough to the past to warrant political activism.

Theoretical Perspectives

Political mobilization, or the process by which masses become politically active, has been addressed often by social scientists. In his landmark study of the phenomenon, Karl Deutsch defined mobilization as "the process in which major clusters of old social, economic and psychological commitments are eroded or broken and people become available for new patterns of socialization and behavior."[17] Deutsch's definition set the pattern for future studies of political mobilization, which tended to focus on the relationship between the modernization and industrialization processes and its impact on the political participation of masses. Early scholars believed that the modernization of states would lead to less conflict among cultures and, therefore, the dissipation of political mobilization along ethnic lines. More recent scholars have pointed to an increase not only in ethnic violence but in the proliferation of ethnic interest organizations in the developed world as evidence that ethnic mobilization has persisted into modernity.[18]

The endurance of ethnic identity into the twenty-first century leaves room for little scholarly debate concerning the relationship between modernization and ethnic identity. Yet a consensus has not been reached concerning the origins of ethnic identity or the ways in which ethnicity is transformed into a political force. The three schools of thought regarding the role of ethnic identity in the political realm—instrumentalism, primordialism, and constructionism—rely on different analytical frameworks for explaining ethnic phenomena. *Instrumentalism* posits that ethnicity is a tool for mobilizing groups for competitive purposes.[19] Advocates of this perspective view ethnic identity as a device used by elites to achieve political goals during societal development. *Primordialism* is the view that ethnicity involves the commonalities inherent in the shared experience of history and culture—these shared communal experiences determine how individuals define themselves. Some priomordialists even contend that ethnic identity is genetically or biologically driven. *Constructionism* eschews the naturalist approach of primordialism, claiming instead that ethnic identity is "constructed" by elites through the processes of state building and is dependent in part upon changes in communication within societies.

If we conceptualize modern ethnic mobilization as involving the formation and activity of ethnic interest organizations, only the constructionist perspective is helpful in explaining the ethnic interest group explosion in the United States.[20] Instrumentalism fails to provide a rigorous explanation for ethnic mobilization because many of these groups are more involved in lobbying government for changes affecting coethnics abroad than for demanding resources for their own communities within the United States. In other words, the "rationality" (i.e., self-interest basis) inherent in instrumentalism often seems absent in U.S. ethnic interest groups. Indeed, American ethnic Serbs have little to gain personally by influencing policy in the Balkans today; only Serbs in Europe and the Balkans benefit directly from such efforts. Primordialism helps illustrate why ethnic identity is important, but the theory does not explain why the significance of ethnic identity varies across states and groups or why some mobilize for political purposes while others do not. Constructionism, however, allows for the examination of multiple variables that may be related to the process of ethnic mobilization. Because constructionists view ethnicity as manufactured over time, they also view ethnicity as transforming in form and strength as changes occur in global or domestic communication abilities, levels of group solidarity, perceived threats to the collective group, manipulation by elites or media, and so on. Although the constructionist school has its detractors, it is important to recognize the function that outside forces have both in the processes of identity formation and in arriving at an explanation for ethnic mobilization over time. Two outside forces play a particularly important role in the development of Serbian identity and in the mobilization of Serbian ethnics: historical group trauma and religion.

The level of importance that ethnic elites place on these forces and whether elites deem these forces as important to increasing mass participation are of key interest to the constructionist perspective on identity and identity mobilization.

Indeed, scholars of identity-based mobilization have noted that memory is an important component of ethnic ideology: "Ethnicity cannot be politicized unless an underlying core of memories, experience, or meaning moves people to collective action."[21] Scholars of the constructionist school point to the importance of group memory in the development of identity and collective myths over time—with particular significance assigned to the role of group trauma in promoting solidarity. Herbert Hirsch has noted that memory is a "distinctly political phenomenon and requires analysis as possibly the most important aspect of political understanding."[22] Hirsch's work has pointed to the state as the actor most responsible for the manipulation of memory, with an explicit role reserved for group elites.[23] I hypothesized here that Serbian-American ethnic elites deem reliance upon traumatic collective memory and religious symbolism as important to their efforts. Additionally, I propose that identification with the historical Serbian state and the perception of continued efforts to destroy the Serbian nation-state are important to Serbian ethnic identity and political mobilization.

Serbian Memory: The Battle of Kosovo and Jasenovac

Two aspects of history are arguably relevant to present-day Serbian politics and Serbian political mobilization: the Battle of Kosovo-Polje and the Ustashe murders symbolized for Serbs by the extermination camp Jasenovac. In efforts to rally antagonism between Serbs and other ethnic groups, nationalist elites in present-day Serbia have continually exploited these memories. Consequently, scholars have noted that Serbs in Serbia see present-day events as simply the continuation of centuries of oppression and persecution of Serbs and suppression of the Greater Serbian state. For centuries, the 1389 Battle of Kosovo has continued to be of importance to Serbian identity. The collapse of the Serbian Empire serves as the model of the "symbolic state" around which Serbs can mobilize. In this sense, the recent conflict in Kosovo takes on extreme importance. In a discussion of the history of Serbs and Croats, Alex Dragnich notes the significance of the battle and the territory of Kosovo:

It had been the center of the Serbian kingdom of the Middle Ages, when Serbia was the strongest empire in the Balkans for more than a hundred years. It is there that the most cherished Serbian Christian monuments, its monasteries and churches, are located. It was there that the Serbian army suffered defeat in 1389 at the hand of the Ottoman Turks, and the Serbian monarch, Prince Lazar, lost his life. In the nearly five hundred years of Turkish rule that followed, the Serbs never stopped dreaming of a resurrected Serbian state.[24]

The battle has become, through the centuries, the symbol of Serbian national-ism. Scholars note that a national myth arose celebrating the sacrifices made by those who died in the battle, and Tim Judah maintains that Serbs may think of the province of Kosovo as the Serbian "Jerusalem."[25]

The dominant story of the Battle of Kosovo asserts that the Ottomans and Serbs met in the Field of the Blackbirds in 1389.[26] Sultan Murad I, the leader of the Ottomans, and Prince Lazar, the leader of Serbian Orthodoxy, were both mortally wounded following political betrayals. The myth includes the notion that the battle was a crushing defeat for the Serbs, who were forced to evacuate the region and subsequently suffered five centuries of Ottoman occupation and the death of the Serbian Empire. Serbian independence was not again achieved until Serbian uprisings began in 1804, with full recognition and independence institutionalized through the Congress of Berlin in 1878. Serbians still celebrate "Vidovdan," the commemoration of defeat by the Turks in the Battle of Kosovo. "This distant battle has great significance for Serbian identity and the ideal of Serbian national unity. On Vidovdan, June 28, Serbian fighters are memorial-ized in a special liturgy, program and dance."[27]

The second, and more contemporary, memory for Serbs is the massacre of be-tween five hundred thousand and seven hundred thousand Serbs during World War II. The genocide of ethnic Serbs during World War II had its origins in the failure of the first Yugoslav state. In 1918, Serbs, Croats, Slovenians, Macedo-nians, and Montenegrins became united in the new Yugoslavia. However, the unification did not erase historical and religious differences. The events that oc-curred during World War II exemplified the divisions between some Serbs and Croats and would eventually become the basis for future hostilities.

When Germany invaded Yugoslavia in April 1941, the Yugoslav military col-lapsed within days. An independent Croatian state (the NDH) was formed by the Ustashe (a profascist, anti-Serb group) with the assistance of the Nazis; Ante Pavlic became its leader. The NDH remained in control of the area until 1945. This Croa-tian state encompassed most of present-day Croatia and Bosnia-Herzegovina, with the Germans occupying Serbia and controlling the country through a mil-itary puppet government.[28]

The Ustashe government resolved to eliminate its Serbian population—about one-third of the total population. Serbs, Jews, and Roma (Gypsies) were to be eliminated from the state through extermination or, for some Serbs, forced con-version or expulsion to Serbia. A war was waged on all things Serbian—includ-ing Orthodoxy and the Cyrillic alphabet. It is estimated that between two hun-dred thousand and three hundred thousand Serbs converted to Catholicism under the duress of the time.[29] The Ustashe also operated a string of concentra-tion camps in which thousands of Serbs, Jews, and Roma were murdered. The largest camp was Jasenovac, located on the Sava River near Bosnia. Jasenovac has similar meaning to Serbs as Auschwitz does to Jews.[30]

The genocide of ethnic Serbs by Croats has contemporary relevance: the emer-gence of ultranationalists in Croatia, the use of nationalist slogans and the Ustashe flag, and the secession of Croatia and Slovenia from Yugoslavia in 1991 were viewed as evidence of a continued conspiracy to undermine not only the Serbian state but the very existence of ethnic Serbs. Dragnich has noted the relevance of the massacres and of Ottoman subjugation of Serbia in the Yugoslav war: "More bloodshed occurred in Croatia, between Croatian militia and armed groups of Serbs representing the 600,000 to 800,000 minority Serbs living in Croatia. These Serbs were the descendants of the survivors of the massacre of 1941 and, going further back, descendants of those who protected Austria-Hungary's citizens (including Croats) on the military border, the Krajina, from the Ottoman Turks."[31]

The Battle of Kosovo and Jasenovac are undoubtedly important historical events in their own right. But how is history relevant to present-day events? For Serbs, the Battle of Kosovo and Jasenovac have great symbolic importance. They signify the loss of the Serbian Empire (the symbolic state) and the continued persecution of Serbs in Europe. Media events commemorating the slaughters of Serbian peoples helped foster the sense of hysteria and oppression that allowed nationalist elites to pursue their consolidation of power and ultimately, war. According to Judah, history provides the explanation for the wars in the former Yugoslavia: "Obviously the history of any people explains why they are where they are today, but in the Serbian case a new look at their history goes far towards explaining how and why they went to war in 1991. When Serbian peasants from villages surrounding Sarajevo began to bombard the city they did so confusing in their minds their former Muslim friends, neighbours and even brothers-in-law with the old Ottoman Turkish viziers and pashas who had ruled them until 1878."[32]

Serbian Religion and Nationalism

The existence of a state religion with deep historical roots is of great importance to Serbian identity. In her study of Serbian settlers in Milwaukee, Wisconsin, Deborah Padgett notes that Serbian Orthodoxy and Serbian nationalism are interwoven. "For Serbs, the Orthodox religion permeates all aspects of organizational life: it is inextricably related to individual and group identity."[33] Padgett insists that religion is at the root of both Serbian and Croatian identity. This relationship between nationalism and religion may be attributed to the evolution of the two institutions of state and church and their common origins. The acceptance of Christianity in Serbia is attributed to Saint Sava, the son of a Serbian prince. The Church became the only truly national institution, and the royal origins of the organization firmly bound church to state. The institution of the Serbian Orthodox Church is tied to the history of the Serbian state as the Church played a powerful role in medieval Serbia. The Turkish invasion put an end to the Serbian state, but the Church survived to become a symbol of Serbian endurance: scholars note that Serbian Orthodoxy became important in developing a tradition of struggle that would come to characterize Serbian identity.[34]

Out of the struggle grew national ballads, poems, and artwork dedicated to the revival of the Serbian nation-state. Orthodoxy provides a moral element legitimizing the goal of national self-determination.

It might be expected that religious cleavages could give rise to political cleavages within the current Serbian-American community. In fact, a 1962 rift between the American and Canadian Serbian Orthodox churches had some basis in political events. When a Serbian Orthodox bishop in the United States argued that the diocese should break from central authority in Belgrade due to the church's subjugation to the communist government in Yugoslavia, the North American church became factionalized. According to Padgett, about one-third of the Serbian Orthodox parishes in the United States and Canada are "Free Serbian Orthodox" parishes, having broken from Belgrade.[35] This factionalism of the Serbian Orthodox Church led to factionalism within other Serbian-American organizations in the 1960s, although thousands supported neither side. According to Milosh Milenkovich, current president of the SUC, the rift in Orthodoxy was resolved with the collapse of communism in the former Yugoslavia. The Serbian Orthodox Church has become somewhat of a refuge for many Serbian immigrants and Serbian-Americans.[36] The war in the former Yugoslavia and the vilification of the Serbs may have resulted in a return to the faith by some who previously did not participate in services or religious organizations.[37]

Three conclusions may be drawn concerning history, religion, and Serbian ethnic identity. First, at a minimum, historical memory is of present-day relevance to Serbian elites in Serbia—if only for the purpose of mobilizing coethnics. Second, the Serbian Orthodox Church has been an important repository of Serbian nationalism throughout history. Third, the merging of Serbian Orthodoxy with Serbian nationalism elevates the vision of "Greater Serbia" to a near sacrosanct vision. Religion legitimizes nationalism, and history provides the myth that preserves the image of the Serbian state.

ETHNIC MOBILIZATION: RESPONSE TO ESCALATION IN KOSOVO

Ethnic conflict in Kosovo preceded the collapse of Yugoslavia and was rekindled following the Bosnian civil war. The Milosevic government resolved to maintain its stronghold on the remaining autonomous territories of the former Yugoslavia (in addition to Serbia)—Montenegro, Vojvodina, and Kosovo. Albanian Kosovars have increasingly demanded outright independence or unification with Albania.

The Battle of Kosovo-Polje, as the pivotal event in Serbian history, has rendered Kosovo a historical symbol of Serbian nationalism. Furthermore, the conflict between Serbs and Kosovar Albanians has modern historical roots as well. During World War II, large numbers of Serbs fled the region under assault by the Albanians. Toward the end of the war, the Partisans promised that "Kosovo would stay within Albania after the war. When in 1944, it was discovered that

Kosovo was again to be part of Yugoslavia, insurrections began and the communist leader Tito was forced to send some 30,000 troops to pacify the region."[38]

Unrest in Kosovo resumed as early as 1968. A period of "Albanianization" followed and led to a mass exodus of Serbs from the area, resulting in a 90 percent Albanian population in the region by the 1990s. Throughout the 1970s and 1980s, Kosovo's economic development lagged behind the rest of Yugoslavia. The collapse of communism and Serbian suppression of Kosovar Albanians resulted in the development of a "second economy" among Kosovar Albanians. As state enterprises collapsed and political oppression of Kosovar Albanians increased, the Albanians responded by developing private businesses that flourished while ethnic Serbs languished in low-paying positions.[39] The growing economic cleavage further fueled tensions between the two groups and allowed nationalists the opportunity to scapegoat Albanians as the source of Serbian misfortune.

Judah describes Kosovo as "the greatest source of political instability in Yugoslavia."[40] He states that a series of Serbian-initiated petitions protesting the situation of Serbs in Kosovo, together with the ability of Slobodan Milosevic to capitalize on the unrest in the region, ultimately led to the demise of the state of Yugoslavia. In a sense, Milosevic's use of nationalism and hard-line policies in Kosovo led to the secession of Slovenia and Croatia as Slovene elites protested Serb policies and the Croatian nationalist party (the Croatian Democratic Union) adopted anti-Serb policies in Croatia.

It is beyond the scope of this chapter to detail the events that led to the wars in Yugoslavia. However, it is important to note that events in Kosovo spurred the conflicts that began in 1991, and Serbian elite resolve to maintain the region may only have strengthened following the economic hardships associated with the war, international isolation as a result of United Nations sanctions, international condemnation of Serbian atrocities, and the tenuous peace established through the Dayton Agreement. The long struggle for Serbs to maintain a stronghold on Kosovo made the escalation of the crisis meaningful for Serbian elites.

The acceleration of tensions in Kosovo provides a useful point for analysis of the mobilization strategies of the SUC. As the Serbian crackdown progressed in Kosovo, the SUC communicated with its membership and attempted to sway the United States and NATO away from military intervention in the region. In order to determine the extent to which Serbian-American elites used historical trauma and religion to mobilize Serbian-Americans, I analyzed SUC press releases, letters to officials in Washington, and SUC bulletins from February 1998 to November 1999 for references to the Battle of Kosovo, Jasenovac, and religious nationalism.[41]

The 1998 Kosovo Crisis

The origins of the crisis in Kosovo stem from the Belgrade regime's stripping of Kosovo's autonomy and separate federal status. Kosovar Albanians formed a shadow government in 1991, headed by Ibrahim Rugova. Rugova's government consistently pressed for Kosovo's autonomy. More radical organizations began to emerge and strengthen with the conflicts in the former Yugoslavia in the 1990s, including the Kosovo Liberation Army (KLA), which has used terrorist methods in an attempt to achieve Kosovo's secession.

In February 1998, tensions in Kosovo escalated as the KLA continued its campaign for independence from the Serbian state. Yugoslav president Slobodan Milosevic responded to the increase in KLA attacks by increasing the presence of the Serbian police forces and military in the region. Serbian forces launched frequent attacks, which included a massacre of twenty-four Albanian civilians in March.[42] It is estimated that between two hundred thousand and four hundred thousand Albanians became refugees as a result of the growing conflict. However, the world's attention did not turn to the growing violence until pictures of the Serb massacre of eighteen Albanian men, women, and children in Gornje Obrinje made the front pages of newspapers in September 1998.

By the end of September, the United States and its NATO allies demanded a Serbian withdrawal from Kosovo. In early October, NATO demands were backed with the threat of force as American B-52 bombers began preparing for airstrikes and the U.S. Sixth Fleet was placed on alert in the Adriatic Sea. In an effort to bring a diplomatic solution to the crisis, U.S. Special Envoy Richard Holbrooke flew to Belgrade and negotiated an agreement whereby Serbia would reduce its forces in the region to March 1998 levels and restore Kosovo's autonomous status. The withdrawal of Serbian troops was to be monitored via U.S. and European aerial surveillance and the placement of two thousand international monitors from the Organization for Security and Cooperation in Europe (OSCE).[43]

For the United States and NATO, the Kosovo question became increasingly difficult. U.S. policymakers were fearful that the conflict would spread to neighboring Macedonia because of the existence of a large Albanian minority in that country. Essentially, the West was faced with supporting one of three policy options: independence for Kosovo as proposed by the KLA, some degree of autonomy for Kosovo within the existing Serbian state, or a maintenance of the status quo. None of these options was particularly appealing to U.S. policymakers. Supporting independence runs counter to the global principles of respecting state sovereignty, and there was hesitancy on the part of many to reward the KLA's use of terrorism. Yet supporting a return to autonomy or the status quo could have been viewed as giving tacit approval to authoritarian rule under Milosevic.

The SUC Response

The SUC responded to the NATO threat of force in Kosovo by issuing statements to the press, sending letters from SUC leadership to Congress and the Clinton administration, and mobilizing constituents to contact members of Congress. In addition, the organization sponsored a demonstration in front of the

State Department on 15 October 1998, with between two hundred fifty and three hundred supporters turning out for the candlelight vigil. How the SUC mobilized members and other sympathetic individuals to act is of chief concern here. It is hypothesized that leaders of the SUC relied on key components of identity, namely, the traumatic group memories of the Battle of Kosovo and Jasenovac, as well as religious symbolism, to convince members to act.

The Use of Memory

Serbian organizational leaders indicated that the genocide of Serbs under the Croatian Ustashe is an exceedingly important component of the SUC's ideology. Joksimovich claimed that he knew nothing of Jasenovac until his emigration in 1965, but the discovery of the Ustashe atrocities had a profound impact on him. "Now," he stated, "I cannot imagine that Croats and Serbs voluntarily could ever live in a joint state."[44] Joksimovich argued that Jasenovac is of importance to all Serbian-Americans to varying degrees—depending on personal family experiences (whether family members were victimized by the Ustashe) and the time of immigration to the United States. Jasenovac, he contends, is relevant to the SUC's goals to the extent that "the truth needs to be told and must prevail."

Interestingly, Joksimovich was less adamant about the importance of Kosovo: "As heritage and significant part of history it is pertinent. However, we take history only as a guide and try to confront contemporary tragic events in the Balkans using approaches appropriate for the nineties of this century." Nevertheless, he maintained, "We are the people proud of Serbian history in its entirety. [The] Battle of Kosovo is of course a battle which profoundly impacted not only the history of [the] Balkans but that of Mid-Europe as well. I happen to think that the Serbs saved parts of Europe from islamization."[45]

Milenkovich's responses differed somewhat from his predecessor's. He asserted that the Battle of Kosovo is important in the development of a "Serbian ethic." For Milenkovich, the Battle of Kosovo provides an operational code for Serbian response to contemporary events when Serbs feel as if they are facing overwhelming odds. Joksimovich and Milenkovich agreed on the role of Jasenovac, however. Milenkovich asserts that the genocide of Serbs by the Ustashe "helps to explain the intolerance and hatred fifty years later in the dismemberment of Yugoslavia. ... [A]trocities by the Serbs [can be] explained by revenge. The sons and grandsons of the victims of World War II are avenging their deaths. ... [Events today] have an element of continuation in the form of revenge by the Serbs."[46]

Although both men perceived historical trauma as pertinent to their own worldviews and to the missions of the organization, they offered remarkably different responses when asked the following: "Do you often refer to the Ustashe massacres or the Battle of Kosovo in your organization's literature?" Joksimovich responded, "No, because we are focused on the existing tragedies of the Serbian nation which is fighting for its bare survival."[47] However, Milenkovich asserted that references to these historical events were made "when it's appropriate" because "it's part of our life." Again, he noted that the Battle of Kosovo brought about the birth of the "Kosovo ethic," which prescribes how Serbs should behave when facing great odds. He compared the events of the Battle of Kosovo to the biblical David and Goliath and declared that the "Kosovo ethic" is a sort of "Kamikaze mentality" in which it is "better to die for a cause" because a better life awaits Serbs after death. Any cause that has to do with Serb freedom is potentially subject to the Kosovo ethic.[48]

It is difficult to account for the differences in the leaders' responses.[49] Regardless, the organization's literature includes multiple references to the Ustashe massacres and the Battle of Kosovo and comparisons of both to present-day events. Often, however, references are made in discussions of particularly historic problems or questions. The most prominent example of this comparison involves the organization's efforts upon the arrest in Argentina of Dinko Sakic, former commander of the Jasenovac concentration camp, in May 1998. The SUC contacted the Clinton administration and issued a press release calling for Sakic's trial to be held in a jurisdiction other than Croatia. The press release announcing the SUC's position noted Croatia's failure to recognize the genocide and the potential emotional trauma for Jasenovac survivors should they have to return to Croatia to testify. Specifically, the SUC asserted that "recent examples of Croatian bad faith rule out a trial in Croatia. These include Croatia's vicious ethnic cleansing of Serbs from the Krajina region in 1995 and Croatia's failure to honor its obligations under the Dayton and Erdut Accords."[50] Nonetheless, Sakic was extradited to stand trial in Croatia, and his wife, who allegedly worked at the concentration camp run by her husband, was extradited in November 1998.[51]

SUC bulletins and the organization's Web sites—two vehicles of Serbian diaspora mobilization—contain explicit references to historical trauma. Its Web sites are rife with references to the genocide in fascist Croatia, and also to Ottoman domination. One section entitled "100 Irrefutable Facts" asserts the following:

1. [The war in Bosnia represented] the resumption of the 1941–1945 civil war in which the Croatian Fascists, collaborators of the Nazi regime, and Muslim religious extremists murdered between 600,000 and 1,200,000 Serbs. The issues are the same, the battlefields are the same, even the flags and army insignia are the same.

2. The dismemberment of Yugoslavia has clearly revealed the reemergence of the old geopolitical ambitions of Germany, and the revival of Germany's alliances with primitive nationalists and religious fanatics in the Balkans. For the third time in this century Germany is trying to expand its influence in this region, and for the third time it is encountering Serbian resistance....

7. Soon after Croatia declared its independence on June 25, 1991, Krajina Serbs were subjected to harsh discrimination by the Croatian government: they began to lose their jobs, their houses were destroyed, their political and cultural rights abrogated, and their national identity threatened. When in the summer of 1991 the Croatian armed forces began to

threaten them, the Serb population either fled to Serbia or took up arms in self-defense. These Krajina Serbs are the children and grandchildren of the Serbs in Croatia that had been systematically persecuted and massacred by the Croat Ustashas and Muslim extremists in World War [II]. Confronted with extreme aggressiveness of the Croatian state and population, the Krajina Serbs were now rising to their self-defense under the motto: "Never Again."[52]

A separate SUC Web page uses pictorial evidence to make direct comparisons between Turkish atrocities, genocide in Croatia, and contemporary events. The site opens with an image of the Skull tower at Nish, Yugoslavia. Constructed in 1809 by Ottoman leader Hursid Pasha, the tower was built with the skulls of between one thousand and two thousand Serbs following a Serbian defeat at an uprising. Approximately fifty skulls are still present in the tower. The caption at the beginning of the site reads: "Twice before in this century there have been well documented attempts by the Croats and Muslims to destroy the Serbian people, and to obliterate their culture, religion and memory. The pictures you will see is their third try."[53] What follows is a pictorial comparative of events from World War II and the wars with Croatia and Bosnia, including death pits, forced marches, dead children, and mutilated bodies from both wars.

It is important to note that most references to the historical events under the Ottoman regime or the fascist Croatian state occurred with respect to the civil wars from 1991 to 1995. Most press releases, bulletins, and letters to the administration and congressional officials on the issue of U.S. or NATO intervention in Kosovo contained little overt reference to Turkish oppression or the Croatian genocide. There are two potential reasons for this. First, it obviously seems more appropriate to point out past Croatian offenses when the Croats are an important party to the policy at stake. This was not the situation with escalation of the crisis in Kosovo. Second, even though Kosovo Albanians are of Muslim descent, there are ethnic differences between Albanian and Bosnian Muslims. In fact, press releases and memoranda on Kosovo made reference to fears of Albanian irredentism, as distinct from the "Muslim problem" in Bosnia. In an August media alert, the SUC noted, "For the time being, the KLA's ambition of achieving independence for Kosovo as a pre-cursor for a new Greater Albanian state incorporating Kosovo, Albania, and parts of Macedonia has been defeated."[54]

Religious Symbolism

Given the explicit tie between religion and Serbian nationalism, it might be expected that the SUC would place a great deal of emphasis on religious symbolism in its mobilization efforts. Joksimovich noted that churches are "extremely important" to his organization and pointed out the role that the Serbian Orthodox Church has played in preserving the nation. In fact, when questioned about possible cooperation with other Serbian organizations, Joksimovich noted that the SUC had "religion, language, love for the Serbian culture and ties to the motherland" in common with other Serbian-American organizations.[55] No mention of the North American cleavage during the communist years was made.

As discussed previously, the use of religious symbolism by ethnic organizations has the potential to legitimize the cause in the eyes of constituents. One study indicated that SerbNet "frequently held propaganda functions in local Serbian churches where political statements from Patriarch Pavle in Belgrade were distributed."[56] In advertising the October 1998 candlelight vigil, the SUC noted that "the prayer vigil for peace in the Balkans and against violence and NATO bombing as an answer to the Kosovo problem" would be led by Bishop Mitrophan and Bishop Artemije of the Serbian Orthodox Church.[57] Milenkovich noted that the Church is "extremely important" because "Serbs consider the church part of them. The Church identifies with the suffering of the people."[58] In addition, the organization's press releases and bulletins note the role of Orthodox leaders within Kosovo in attempting to achieve peace.[59]

Perhaps because the civil war in Yugoslavia has been deemed a "religious war" by some, a number of references to the role of the Roman Catholic Church and Islamic Fundamentalism exist in the tract "100 Irrefutable Facts."[60] The complicity of the Roman Catholic Church, as evidenced by the actions of Pope John Paul II, and Bosnian Muslim leader Alija Izetbegovic's ties to Islamic fundamentalism are important points in the tract:

8. In August 1991, in the Hungarian city of Pecs, Pope John Paul II, speaking in Croatian, urged the world to "help legitimate the aspirations of Croatia." ("Everything that has happened in Eastern Europe in the last few years would not have been possible without the presence of Pope [John Paul]" said Mikhail Gorbachev in an article published in Stampa of Turin on March 3, 1992).

9. The Vatican has an intelligence chief, Jean-Louis Tauran, an efficient diplomat, who also involved himself in the dismemberment of Yugoslavia. He was, moreover, instrumental in organizing the recognition of Slovenia and Croatia....

12. On December 25, 1991, Germany recognized Slovenia and Croatia. It did so on the very day after German Foreign Minister Genscher visited Pope John Paul II at the Vatican....

14. On January 13, 1992, the Vatican recognized Slovenia and Croatia. Prior to this recognition Pope John Paul II rejected many appeals to use his moral power and responsibility to encourage and inspire a climate for peaceful coexistence in Yugoslavia, in fact, he welcomed the move toward secession.

And with respect to Izetbegovic and Islam:

17. In the spring of 1943, as leader of the Muslim youth in Sarajevo, he [Izetbegovic] welcomed Amin-el Husseini, the Grand Mufti of Jerusalem, a well known friend of Hitler. In the same year, Izetbegovic was one of the organizers in the formation of the notorious Waffen SS "Handzar Division" (Handzar in Arabic means "to slit the throat"), consisting entirely of Bosnian Muslim volunteers. This division (peak strength 25,000), officered by Germans and wearing German uniforms and insignia, committed such atrocities against the Bosnian Serbs that even the hardened German officers were shocked....

18. In his book, *The Islamic Declaration*, published in 1970 and republished in Sarajevo in 1990, A. Izetbegovic makes a clear and ringing statement for the absolute validity and dominance of the Islamic religion: "There can be neither peace nor coexistence between the Islamic religion and non-Islamic social and political institutions."

While these references are evidence of the belief that religion is an important factor in the war, they also demonstrate the role of historical memory by underlining the importance of fascism and German complicity. "Irrefutable Fact 25" notes the irony that "[on] April 6, 1992—the anniversary of Hitler's 'Operation Punishment' when successive waves of German bomb attacks wreaked the virtual destruction of Belgrade in 1941—the E.C. [European Community] abruptly recognized the sovereignty and independence of Bosnia-Hercegovina."[61]

Summation

A review of SUC literature indicates that SUC organizers view traumatic memory as an important point of comparison. Use of traumatic memory is most often evident in those areas most likely to mobilize constituents (i.e., the use of such rhetoric is less evident in letters to members of the Clinton administration, congresspersons, and other policymakers).[62] Because religion is an important component of Serbian nationalism, it is not surprising that the SUC mentions the leading role of Orthodox clergymen and refers to the importance of religious history to current international conflict.

CONCLUSION

Despite the efforts of the SUC, there is little evidence to suggest that the Serbian lobby was effective in influencing U.S. foreign policy. Ultimately, Western powers, with U.S. backing, bombed Serbia in an effort to halt Serbian atrocities in Kosovo, and NATO-led peacekeeping troops were introduced in the region, effectively detaching Kosovo from Serbia-proper. However, the study of SUC ethnic mobilization efforts sheds light on the importance of history in the development and political agendas of ethnic interest groups. As increasing numbers of ethnic groups organize to influence foreign policy decision making, U.S. policymakers are faced with the daunting task of separating current political crises from their historical roots in efforts to develop a pragmatic national policy. Although atrocities committed decades or centuries earlier may seem irrelevant to contemporary international crises, they are clearly relevant to increasingly powerful ethnic lobbies—whether Serbian, Irish, Cuban, Jewish, or Armenian.

In attempting to devise policies to deal with ethnic conflicts, policymakers must not disregard the role of historical memory; memories of trauma are part and parcel of ethnic identity. There is an inherent conflict between espousing the maxim "never again" and yet disputing the importance of history. Policymakers, nonetheless, do routinely deny the significance of history in contemporary conflicts. Judah wrote of the war in Bosnia: "During the Bosnian war such a view [that history mattered] was considered politically incorrect by western liberal circles. Serbia and the Serbs were the aggressors and to make reference to history in this way was considered the sin of 'moral relativism'.... This was wrong. Reference to history is essential because otherwise all the crimes that were committed seem as random as those of a mad sniper taking pot shots in a western city. It does not, however, absolve anyone of guilt."[63] Morality must be a consideration when attempting to strike a balance between preserving memory for the prevention of future atrocities and preventing nationalist elites from using past persecution to justify contemporary vengeance and violence. Understanding the importance of historical trauma and religion as symbols of ethnic identity is imperative to developing sound policies concerning age-old conflicts that persist into the twenty-first century.

NOTES

1. This paper was originally part of a larger study that examined the ethnic mobilization of diaspora groups in the United States. I wish to thank Clyde Brown, Sheila Croucher, Dan Jacobs, and my husband, David Paul, for their suggestions.

2. See the Selected Bibliography at the end of this volume.

3. Brad Blitz, "Serbia's War Lobby: Diaspora Groups and Western Elites," in *This Time We Knew: Western Responses to Genocide in Bosnia*, ed. Thomas Cushman and Stjepan G. Mestrovic (New York: New York University Press, 1996).

4. During the course of the study, Milosh Milenkovich replaced Vojin Joksimovich as SUC president. The SUC held its presidential election at the Ninth Annual Serbian Unity Congress Convention in Washington, D.C., September 18–20, 1998. Consequently, both Dr. Joksimovich and Mr. Milenkovich were interviewed for this study.

5. Vojin Joksimovich, written interview responses, 1998.

6. Blitz, "Serbia's War Lobby," 204. Interestingly, SUC president Milenkovich contends that the SUC is not a political organization. He argued that it is instead "educational.... [W]e don't belong to political parties. We try to educate and see that Serbian people are properly represented here." According to Blitz's analysis, the SUC, established as a nonprofit organization in the state of Nebraska, cannot legally engage in lobbying. It is possible that the emphasis by SUC members that their organization is "not political" is related to their questionable status. When I first contacted the SUC for information, I was informed quite firmly that they no longer engaged in lobbying and no longer had a political agenda. Milosh Milenkovich, telephone interview, October 1998.

7. This perception stems from the failure of U.S. leaders to call explicitly for the removal of Milosevic from power, especially given his antidemocratic stance and mass demonstrations against his regime in 1997. The SUC asserts that the United States has continued to foster the perception that Milosevic is viewed as a principle in the negotiations in the Balkans—a fact that Milosevic uses to his advantage to maintain power in Serbia.

8. SUC president Milosh Milenkovich claimed that the membership is at least five thousand and growing as the organization is focusing on bringing inactive members back into active membership.

9. Joksimovich, interview.

10. According to Milenkovich, SerbNet disbanded following the death of its member Serbian National Federation leader Robert Stone.

11. Sidney Tarrow, *Power in Movement* (New York: University of Cambridge, 1994), 18.

12. Milton J. Esman, *Ethnic Politics* (Ithaca, NY: Cornell University Press, 1994).

13. Milenkovich, interview.

14. Joksimovich, interview.

15. Blitz, "Serbia's War Lobby," 202.

16. U.S. Bureau of the Census, *Statistical Abstract of the United States: 1990* (Washington, DC: U.S. Bureau of the Census, 1990).

17. Karl W. Deutsch, "Social Mobilization and Political Development," *American Political Science Review* 55, no. 3 (1961): 493–514.

18. See Cynthia Enole, *Ethnic Conflict and Political Development* (Lanham, MD: University Press of America, 1986); and Joseph Rothschild, *Ethnopolitics: A Conceptual Framework* (New York: Columbia University Press, 1981).

19. For more on the instrumentalist approach to explaining political mobilization, see John D. McCarthy and Mayer N. Zald, "Resource Mobilization and Social Movements: A Partial Theory," *American Journal of Sociology* 82, no. 6 (1977): 1212–41; Joane Nagel and Susan Olzak, "Ethnic Mobilization in New and Old States: An Extension of the Competition Model," *Social Problems* 30, no. 2 (1982): 127–43; and Susan Olzak, "Contemporary Ethnic Mobilization," *Annual Review of Sociology* 9 (1983): 355–74.

20. Milton Esman, *Ethnic Politics*, provides a convincing argument that studies of ethnic mobilization should focus on their organizations. He proposes seven variables that are important to the study of ethnic interest groups: political opportunity structure, leadership, strategies and tactics, ideology, organization, goals, and resources.

21. Ibid., 14.

22. Herbert Hirsch, *Genocide and the Politics of Memory* (Chapel Hill: University of North Carolina Press, 1995), 10–11.

23. John R. Gillis, ed., *Commemorations* (Princeton, NJ: Princeton University Press, 1994); Paul Connerton, *How Societies Remember* (Cambridge, England: Cambridge University Press, 1989).

24. Alex N. Dragnich, *Serbs and Croats* (San Diego: Harcourt Brace, 1992), 162.

25. Judah also notes the irony in the fact that this memory of defeat has such significance when historical records indicate that the battle may not have been the decisive moment that ushered in Ottoman rule. He contends that the Serbian Empire was already in decline and that some archives indicate that the Serbs may have emerged victorious from that particular battle. Nevertheless, Kosovo has important symbolic meaning for Serbs. Tim Judah, *The Serbs* (New Haven, CT: Yale University Press, 1997).

26. Judah notes that the loss at the Maritsa River in Bulgaria may have had more factual impact on the Serbs than did the Battle of Kosovo. He writes: "The Battle on the Maritsa was a crushing victory for the Turks, and as a consequence Bulgaria, Macedonia and parts of southern Serbia fell under their sway. In strategic terms its consequences were far greater than those of the Battle of Kosovo in 1389, but because of the myths and legends that have grown up around the latter the first has tended to be forgotten." Judah, *The Serbs*, 26.

27. Deborah Padgett, *Settlers and Sojourners: A Study of Serbian Adaptation in Milwaukee, Wisconsin* (New York: AMS Press, 1989), 66–67.

28. Ibid.

29. Judah, *The Serbs*, 126.

30. Ibid.

31. Dragnich, *Serbs and Croats*, 160–61.

32. Judah, *The Serbs*, xi.

33. Padgett, *Settlers and Sojourners*, 46.

34. In addition to Padgett, *Settlers and Sojourners*, and Judah, *The Serbs*, see also Joel Halpern and Barbara Kerwsky Halpern, *A Serbian Village in Historical Perspective* (New York: Holt, Rinehart and Winston, 1972).

35. Bishop Dionisije, the leader of the faction, was defrocked by Belgrade church officials. According to Padgett, as of 1989, no other religious body recognized or affiliated itself with the "Free" faction of the Serbian Orthodox church, despite attempts by Dionisije to gain recognition from the Russian Patriarch in 1966.

36. Jyoti Thottam, "Church Provides Refuge for Serbs in New York," *Christian Science Monitor*, 9 October 1996, 12.

37. Jyoti Thottam noted the growth of Saint Sava Parish in Manhattan where, according to Pastor Ljubomir Josimovic, many of those joining the parish are unfamiliar with church beliefs and traditions—some not even knowing how to cross themselves. Thottam, "Church Provides Refuge for Serbs," 12.

38. Judah, *The Serbs*, 132.

39. Miranda Vickers, *Between Serb and Albanian: A History of Kosovo* (New York: Columbia University Press, 1998).

40. Judah, *The Serbs*, 156.

41. This period covers the escalation of the conflict marked by an increase in killings and massacres and ending with the October 1998 agreement negotiated by U.S. envoy Richard Holbrooke. This agreement provided only a brief resolution to the crisis that ultimately led to NATO airstrikes in spring 1999. However, this escalation does represent a "disturbance" point with a definite endpoint—a necessity for the analysis.

42. Gary Dempsey, "Kosovo's Conflict … Rooted in Quicksand," *Washington Times*, 12 March 1998, A-14.

43. Through their seat on the United Nations Security Council, the Russian government voiced extreme opposition to the use of force against the Serbs. The presence of Russians on the OSCE monitoring team is deemed by some as a possible symbol of conciliation for the Serbs.

44. Joksimovich, interview.

45. Ibid.

46. Milenkovich, interview.

47. Joksimovich, interview.

48. Milenkovich, interview.

49. It is of course possible that the respondents simply replied as they thought they should, rather than making an honest assessment—a danger inherent in the gathering of interview-based data. The fact that current and previous literature is rife with references to history indicates that there has not been a change in SUC tactics with the change in leadership. I suspect that Joksimovich was concerned about the way in which Serbs and Serbian-Americans would be portrayed in my analysis, particularly given his insistence on written responses to my questions. This is understandable given the unflattering picture painted of the SUC by Brad Blitz and of Serbs in general by the mass media.

50. Serbian Unity Congress, "Serious Trial Needed for Croatian Death Camp Commander," SUC Archive No. 18/98, 1 May 1998.

51. "Argentina Extradites War Crimes Suspect," *New York Times*, 2 November 1998, A13.

52. Serbian Unity Congress, "100 Irrefutable Facts," <http://www.suc.org/politics /100facts/index.html> (accessed October 2001).

53. Serbian Unity Congress, "Forbidden Pictures," <http://www.serbianunity.net /politics/forbidden_pictures/> (accessed October 2001).

54. Serbian Unity Congress, "Propaganda on Kosovo: Media Alert for Foreign News Editors," SUC Archive No. 23/98, 6 August 1998.

55. Joksimovich, interview.

56. Blitz, "Serbia's War Lobby," 202.

57. Serbian Unity Congress, "No Bombs," SUC Action Alert, Archives of SUC, October 1998.

58. Milenkovich, interview.

59. Serbian Unity Congress, "Appeal of the Orthodox Diocese of Raska and Prizren," SUC Archive No. 148, 1 May 1998.

60. Edmond Paris, *Genocide in Satellite Croatia, 1941–1945* (Chicago: American Institute for Balkan Affairs, 1961).

61. Serbian Unity Congress, "100 Irrefutable Facts."

62. It is of interest to note that an effective means for mobilizing ethnic constituents is deemed inappropriate and perhaps ineffective in influencing policymakers. Both Joksimovich and Milenkovich noted that members of Congress and the executive branch had little interest in the trials of Serbs throughout history.

63. Judah, *The Serbs,* 74.

Chapter 6

Latinos and Latin America: A Unified Agenda?

Michael Jones-Correa

As the Hispanic population in the United States expands, Latinos are likely to become more active players in foreign policy debates, particularly on U.S. relations with Latin America. But there are important differences among Latinos in how much weight to give foreign policy issues, which issues to emphasize, and along which avenues to pursue them. Foreign policy approaches will be shaped not only by differences in national origin but also in generation. Two sets of Latino actors are involved in U.S. foreign policy: one, a largely native-born elite that mobilizes sporadically around issues in U.S.–Latin American relations through formal policy channels, and the other composed of Latin American immigrants who are engaged in constant, informal contact with their countries of origin. These two sets of actors have only rarely overlapped substantively or organizationally, with one recent exception: immigration policy.

TWO TRENDS

The potential weight of Latinos in U.S. foreign policy is predicated on their numbers. There are currently more than thirty million persons of Hispanic origin in the United States, and these numbers are rapidly increasing (see table 6.1). By 2025 only two countries will have more persons of Latin American descent living within their borders—Mexico and Brazil. In a few years, then, the United States. will become the third-largest Latin American state. The expectation is that these numbers alone will give Latinos a stake in U.S. relations with Latin America.

Table 6.1
Latinos in the United States, Selected Countries of Origin

Mexico	19.8 million
Cuba	1.3 million
El Salvador	.6 million
Dominican Republic	.6 million
Colombia	.6 million
Guatemala	.4 million
Nicaragua	.3 million
Ecuador	.3 million
Peru	.3 million
Total	30.0 million

Sources: U.S. Bureau of the Census, "The Hispanic Population in the United States: Population Characteristics," *Current Population Reports* P20-527, February 2000; U.S. Bureau of the Census, *We the American ... Hispanics* (Washington, DC: Government Printing Office, 1993), 4.

Moreover, a good deal of the Latino population growth is due to immigration. Some 40 percent of all Hispanics are now foreign born, many relatively recent arrivals.[1] This foreign-born Latino population is growing by almost 5 percent each year. The foreign-born population from Mexico alone increased from 0.8 million in 1970 to 2.2 million in 1980 to 4.3 million in 1990 and to 7 million in 1997.[2] The recent arrival of these immigrants suggests that they are likely to maintain close ties with their countries of origin and to have an active interest in seeing U.S. policy reflect those ties. That this is the case is illustrated by the plethora of first-generation immigrant organizations that have sprung up in cities such as Los Angeles, New York, Chicago, and other centers of Latino immigrant settlement.

Along with the rising numbers of Hispanics, there has also been a dramatic increase in the numbers of Latino elected officials, appointees, and civil service employees at all levels of government in the United States. In 1999 there were nineteen Hispanics elected to the U.S. House of Representatives, twenty-seven states had Latinos holding statewide office, and there were more than six thousand Hispanics elected to office at the local level. In 1996 2.5 percent of federal appointees were Latinos, as were 8.4 percent of the appointees to the U.S. Court of Appeals in 1993 and 1994. From 1973 to 1997, Latinos more than tripled their numbers in civil service positions, making up 7.5 percent of all those employed in state and local government in 1997.[3] Together with the staff of nonprofit advocacy groups such as the Mexican-American Legal Defense and Education Fund and the Southwest Voter Registration Project, these officials and civil service employees form the backbone of a Latino policy elite, a group of individuals who can mobilize and lobby effectively within the American political system.

The rapidly growing Hispanic population, much of it foreign born, and the expanding Latino policy elite both point toward increasing Latino influence in the foreign policy arena. But will Latinos speak with one voice? The evidence seems to indicate that immigrants and native-born elites display significant differences in how, and how much, they emphasize their foreign policy interests.

THE FOREIGN POLICY INTERESTS OF LATINO ELITES

The largely native-born policy elite ranks foreign policy issues far from the top of their policy agendas. For example, in a 1997 survey, 454 Hispanic elites (public officials, academics, business leaders, and activists) gave their views on foreign and domestic policy issues. Respondents were asked to rank eighteen domestic and foreign policy issues (see table 6.2).[4] Five of the top six issues ranked "very important" were domestic rather than international policy issues (the exception being "international terrorism"). More than 85 percent of Latino leaders responded that Latinos in the United States should be most concerned with the well being of the Latino community in the United States. Three out of four agreed with the statement: "What happens in the Hispanic/Latino community in the U.S. is more important to me than the state of U.S. relations with Latin America."[5] Regardless of national origin, Latino elites' political interests and agendas were primarily domestic, not international, in focus.[6]

It should be noted that the overwhelming preference Latino elites show for domestic issues over foreign policy concerns does not mean that foreign policy is neglected entirely. In their 1997 survey, for instance, Pachón and Pantoja found that despite their domestic inclinations, Cuban- and Mexican-American elites still followed developments in their countries of origin. Eighty-five percent felt the United States should pay more attention to its relations with Latin America. Seventy-one percent thought that increased U.S. involvement would be good for the region, 56 percent gave top priority to increasing trade and economic growth and development in the region, and 52 percent gave priority to democracy and human rights. On trade, 69 percent thought that the model of the North American Free Trade Agreement (NAFTA) should be extended to the rest of Latin America.[7]

Table 6.2
Rankings of Foreign versus Domestic Policy Priorities

Percent Ranking Issues "Very Important"

U.S. Education	94.5
U.S. Race & Ethnic Relations	79.5
U.S. Economic Growth	75.3
U.S. Crime	60.4
U.S. Environment	59.9
International Terrorism	40.1
U.S. International Relations	39.6
Strengthen U.S.	18.7
Protect U.S. Jobs	38.5
Nuclear Proliferation	62.7
Flow of Illegal Drugs	53.7
Illegal Immigration	13.7
Trade Deficit	20.3
World Hunger	39.6
U.S. Military Superiority	20.3

Source: Henry Pachón and Adrián Pantoja, "Domestic vs. Foreign Policy Concerns of Latino Leaders in the U.S." (paper prepared for the Latin American Studies Association Meeting, Miami, Florida, 17 March 2000), 21.

However, active mobilization by these Latino policy elites in the foreign policy arena has been episodic. The 1993 NAFTA debate is a key example. Beginning in 1991, the Salinas administration in Mexico began courting Mexican-American elite opinion with the purpose of generating a domestic lobby to influence the U.S. congressional vote on the treaty. Delegations of Mexican-American leaders were flown to Mexico City for briefings, preparing them for their role as advocates for NAFTA.[8] As the Clinton administration grew increasingly desperate to find votes in support of the measure, Esteban Torres (D-Calif.) organized a group of dissidents (some, but not all, of whom were Hispanic) to hold out for concessions from the administration. By keeping the group together, and offering their votes to the administration as a bloc, Torres was able to receive, in return, the Clinton administration's backing on six of the nine conditions he had wanted added to the treaty, including a solid commitment for funding a North American Development Bank. It is instructive to note that while in the end, the majority of Latinos in Congress supported NAFTA, they did so only in return for concessions on domestic, not international, issues. After the passage of NAFTA, the free trade issue diminished once again in importance for Latino policy elites.

In practice, the only consistent and sustained foreign policy involvement by Latinos in the United States has been Cuban-American lobbying for sanctions against Castro-led Cuba. Here, however, Cuban-Americans may be the exception that proves the rule. Unlike most other Latino residents of the United States, Cuban-Americans arrived as political asylees, fleeing a newly established communist regime in Cuba. As a result, many Cuban migrants felt their decision to come to the United States as one of coercion rather than choice, and their stay in this country as one of exile rather than permanent settlement. Instituting a change of regime in Cuba has been the number-one policy goal of Cuban-Americans ever since. However, once this central policy preference is taken into account, Cuban-Americans rank other foreign policy issues about as low as do other Latinos in the United States.

In general, interventions by Latinos in the formal foreign policy arena are still quite rare. When interventions have occurred, they have not mobilized all Latino groups but rather have involved specific national subgroups on an issue-by-issue basis (i.e., Cubans on Cuba policy, Mexicans on trade issues, Central Americans on the extension of Temporary Protected Status for Central American refugees).[9]

THE FOREIGN POLICY INTERESTS OF LATIN AMERICAN IMMIGRANTS

Whereas native-born Hispanic elites traditionally have been less interested in foreign policy issues, even those issues directly affecting Latin America, recent Latin American immigrants have followed their own agendas. In many ways, the involvement of these immigrants in Latin America has been much more sustained than that of policy elites, building on day-to-day contacts with family, friends, organizations, and governments abroad. Some of their foreign policy impact is the result of the indirect consequences of these daily interactions, as in the case of remittances, rather than immigrants' active engagement in formal policymaking arenas. In other areas, such as campaign contributions and dual nationality, immigrant activists have pressed for concrete outcomes through more formal channels.

Remittances

A significant number of immigrants remit a portion of their income, in some cases a substantial portion, back to their home country.[10] Because of the increasing numbers of immigrants in the United States, remittances today are ten times what they were in 1980. Flows just to Central America and Mexico increased from nearly $1 billion in 1980 to $3.7 billion in 1990 to more than $11 billion in 1999.[11] Annual remittances in 1999 totaled more than $5.9 billion for Mexico, $1.4 billion for El Salvador, about $1.5 billion for the Dominican Republic, and more than $500 million each for Colombia and Guatemala.[12] Remittances to Mexico account for the greatest dollar amount, but as a percentage of the sending countries' exports, they are more crucial for other countries. In El Salvador, remittances equaled more than 100 percent of the value of exports in 1993, in Nicaragua over 80 percent of the value of exports in 1998, and in the Dominican Republic over 70 percent of the value of exports, whereas in Mexico remittances equal only 10 percent of the value of exports—although still almost equal to the total amount of foreign investment.[13]

Given the size of the flows, remittances may be expected to have a significant impact on sending countries' economic development. This explains why sending country governments are increasingly involved in actively maintaining ties to their expatriate communities. Several Latin American governments, for example, have established programs to organize their immigrant communities in the United States. The most fully developed are those of the Mexican government, which are designed to encourage Mexican immigrants to form associations and to prompt the membership of these organizations to remit funds and invest in their local communities of origin.

The Paisano program[14] and the Program for Mexican Communities Living Abroad (PCMLA) are two such examples. The Paisano program seeks to improve the treatment that the returning migrants receive at the hands of Mexican officials by reducing corruption and abuse.[15] Established in 1990, the PCMLA provides a wide range of services to Mexican immigrants in the United States through the Mexican consular network and first-generation immigrant organizations sponsored by the consulates, as well as channeling remittances toward local development projects.[16] Hometown associations have served as platforms for matching fund schemes that pool remittance monies with government funds and expertise, and occasionally with private sector contributions, for locally focused economic development projects.[17]

There have been similar, though weaker, efforts on the part of other sending countries' governments as well. The Dominican Republic has begun a program of cooperation with Dominican immigrant organizations in the United States, helping to establish the Dominican American Roundtable in 1997 to help coordinate and promote a common agenda for Dominicans in the United States.[18] El Salvador has also begun to conduct outreach to immigrant groups in the United States through its embassy and consulates. The Consejo Nacional para la Cultura y el Arte, the Salvadoran government agency that oversees the activities of Casas de la Cultura in El Salvador, is now working to open similar branches in the United States.[19] In fact, the Salvadoran government has made outreach one of its foreign policy objectives since the late 1990s.[20] The Guatemalan embassy is considering initiating similar outreach efforts.[21] The Colombian Ministry of Foreign Relations established the Program for the Promotion of Colombian Communities Abroad in 1996, which was intended at least initially to survey the Colombian population abroad and its needs.[22] Most of these programs are still in their beginning stages.

Campaign Fund-Raising

Political candidates from Latin America now routinely come to the United States to raise money for their campaigns in the home countries and build ties with the immigrant community abroad. For years Dominicans residing in New York have been an important source of contributions for political campaigns in the Dominican Republic. One source estimates that as much as 15 percent of the campaign funds for Dominican general elections is raised among immigrants abroad.[23] Dominican politicians routinely make trips to the city to hold fundraisers and emphasize the ties between the two communities. For instance, while running for president in 1996, Leonél Fernández capitalized on his New York upbringing, proclaiming, "I am a product of New York City."[24] The importance of these campaign funds has only increased as the Dominican community in New York has become larger, more established, and more prosperous. Incomes that, in absolute terms, are several times the norm for their compatriots in their country of origin make Dominicans resident in New York significant potential campaign donors. They probably raise hundreds of thousands of dollars for Dominican politicians, much of it raised at $150-a-head dinners in Washington Heights, Corona, or the Bronx. Peña-Gomez, one of the two front-runners in the 1996 presidential race, declared that the role of Dominicans in New York was "absolutely decisive."[25]

For politicians in the home country, the immigrant community is seen as worth placating. The possibility that immigrant campaign contributions could go to the opposing party stirs party competition and strengthens immigrants' hands in pressing their own demands. For example, by the time of the 1988 presidential elections, New Mexico, California, and Texas were well-established campaign stops for Mexican politicians in the opposition and increasingly, for the governing party of the Partido Revolucionario Institucional (PRI) as well. Governors of Mexican states met regularly with residents abroad for consultations, support, and contributions.[26] For the first time, Mexican opposition parties directly appealed to the emigrant vote in the 1988 campaign by promising dual nationality and the ability to vote from Mexican consulates in the United States. The Frente Democrático Nacional (the forerunner of the current opposition party, the Partido Revolucionario Democrático, or PRD) launched a petition drive to collect signatures from Mexican nationals in California supporting the voting rights of Mexicans in the United States.[27] The 1988 elections were a warning signal to the ruling PRI party that the Mexican expatriate electorate was up for grabs. In response, the PRI backed reforms that were high on migrants' agendas, such as dual nationality.

Dual Nationality

One of the reforms most desired by Latin American immigrants has been the recognition of dual nationality by their countries of origin. Eleven Latin American countries now allow individuals to belong as nationals to more than one country, seven of them since 1992 (see table 6.3). The increasing recognition of dual nationality in Latin America has largely been due to the fact that immigrants in the United States used their financial clout—reflected in remittances and campaign contributions—to successfully lobby the governments of their home countries. This was certainly true in the Colombian, Ecuadorian, Dominican, and Mexican cases.[28] Immigrants won concessions from political parties and legislatures in their countries of origin to regularize their status as citizens, their ownership of land, and their ease of access when returning, among other things. Dual nationality is increasingly seen as a win-win situation for both immigrants and sending countries: immigrants can regularize and formalize their ties to both sending and receiving countries, and sending states can retain ties with the citizens or ex-citizens abroad.

These successes have inspired other immigrant groups to petition and lobby for additional rights and benefits. For instance, there is increasing discussion of giving immigrants direct participation in national elections.[29] Colombia and Peru have had a system of voting through their consulates for some time; Mexico and the Dominican Republic have talked of putting similar systems into place.[30] However, Latin American governments have yet to extend political rights such as voting and election to office for their nationals abroad. The Mexican government, for instance, has drawn a clear distinction between the recognition of dual *nationality* and dual *citizenship*—the latter being nationality plus political

Table 6.3
*Recognition of Dual Nationality among Selected Countries
in the Western Hemisphere*

Country	Year
Brazil	1996
Colombia	1992
Costa Rica	1995
Dominican Republic	1994
Ecuador	1995
El Salvador	1983
Guatemala	1996
Mexico	1997
Nicaragua	2000
Panama	1972
Peru	1980
Uruguay	1919

Source: Michael Jones-Correa, "Under Two Flags: Dual Nationality in Latin America and Its Consequences for Naturalization in the United States," *International Migration Review* 35, no. 4 (2001): table 1.

rights. Although Colombia and Peru allow voting from their consulates overseas, other Latin American countries exploring the option of expatriate voting have postponed making any commitments.[31] Mexico, the Dominican Republic, and Haiti, for instance, all of which had talked of allowing voting abroad at some point, seem to have shelved the implementation of these plans indefinitely.[32] Because immigrants are important sources of campaign contributions, political candidates and parties from sending countries will continue to court them. By the same token, however, the independent power base that their financial resources allow them may be one of the reasons that sending country governments are reluctant to allow them full political citizenship. Sending countries may fear that immigrants may become political "loose cannons."[33]

ONE AREA OF OVERLAP: IMMIGRATION POLICY

The one area of collaboration (or at least joint mobilization) between Latino immigrants and U.S. native-born Latinos has been in the area of immigration policy. Until the early 1980s, native-born Hispanic policy elites were generally quiescent on immigration issues. This changed with the debate in Congress over immigration restrictions. Hispanic civil rights organizations, together with elected officials and activists, joined broader liberal coalitions seeking to block more restrictionist reforms (in particular, employer sanctions making it illegal to hire undocumented workers). In the 1984 battle over immigration, Mexican-Americans were widely perceived as being instrumental in preventing the passage of Simpson-Mazzoli Immigration Reform Act in the U.S. House of Representatives.[34] However, when the next version of immigration reform came to a vote in 1996, the Mexican-American coalition was split. Employer sanctions were still present in the bill but were tempered by legalization programs for undocumented immigrants. The first applied to illegal residents who had been in the United States since 1 January 1982, and the second was a special program for agricultural workers. The bill included safeguards "designed to prevent employment discrimination against foreign-looking and foreign-sounding citizens and legal aliens," and existing prohibitions against employment discrimination were expanded to prohibit discrimination on the basis of citizenship status.[35] The Immigration Reform and Control Act of 1986 (or IRCA, as it became known) passed with the votes of five Latino members in favor, six against.[36]

Eight years later, Hispanic policy elites were galvanized by the passage of Proposition 187 in California, which proposed barring undocumented aliens from receiving any kind of state benefits, including education and health services. Hispanic elites interpreted the proposition as a direct attack on all Latinos, whether citizens or noncitizens. Three events in 1996 cemented Latino elite opinion on immigration. The first was the run for by presidency by then Governor Wilson of California, who based his campaign largely on an anti-immigrant platform. The second was Congress's passage of the 1996 Welfare Reform Act, which sought to keep undocumented immigrants from accessing federal public benefit programs. More drastically, it also barred permanent legal residents from participating in Social Security and food stamp programs, and it banned all new resident noncitizens from federal means-tested programs such as AFDC (Aid for Dependent Children).[37] The third event was the passage that same year of a new Immigration Act by the Republican-controlled Congress, which heightened the penalties for illegal stay in the United States and increased the provisions under which permanent residents as well as undocumented aliens could be deported.

By the late 1990s, Hispanic policy elites were active and regular participants in the ongoing immigration debates in Congress.

The 1990s were a key period for immigrant groups as well. Anti-immigrant initiatives spurred the formation of immigrant umbrella groups and alliances, particularly with labor unions and the Catholic Church, to make their case for reduced immigration restrictions. Central American immigrants, for instance, with the backing of the Catholic Church, U.S. Hispanic organizations, and sending-country governments, began lobbying for the extension of Temporary Protected Status for Central Americans who had been residing in the United States since the 1980s. The prospect of California's Proposition 187, together with Propositions 209 (scrapping state affirmative action programs in California) and 227 (ending the state's bilingual education programs in public schools) stimulated new coalitions across ethnic and racial lines. The formation of alliances among immigrants, and then between immigrants and other actors, is relatively new. However, these new coalitions have arguably already had a significant impact on recent immigration debates.

The success of these alliances, and the extent to which, at least on the immigrant restriction issue, Hispanic elites and Latin American immigrant groups are on the same page is illustrated by the rapidity with which support snowballed in support for a new immigrant amnesty. Within six months, a coalition was formed joining immigrant organizations and Latino advocacy groups, together with unions, churches, and other civil rights advocates. This coalition supported an immigrant amnesty proposal introduced by Latino legislators known as the "Latino Immigration Fairness Act" (S. 2912). The act would have allowed tens of thousands of refugees who had escaped from political unrest in El Salvador, Guatemala, Haiti, and Honduras to apply for permanent residence under a process now open to Nicaraguans and Cubans. It also proposed that illegal immigrants who had lived in the United States prior to 1986 be given the chance to apply for permanent residence (the current cutoff date is 1972) and that certain undocumented aliens be allowed to stay in the United States with their families while applying for permanent residence.[38] In November 2000, immigrant groups in New York, Houston, Los Angeles, Dallas, San Francisco, Boston, Chicago, Washington, D.C., and other cities with large Latino immigrant populations held rallies in favor of the measure.[39] However, the proposal was largely rejected by the 106th Congress, which passed a much-reduced immigration reform package, in particular setting aside any question of amnesty. Nonetheless, it is around the amnesty question that future coalitions will continue to form.

CONCLUSION

Latino approaches to foreign policy issues are divided along generational lines. With the possible exception of Cuban-Americans, the native-born Hispanic policy elite gives much greater weight to domestic policy issues than to foreign policy issues. Latino immigrants, on the other hand, have a sizable impact on their home countries through remittances and campaign funding and have translated this leverage into concrete policy gains, as in the case of dual nationality. For the most part, the approach and the agendas of Hispanic policy elites and Latino immigrants remain separate and distinct. If recent events are any indication, only the issue of immigration bridges the gap between these two sets of Latino foreign policy actors. Only here can the domestic focus of the mostly native-born Latino policy elites and the international focus of new immigrants come together comfortably.

U.S. immigration policy engages both immigrants and Latino policy elites because it has both domestic and foreign policy components. Hispanic policy elites see immigration primarily as a domestic issue, fitting in with their traditional emphasis on civil rights. Immigrants see immigration policy as a foreign policy issue, one often involving their home countries as well as the United States. Even in this area of overlap, then, there are still differences in perspectives. Furthermore, although there is agreement on the ends to be achieved, the organizational networks of Latin American immigrants and Latino elites remain, for the most part, separate. Mexican hometown associations in Los Angeles, for instance, rarely interact with the Mexican-American Legal Defense and Education Fund, which is based in Los Angeles.

A unified Latino foreign policy agenda would require, at the very least, bringing Latin American immigrant organizations into regular contact with national Hispanic policy organizations based in Washington, D.C. Some of these contacts have been initiated but would have to be sustained beyond the limited mobilization around immigration, and immigrant amnesty in particular. Whether this is likely is still far from certain. Other alliances, with unions for instance, may carry immigrant organizations away from ethnic-specific coalitions. In another scenario, contacts between national Hispanic policy elites and immigrant organizations might be strengthened and sustained, but their interests would converge around domestic issues, not foreign policy. Research shows that as the first-generation Latin American immigrants spend more time in the United States, their contributions and remittances to their countries of origin drop off precipitously. It may be that a united Latino foreign policy is a chimera—tantalizingly tempting in the distance, it will always slip away just as it lies within reach.

NOTES

1. About half of all foreign-born Latinos in 1990 arrived since 1980. The median length of residence for foreign-born Latinos in the United States in 1998 was twelve years. See U.S. Bureau of the Census, *We the American ... Hispanics,* 6.

2. Immigrants from Mexico accounted for 28 percent of the total foreign-born population in 1997. The foreign-born population from Mexico that year was about six times as large as the next-largest immigrant population.

3. For additional details and sources, see Michael Jones-Correa, "Latinos in the 21st Century" (paper commissioned by the Inter-American Dialogue and the Embassy of Japan, Summer 2000).

4. Henry Pachón and Adrián Pantoja, "Domestic vs. Foreign Policy Concerns of Latino Leaders in the U.S." (paper prepared for the Latin American Studies Association Meeting, Miami, Florida, 17 March 2000), 21; see also Public Agenda and the Tomás Rivera Policy Institute, *Here to Stay: The Domestic and International Priorities of Latino Leaders* (Claremont, CA: Tomás Rivera Policy Institute, May 1998).

5. Pachón and Pantoja, "Domestic vs. Foreign Policy Concerns."

6. Although Latino elites born in the United States tended to agree with the statement quoted here more often than those born in Latin America (81 percent versus 64 percent), a solid majority of both groups saw the policy priority of Hispanics primarily in domestic rather than international concerns. But the 'n' for foreign-born policy elites (apart from Cuban-Americans) is very small.

7. Pachón and Pantoja, "Domestic vs. Foreign Policy Concerns," 8.

8. See Arturo Santamaria Gomez, "Chicano Lobby, Indocumentados, y el TLC," *La Jornada*, 12 May 1991, cited in Denise Dresser, "Exporting Conflict: Transboundary Consequences of Mexican Politics," in *The California-Mexico Connection*, ed. Abraham Lowenthal and Katrina Burgess (Stanford, CA: Stanford University Press, 1993), 102.

9. Some, however, have argued that trade and immigration issues could form the backbone of a true Hispanic foreign policy agenda. See, for instance, Michael Jones-Correa, "New Directions for Latinos as an Ethnic Lobby in U.S. Foreign Policy," *Harvard Journal of Hispanic Policy* 9 (1995–1996): 47–49; and *Latinos, Foreign Relations and the National Interest, Second Interim Report* (Claremont, CA: Tomás Rivera Policy Institute, 28 January 2000).

10. In 1989, for example, Colombian immigrants in the United States were remitting an astonishing 17 percent of their incomes back to Colombia. Recent figures for other Latin American immigrant groups are equally impressive: Dominicans remitted 11 percent, Salvadorans 10 percent, Mexicans 8 percent, and Guatemalans 6 percent of their annual incomes. See Rodolfo de la Garza, Manuel Orozco, and Miguel Baraona, "Binational Impact of Latino Remittances," Tomás Rivera Policy Institute Brief, March 1997, 4 (table 4).

11. Manuel Orozco, "From Family Ties to Transnational Linkages: The Impact of Family Remittances to Latin America," *Pensamiento Propio*, July–December 2000, 66; Deborah Waller Meyers, "Migrant Remittances to Latin America: Reviewing the Literature," working paper, Inter-American Dialogue and Tomás Rivera Policy Institute, 1998. The Mexican state of Zacatecas, which has more than a third of its population abroad, receives more money in remittances than it does from the federal government of Mexico. Chris Kraul, "Tapping Generosity of Emigrants" *Los Angeles Times*, 8 June 2000, 1.

12. Because these estimates are based on the World Bank's figures collected from central bank data, they almost certainly underestimate the total amount of remittances to these countries.

13. See Orozco, "From Family Ties to Transnational Linkages."

14. See the Paisano program Web page, <http://www.paisano.gob.mx/> (accessed 9 February 2000). See also Patrick McDonnell, "Mexico Vows to Curb Abuses against Returning Citizens," *Los Angeles Times*, 1 December 1995, B3.

15. Manuel Orozco, "Remittances and Markets: New Players and Practices," working paper, Inter-American Dialogue and Tomás Rivera Policy Institute, 2000, 12.

16. Carlos González and Maria Esther Schumacher, "La Cooperación Internacional de México con los Mexicao-Americanos en los Estados Unidos: El Caso de PCME" in *México y Estados Unidos: Las rutas de la cooperación,* ed. Olga Pellicaer and Rafael Fernández de Castro (México D.F.: Instituto Matias Romero 1998).

17. Orozco, "Remittances and Markets," 15. Interestingly, many outreach programs in Mexico are being conducted by various state, rather than federal, governments. The governments of Zacatecas, Jalisco, and Oaxaca have all established matching programs for remittances originating from Zacatecan clubs in the United States. See R. Marquez, "Seminario Sobre Migración Internacional y desarollo en Norte y Centro América," Programa Dos Por Uno, Gobierno de Zacatecas, Mexico, May 1998, cited in Orozco, "Remittances and Markets," 18. Indeed, federal programs were implemented partly to reestablish central control over autonomous state level initiatives, like the Program for Zacateños Abroad.

18. See the Dominican American Roundtable Web site, <http://www.danr.org/register /register.html> (accessed 9 February 2000).

19. Patricia Landolt, "Salvadoran Transnationalism: Towards the Redefinition of the National Community," Working Paper 18, Program in Comparative and International Development, The Johns Hopkins University, 1997, 18. The branch in Los Angeles opened in 1996. The Salvadoran outreach effort, like the Mexican, was initiated at least as a way to reincorporate the self-mobilization of Salvadoran organizations abroad into a government-sponsored program. In Los Angeles, for instance, about forty Salvadoran organizations formed a nongovernmental umbrella group COMUNIDADES, separate from any involvement by the Salvadoran government.

20. Dirección General de Atención a la Comunidad en el Exterior, December 2000, <http://www.rree.gob.sv/sitio/sitio.nsf/pages/dgrace> (accessed February 2000).

21. Orozco, "Remittances and Markets," 14.

22. Luis Eduardo Guarnizo, "On the Political Participation of Transnational Migrants: Old Practices and New Trends" (paper presented at the Social Science Research Workshop on Immigrants, Civic Culture and Modes of Political Incorporation: A Contemporary and Historical Comparison, Santa Fe, New Mexico, 1–4 May 1997), 4.

23. Pamela Graham, "Reimagining the Nation and Defining the District: Dominican Migration and Transnational Politics," in *Caribbean Circuits: New Directions in the Study of Caribbean Migration,* ed. Patricia Pessar (New York: Center for Migration Studies 1997), 101.

24. Larry Rohter, "New York Dominicans Taking Big Role in Island Elections," *New York Times,* 29 June 1996, 21.

25. Ibid.

26. During 1990 and 1991, the governors of the states of Zacatecas, Chihuahua, Jalisco, Nayarit, Sinaloa, and Baja, California visited Los Angeles (most of them more than once) to meet with their respective *colonias.* Communities of people from Oaxaca, Durango, Michoacán, and Colima are also working to establish relationships with the governments of their home states. See Carlos Gonzalez Guttierez, "The Mexican Diaspora in California: Limits and Possibilities for the Mexican Government" in *The California-Mexico Connection,* ed. Abraham Lowenthal and Katrina Burgess (Stanford, CA: Stanford University Press 1993), 229.

27. Denise Dresser, "Exporting Conflict: Transboundary Consequences of Mexican Politics," in *The California-Mexico Connection,* ed. Abraham Lowenthal and Katrina Burgess (Stanford, CA: Stanford University Press, 1993), 100. See also "A Mexican Right

to Vote from Abroad: A Key Strategy for Expanding Mexican Democracy" (proposal presented to the Statewide Meeting of the Partido Prevolucionario Democrático, Riverside, California, 1 July 1991).

28. Michael Jones-Correa, "Under Two Flags: Dual Nationality in Latin American and Its Consequences for Naturalization in the United States," *International Migration Review* 35, no. 4 (2001): table 1.

29. See, for example, the series of articles by Raul Ross Pineda, director of Mexican Affairs, Comité de Servicio de los Amigos Americanos, Chicago, appearing in *La Jornada* during 1998.

30. See the studies commissioned by the Mexican Institute Electoral Federal on the subject, <http://www.ife.org.mx/> (accessed 9 February 2000).

31. In Colombia, the right to vote abroad preceded recognition of dual nationality. Voting for presidential candidates through Colombian consulates began in 1958.

32. Mexican proposals for allowing voting from abroad, although supported by President Vicente Fox, have not been passed as yet by the Mexican Congress. The Mexican Congress did approve an amendment in 1996 that removed a requirement that Mexicans travel to their hometowns to register to vote, which for decades effectively barred emigrants in the United States from taking part in Mexican elections (Sam Quiñones, "Death of Voting-Abroad Bill in Mexico Was Simple Math," *San Diego Union Tribune*, 3 July 1998; Sam Dillon, "Don't Be a Stranger Mexico Says to Émigrés in the U.S.," *New York Times*, 10 December 1996, 5). Since 1994 the Dominican Republic has allowed immigrants to vote in Dominican elections but still requires them to return to the island to vote, although the main parties apparently have begun setting aside at least some spots on their parties' electoral slates for Dominicans overseas (Guarnizo, "On the Political Participation of Transnational Migrants," 10). Although Haitians abroad were referred to as the 'Tenth Department' by President Aristide when he was in exile in the United States in the early 1990s, after the departure of the military government, Haiti has not implemented dual nationality, much less voting abroad. See Linda Basch, Nina Glick Schiller, and Cristina Szanton-Blanc, *Nations Unbound: Transnational Projects, Postcolonial Predicaments, and Deterritorialized Nation-States* (Basel, Switzerland: Gordon and Breach, 1994), 146–47.

33. Benedict Anderson, for instance, writes of his worries that this long-distance dabbling in home country politics could have consequences much worse than just the blurring of national political systems and an opening for opportunists. It creates, he says, "a serious politics that is at the same time unaccountable. The participant rarely pays taxes in the country in which he does his politics; he is not answerable to its judicial system; he probably does not cast even an absentee ballot in its elections because he is a citizen in a different place; he need not fear prison, torture, or death, nor need his immediate family. But, well and safely positioned in the First World, he can send money and guns, circulate propaganda, and build intercontinental computer information circuits, all of which can have incalculable consequences in the zones of their ultimate destinations." Benedict Anderson, "Exodus," *Critical Inquiry* 20 (Winter 1994): 327. These concerns have been raised from the point of view of receiving countries as well, as commentators have pointed out what they feel is the undue influence of ethnic lobbies.

34. David Ayón and Ricardo Anzaldua Montoya, "Latinos and U.S. Foreign Policy toward Latin America," in *Latin America and Caribbean Contemporary Record: vol. 5, 1985–1986*, ed. Abraham Lowenthal (New York: Holmes and Meier Publishers, 1988), 130. For another view of the Mexican-American role, see Harris N. Miller, "The Right

Thing to Do': A History of Simpson-Mazzoli," in *Clamor at the Gates: The New American Immigration,* ed. Nathan Glazer (San Francisco: Institute for Contemporary Studies 1985), 49–71, especially 64 and following.

35. Frank Bean, George Vernez, and Charles Keely, *Opening and Closing the Door: Evaluating Immigration Reform and Control* (Lanham, MD: The Rand Corporation and the Urban Institute, 1989), 25–27.

36. Christine Marie Sierra, "Latinos and the New Immigration: Responses from the Mexican American Community," in *Renato Rosaldo Lecture Series Monograph: vol. 3 1985–1986,* ed. Ignacio M. Garcia (Tucson: Mexican American Studies and Research Center, University of Arizona, 1987), 53.

37. Although there were numerous exceptions including emergency Medicaid, disaster relief, child nutrition, and some training and education, the legislation also allowed states to deny state and local benefits to some categories of immigrants if they so wished. Peter Schuck, "The Re-Evaluation of American Citizenship," *Georgetown Immigration Law Journal* 12, no. 1 (1997): 27.

38. Larry Lipman, "Striking Partisan Note, Democrats Push Immigration Bill," *St. Louis Post-Dispatch,* 27 July 2000; Nick Anderson, "Immigration Issues Top Agenda as Term Wanes," *Los Angeles Times,* 25 September 2000.

39. "Rallies Aim to Spur Republican Support for Immigrant Bill," *EFE,* 24 October 2000.

Chapter 7

Asian-Americans and U.S.-Asia Relations

Paul Y. Watanabe[1]

In pursuit of markets, raw materials, military bases, or lost souls, the United States' Pacific crossings have had a substantial impact on shaping Asia, the United States, and relations between the two. It is in these encounters as well that the foundations of the Asian-American community can be located. "The very beginning of modern Asian America," David Palumbo-Liu has written, "may be given context within a respatialization of the nation—the United States' increased involvement in the Pacific, specifically its annexation of the Philippines and Hawai'i. America's interest in the Sino-Japanese War, its war in the Pacific (and its postwar relations in that area), its concern with China's and Taiwan's position in the Cold War, its wars in Korea and Indochina, have all affected Asian-Americans profoundly, both in terms of Asians already in America and Asians who migrated to the United States."[2]

This chapter addresses Don T. Nakanishi's recent call for "renewing a search for a paradigm of Asian Pacific American politics" that takes into account "nondomestic political experiences and relationships."[3] In his contribution to an important new collection on Asian-American politics, he challenges scholars to consider "efforts by Asian Pacific Americans to influence U.S.–Asia relations, especially in advocating changes in American foreign policy toward their countries of origin; the ways in which international processes and policies related to the flow of people, money, goods, and ideas impinge on the political behavior and status of Asian Pacific Americans; and the impact of international political conflicts and domestic political crises involving Asian homelands on interethnic and intracommunity political relations involving Asian Pacific American communities."[4]

FOREIGN POLICY, INTERNATIONAL RELATIONS, AND THE MAKING OF ASIAN AMERICA

Perhaps the most important way that foreign policy and global forces have shaped the Asian-American community is through their impact on immigration. The influence, in turn, of immigration on the countries involved, on their relations with each other, and on the immigrants and their communities has been substantial. According to Michael S. Teitelbaum, "Foreign policies have both stimulated and restrained international migrations, and migrations in turn have had important impacts upon foreign policies. In the recent past, such effects have been far more important than generally perceived, and they show every sign of being on the increase."[5] Indeed, Nathan Glazer and Daniel P. Moynihan have argued that "the immigration process is the single most important determinant of American foreign policy. This process regulates the ethnic composition of the American electorate. Foreign policy responds to that ethnic composition. It responds to other things as well, but probably first of all to the primal facts of ethnicity."[6]

The histories of the groups that constitute Asian America are replete with illustrations of the ties between foreign and immigration policies. Over one hundred thirty years ago, for instance, the United States and China negotiated the Burlingame Treaty, which called on the Chinese government to facilitate the immigration of Chinese and obligated the American government to protect Chinese workers from local and state laws that persecuted them.[7] The Gentlemen's Agreement with Japan (1907–1908) influenced immigration and the well-being of Japanese living in California.[8] The relationship between foreign policy decisions and the status of Asian-Americans was also evident in the Tydings-McDuffie Act (1934), which granted future independence to the Philippines and allowed the United States to immediately designate Filipinos as aliens ineligible for citizenship who were then subjected to the prevailing limitations on passage to the United States.[9]

In his 1943 remarks to Congress, calling for repeal of Chinese exclusion, President Franklin D. Roosevelt stressed foreign policy considerations and China's role in the war effort: "We regard China not only as a partner in waging war but ... shall regard her as a partner in days of peace."[10] World War II and its aftermath have been aptly described as "the major watershed for the Asians in America"[11] that "brought about the first cracks in the wall of Asian exclusion."[12] Sucheng Chang has delineated the importance of this watershed:

World War II affected the lives of all Americans, but it had an especially profound impact on Asian immigrants and their America-born children. The lot of persons of Chinese, Korean, Filipino, and Asian Indian ancestry improved because their ancestral lands were allies of the United States. Four positive changes took place: the images held by the general public of these groups improved, some of their members finally managed to get jobs in the technical professions and skilled trades, sizable numbers of Chinese and Filipinos joined and served in the armed forces, and immigration exclusion was lifted for the Chinese in 1943 and for Filipino and Asian Indians in 1946 after the war ended. Individuals of Japanese ancestry along the Pacific Coast, in contrast, were confined in concentration camps, even as a very large percentage of draft-age Nisei served with distinction in the army and died for their country.[13]

The aftermath of World War II and the immediate onset of the Cold War continued to mold the contours of the Asian-American community. In many respects, the nature of the relationships established during World War II flip-flopped, as, for example, "defeated Japan became America's 'junior partner' in 'containing' communism, while China went Communist and became a feared enemy."[14] During the Cold War, for many of the nations linked to Asian-Americans, the hot wars persisted.

These engagements—both cold and hot—have dramatically affected the size and diversity of Asian America. They and other forces active in the international milieu—such as the rapidly globalized world economy—have resulted in refugees and immigrants from traditional sources of immigration, such as China, the Philippines, Korea, and India, and from newer points of origin such as Southeast Asia, Pakistan, and Bangladesh.[15] Viewed in this manner, "the influx of Indochinese refugees to the United States was part and parcel of a larger ideological effort to lean the balance of the Cold War toward the Free World, the insertion of those Indochinese refugees into America took place within a narrative of Americanization and global politicking."[16]

Even before the large-scale arrival of Southeast Asians beginning in the 1970s, the 1965 Immigration Act's removal of national and de facto racial restrictions on immigration was partially intended to portray the United States in the midst of the Cold War as open and free of discrimination. In a related argument, Robert G. Lee has asserted that the popular designation of Asian-Americans as a "model minority" had its origins in Cold War posturing. "The representation of Asian-Americans as a model minority, although popularly identified with the late 1960s and 1970s, originated in the racial logic of Cold War liberalism of the 1950s. The image of Asian-Americans as a successful case of 'ethnic' assimilation helped to contain three spectres that haunted Cold War America: the red menace of communism, the black menace of racial integration, and the white menace of homosexuality."[17]

As the Japanese-American internment and other experiences have demonstrated, the fate and well-being of Asian-Americans have been connected to foreign events and actions in more ways than immigration and naturalization policies. From the internment and the campaign finance hysteria to the hounding of Wen Ho Lee, the fate of Asian-Americans has been affected in substantial and often damaging ways by what has been happening in U.S. foreign relations. At times, this has led to limits on immigration and outright exclusion, restrictions on legal rights, and anti–Asian-American violence. In the new world of an emergent Asia, for example, many of the concerns about the United States' relative standing in the global economic picture have been blamed on Asian competitors.

Much of this suspicion and blame has been easily redirected at Asian-Americans because of the pernicious tendency to blur the line between Asian-Americans now (i.e., residents of the United States) and their ancestors' country of origin, no matter how long they have lived in America.[18] Talk show hosts and commentators calling for boycotts of Chinese-American businesses during the 2001 spy plane flap with China were singing a sorry, but familiar tune.

Asian-Americans, of course, have been affected at times not only by relations between the United States and Asian countries specifically but also by the machinations of U.S. foreign relations generally. Among the most disturbing legacies of the September 11 tragedy, for example, has been the targeting and abuse of Sikh-Americans and other South Asians by individuals and governmental officials. These groups have been caught up in a broad net of suspicion and harassment that has been driven either by their being misidentified as Arab or Muslim or by willful efforts by some to lump all immigrants together as prospective terrorist sympathizers.

ASIAN-AMERICANS AND THE MAKING OF FOREIGN POLICY

According to a popular conception, immigrant communities, early in their experience, are focused on politics abroad, but in succeeding generations interest and involvement in nondomestic issues wane considerably. Assuredly, for some Asian-American immigrants, the passage of time and experience in the United States has resulted in the loosening of their attachments to their homelands. However, for Asian-Americans in the decades to come, Nakanishi maintains that the likelihood of declining interest will be mitigated by "the changing political economic conditions in states such as California, Washington, and Hawaii for Asian Pacific Americans and other groups. For example, large numbers of second- and third-generation Asian Pacific Americans, particularly those in business, law, journalism, high technology, and academics, are visibly involved in emerging Pacific Rim affairs and, more generally, in the structural transformations stemming from the internationalization of the political economies of many states."[19]

Over the years, Asian-American activism on foreign policy considerations has been irregular, but far from nonexistent.[20] Around the passage of the Burlingame Treaty of 1868, mentioned earlier, the fabled Chinese Six Companies engaged in intense lobbying. Chinese-Americans have been active as well on both sides of the China question. The Asian Indian community was engaged in foreign policy, particularly concerning the issue of Indian independence, through the efforts of associations such as the Ghadar Party, the Indian Welfare League, the Friends for the Freedom of India, the India Home Rule League, and the India League of America.[21] Filipino-Americans were involved early in the Philippine independence movement and much later in efforts to curtail the United States' support of the Marcos regime.[22] Korean-American activists have supported Korean nationalism or, in the case of organizations such as Young Koreans United, reunification.[23] Among the more recent immigrants from Southeast Asia, many Vietnamese-Americans mobilized around the issue of U.S. recognition and reconciliation, and they remain heavily focused on economic, political, and cultural relations with Vietnam. Cambodian-Americans have sought support for measures aimed at restoring Cambodia's economic health and political order after the ravages imposed by Pol Pot. Their most recent activism has been aimed at garnering support from the United States and other nations for free and fair elections. The Bush administration's post–September 11 "war on terrorism" has been accompanied by Asian-American communities, including Pakistanis and Sikhs, diligently monitoring the content and consequences (both foreign and domestic) of the United States' actions.

Contemporary efforts by activists to influence foreign policy discourse have relied increasingly on information technologies unavailable to earlier generations. The Internet and e-mail, for example, have allowed activists to communicate their messages more rapidly, broadening their reach considerably. For Asian-Americans especially, the Internet has been a particularly useful tool. According to a survey conducted by the Pew Internet and American Life Project, "Asian Pacific Americans who speak English are among the heaviest users of the Internet."[24]

Asian-American efforts to influence foreign policy have not always been welcomed and at times have met with determined resistance. Without too much exaggeration, it can be said that foreign policy activism by Asian-Americans on balance has been more discouraged than encouraged, more derided than applauded. Indeed, Asian-Americans have been promoted as a "model minority" despite an uneven record of political involvement in general and especially in the foreign policy realm.

This treatment is consistent with a general tendency of the public and policymakers to view ethnic group involvement in matters of external policy with concern and suspicion.[25] In an article in *Foreign Affairs*, former U.S. Senator Charles McCurdy Mathias, Jr., conveyed the well-established concern about ethnic group activism and foreign policy: "The desirable alternative is the encouragement on the part of ethnic groups of an entirely voluntary appreciation of what Irving Howe has called the 'limits of ethnicity' and the 'grandeur of the American idea.' Ethnicity enriches our life and culture, and for that purpose should be valued and preserved; but the problems of the modern world and their solution have broken past the boundaries of ethnic group, race and nation."[26] In a more recent piece also in *Foreign Affairs*, Samuel P. Huntington noted disapprovingly that since the end of the Cold War, demographic changes in the United States have meant that "Americans have become unable to define their national interests," and consequently, "transnational and nonnational ethnic interests have come to dominate foreign policy."[27]

Asian-Americans, who have been consistently racialized as disguised foreigners, have been especially discouraged from foreign policy–related interests and activities, and they have been forced to confront a double-barreled assault.

They were once barred from naturalizing, and they faced exclusion and de-meaning discrimination. Everything possible has been done to treat them as out-siders regardless of whether they wished to assimilate.[28] Simultaneously, these Asian immigrants and their successors have also been condemned for "behav-ing foreign" and displaying any inkling of interest in the politics of and U.S. pol-icy toward their nations of origin. As Arif Dirlik has noted:

This discourse rendered Asians into permanent foreigners, culturally and even geneti-cally incapable of becoming "real" Americans, an attitude that would serve as a justifi-cation for their exclusion from 1882 through World War II. This exclusion did not extinguish memories of ties to their native origins, or even their involvement in poli-tics in their nations of origin, but it did turn affirmation of such ties into a further liability. Even where consciousness of origins was weak, as with generations born in the United States, the very "Asianness" of Americans of Asian descent was deemed to preclude their becoming "real" Americans.[29]

At times, the government's efforts to combat Asian-Americans suspected of harmful foreign policy activities have been ruthless. In the case of Chinese-Americans after the communist victory in 1949, for example, although it was difficult to gauge the Chinese-American community's political support for the new mainland government, the United States took no chances. According to Robert G. Lee:

The fear of Red China extended to the Chinese-American community. ... The pro-Chiang Kai-shek Chinatown elite, working with the FBI, launched a systematic at-tempt to suppress any expression of support for the new communist regime in China. The Trading with the Enemy Act, which prohibited any currency transfers to the Peoples Republic of China, including remittances to family, was used as a tool to at-tempt to deport suspected communist sympathizers. Although only a few leftists and labor leaders were actually deported, the threat of deportation had a deeply chilling effect, since many hundreds of Chinese had come to the United States as "paper sons" during the long decades of exclusion and were in the United States under false pre-tenses.[30]

Similarly, the U.S. government, in support of its British ally, deported several anticolonial activists in the Indian-American community.[31]

TRANSITIONS AND TRANSNATIONALISM

The economic, political, social, and cultural ties between the United States and Asian nations and conditions in the United States and those countries have com-bined to shape the complex and perhaps contradictory construction of contem-porary Asians in America.[32] Recently, globalization has joined with other forces to stimulate what some scholars describe as a process of transition from a col-lective Asian-American identity grounded in domestic experiences to separate Asian-American ethnic identities molded largely by transnational factors. Asian-

Americans are left to struggle with what Arif Dirlik has called "the contradiction between the global and the local as structuring moments in contemporary society."[33] "The emergence of Pacific Asian economies as key players in the global economy has had a transformative effect on the Asian-American self-image, as well as on the perceptions of Asian-Americans in the society at large," Dirlik has observed. "This has introduced new burdens on being Asian-American and has complicated the very notion of Asian America to a point at which it may break apart under the force of its contradictions. Especially important, I suggest, is the increasing ambiguity in the conceptualization of Asian America of Asian populations as members of grounded communities versus as diasporic 'Rimpeople.'"[34]

The manner in which these myriad transformations work themselves out is critically important to Asian-Americans. Certain identifications spurred on by globalization, for example, may result in enhanced involvement in external affairs, potentially jeopardizing the community-centered orientations that have been driving forces in Asian-American politics. Although it remains highly debatable whether the prospects for pan–Asian-American political activities in the domestic realm will be permanently damaged, it does seem likely that in the future as in the past, it will be exceedingly difficult to achieve Asian-American unity around a shared foreign policy agenda.

Indeed, foreign politics and policies have often fed lingering hostilities. Perhaps nothing has contributed more to the promulgation of "nationally defined ethnic self-perceptions" than foreign policy.[35] Whether because of tenacious historical antagonisms or prevailing national differences, Asian-Americans generally have become interested and involved in foreign policy not as a collective body, that is, as Asian-Americans, but as particular Asian-American ethnic groups, such as Chinese-Americans, Korean-Americans, and Vietnamese-Americans. Issues such as the status of Kashmir and Tibet and responses to the legacy of Japanese imperialism in the first half of the twentieth century have considerably strained any attempts to establish a pan–Asian-American foreign policy consensus. When it comes to bridge building, therefore, Asian-Americans face challenges in spanning their differences over foreign policy.

Furthermore, external matters may exacerbate divisions not only between but also within specific Asian-American groups. In his examination of the workings of the Kuomintang Party in the United States, Him Mark Lai observed that "the concern of the party with events in China frequently led to the injection of homeland political conflicts and struggles into the Chinese-American communities, which often proved divisive and prevented cooperation for the common good."[36] In sizing up the more recent landscape, Yen Le Espiritu has written, "The Chinese, Filipino, Korean, Asian Indian, and Vietnamese American communities continue to be divided among themselves over the politics of their countries of origin. Some of these political differences have sparked violence."[37]

Espiritu, however, has contested the view that schisms engendered by international forces must continue to manifest themselves in unbridgeable divisions among Asian-Americans. Although mindful of the powerful centrifugal forces at play, she nonetheless has argued that with the passage of time and experience in the United States, the saliency of divisive tendencies recedes, allowing centripetal forces to emerge: "As various groups in the United States interacted, they became aware of common problems and goals that transcended parochial interests and historical antagonisms."[38]

The problematic identifications of Asian-Americans have had an impact on how Asian-Americans have seen themselves and also on how outsiders have treated them. Governmental agencies, for example, have at times dealt with Asian-Americans in a disaggregated fashion with disintegrative ends, selectively wooing and abusing certain communities as their interests dictate. Reflective of one formulation, to use General John DeWitt and others' language to justify the internment of Japanese-Americans, "a 'Jap' is a 'Jap.'" At other times, in what Espiritu describes as "Asian lumping," Asian-Americans have been accounted for as an undifferentiated mass.[39] Anti–Asian-American violence, for example, has targeted Asian-Americans broadly.[40] Here the stance seems to be "all Asian-Americans are 'Gooks.'"

Some observers have maintained that in the long run, transnationalism will contribute to the loosening up of the nation-state, fostering a more receptive attitude toward differences. There is ample evidence to indicate, however, that enhanced global linkages do not necessarily hasten the liberalization of attitudes and policies toward immigrants and immigration. In the period after World War I, for example, when the United States emerged as a significant world power, nativists and immigration restrictionists succeeded in making the argument that the United States' new role required greater nationalism, internal unity, and as a consequence, greater suspicion of immigrants and greater opposition to immigration. This culminated in the passage of the 1924 Immigration Act, which significantly controlled large-scale immigration and virtually curtailed all Asian immigration, which already had been greatly reduced by earlier legislation.[41] More recently, the anti-immigrant fervor of the last two decades reflects a similar relationship between rising tides of immigration from Asia and Latin America and determined reactionary responses.

In analyzing the knotty problem of racial and ethnic identities, one should remember that those identities are often imposed rather than chosen. "Asian/American identity politics," Palumbo-Liu has noted, "is therefore not a matter of simple choice between Asia or America, but rather produced within a complex set of material histories."[42] The nature of the attributes and attachments assigned has important consequences. As Rick Bonus has noted in his important study of Filipino-Americans, "Many Filipino-Americans contend that years of formal and covert exclusion from mainstream political, social, and economic institutions on the basis of their race and placement in the global capitalist system have perpetuated racist stereotypes about them, ignored their colonial immigration history, and prevented them from becoming fully recognized citizens of the nation."[43]

CONCLUSION

It cannot be stressed too much that the critical question of Asian-American identity is important because of its role in defining political behavior, especially in
the foreign policy area, and formulating policy agendas. Rather than permanently selecting one identity over another—for example, globalized versus lo-
calized—it seems that many Asian-Americans, if allowed to do so, have been
flexible, choosing or operationalizing a particular dimension dependent upon
particular political interests, objectives, and conditions. Bill Ong Hing has characterized this process as "situational political mobilization,"[44] and he asserts that
"the flexibility of the situational model permits more than one mobilization response without foreclosing the possibility of others in different contexts, in light
of different issues."[45] In a similar vein, L. Ling-chi Wang has argued that Asian-
Americans may assume multiple identities. In his examination of the Chinese
community in the United States, for example, Wang observed that there are different "types of Chinese-American identity" that are "brought about by changes
in China, in the United States, in US-China relations, and in Chinese perceptions of themselves in relation to these changes."[46]

One should not exaggerate the notion that Asian-Americans can choose and
act in accordance politically with their desired identities. Although the hope of
Asian-Americans is to fashion their own fundamental identities, experience indicates that assigned attributes such as permanent outsider status built on the
twin pillars of racism and nativism will continue to define and delimit their political activities and societal well-being. "The history of Asians in America,"
Sucheng Chan has reminded us, "can be fully understood only if we regard them
as both immigrants and members of nonwhite minority groups. As immigrants,
many of their struggles resemble those that European immigrants have faced,
but as a people of nonwhite origins bearing distinct physical differences, they
have been perceived as 'perpetual foreigners' who can never be completely absorbed into American society and its body politic."[47] At the same time, one
should pay heed to Rick Bonus's observations, which, although they focus on
Filipino-Americans, could apply as well to other Asian-Americans:

Filipino-Americans who want to be included also want a *different* kind of inclusion, on
terms other than full assimilation. They want to be assimilated and integrated, but in
ways that will not erase their identities as Filipinos. They want to be included, but in
ways in which their representations will also amount to a recognition of them as citizens entitled to an equal share of power. As their identities are transformed in the new
place of settlement, they want to transform the ways in which the nation incorporates
them.[48]

In a curious way, therefore, American society's proclivity to marginalize Asian-
Americans may coincide with a desire of Asian-Americans to seek "a different
kind of inclusion." Perhaps Asian-Americans can navigate through the puzzle
of their many selves by fully rejecting none of them and by reconceptualizing

all of them. The challenge for the United States, in turn, is to rethink and re-formulate its politics and practices to make room for the diverse attachments ac-companying persistent local and pressing global exigencies that continually tug at Asian-Americans from many directions.

NOTES

1. A version of this chapter originally appeared in *PS: Political Science & Politics* 34, no. 3 (2001): 639–44.

2. David Palumbo-Liu, *Asian/America: Historical Crossings of a Racial Frontier* (Stanford, CA: Stanford University Press, 1999), 218.

3. Don T. Nakanishi, "Beyond Electoral Politics: Renewing a Search for a Paradigm of Asian Pacific American Politics," in *Asian-Americans and Politics: Perspectives, Experiences, Prospects,* ed. Gordon H. Chang (Washington, DC: Woodrow Wilson Center Press; Stanford, CA: Stanford University Press, 2001), 106.

4. Ibid., 106–7.

5. Michael S. Teitelbaum, "International Relations and Asian Migration," in *Pacific Bridges: The New Immigration from Asia and the Pacific Islands,* ed. James T. Fawcett and Benjamin V. Carino (Staten Island, NY: Center for Migration Studies, 1987), 72–73.

6. Nathan Glazer and Daniel Patrick Moynihan, eds., introduction to *Ethnicity: Theory and Practice* (Cambridge, MA: Harvard University Press, 1975), 23–24.

7. L. Ling-chi Wang, "Roots and Changing Identity of the Chinese in the United States," *Daedalus* 120 (1991): 181–206.

8. Roger Daniels, *The Politics of Prejudice: The Anti-Japanese Movement in California and the Struggle for Japanese Exclusion* (Berkeley and Los Angeles: University of California Press, 1962); Akira Iriye, *Pacific Estrangement: Japanese and American Expansion, 1897–1911* (Cambridge, MA: Harvard University Press 1972).

9. John M. Liu, Paul M. Ong, and Carolyn Rosenstein, "Dual Chain Migration: Post-1965 Filipino Immigration to the United States," *International Migration Review* 25 (1991): 487–513.

10. Quoted in Roger Daniels, "Changes in Immigration Law and Nativism since 1924," in *The History and Immigration of Asian-Americans,* ed. Franklin Ng (New York: Garland, 1998), 71.

11. Franklin Ng, ed., introduction to *The History and Immigration of Asian-Americans* (New York: Garland), x.

12. Bill Ong Hing, *Making and Remaking of Asian America through Immigration Policy, 1950–1990* (Stanford, CA: Stanford University Press, 1993), 36.

13. Sucheng Chan, *Asian-Americans: An Interpretive History* (Boston: Twayne, 1991), 121.

14. Ibid., 142.

15. See Illsoo Kim, "Korea and East Asia: Premigration Factors and U.S. Immigration Policy," in *Pacific Bridges: The New Immigration from Asia and the Pacific Islands,* ed. James T. Fawcett and Benjamin V. Carino (Staten Island, NY: Center for Migration Studies, 1987); and Urmil Minocha, "South Asian Immigrants: Trends and Impacts on the Sending and Receiving Societies," in *Pacific Bridges: The New Immigration from Asia and the Pacific Islands,* ed. James T. Fawcett and Benjamin V. Carino (Staten Island, NY: Center for Migration Studies, 1987).

16. Palumbo-Liu, *Asian/American*, 238–39.

17. Robert G. Lee, *Orientals: Asian-Americans in Popular Culture* (Philadelphia: Temple University Press, 1999), 10.

18. Claire Jean Kim, "The Racial Triangulation of Asian-Americans," in *Asian-Americans and Politics: Perspectives, Experiences, Prospects,* ed. Gordon H. Chang (Washington, DC: Woodrow Wilson Center Press; Stanford, CA: Stanford University Press, 2001); Setsuko Matsunaga Nishi, "Asian-Americans at the Intersection of International and Domestic Tensions: An Analysis of Newspaper Coverage," in *Across the Pacific: Asian-Americans and Globalization,* ed. Evelyn Hu-DeHart (Philadelphia: Temple University Press, 1999).

19. Nakanishi, "Beyond Electoral Politics," 120.

20. Paul Y. Watanabe, "Asian-American Activism and U.S. Foreign Policy," in *Across the Pacific: Asian-Americans and Globalization,* ed. Evelyn Hu-DeHart (Philadelphia: Temple University Press, 1999).

21. See Gary R. Hess, "The Forgotten Asian-Americans: The East Indian Community in the United States," *Pacific Historical Review* 43 (1974): 576–96; Sanjeev Khagram, Manish Desai, and Jason Varughese, "Seen, Rich, but Unheard? The Politics of Asian Indians in the United States," in *Asian-Americans and Politics: Perspectives, Experiences, Prospects,* ed. Gordon H. Chang (Washington, DC: Woodrow Wilson Center Press; Stanford, CA: Stanford University Press, 2001); Karen Isaksen Leonard, *The South Asian-Americans* (Westport, CT: Greenwood Press, 1997); Minocha, "South Asian Immigrants."

22. Karin Aguilar-San Juan, "Linking the Issues: From Identity to Activism," in *The State of Asian America: Activism and Resistance in the 1990s,* ed. Karin Aguilar-San Juan (Boston: South End Press, 1994); Madge Bello and Vincent Reyes, "Filipino Americans and the Marcos Overthrow: The Transformation of Consciousness," *Amerasia* 13, no. 1 (1986–1987): 73–83; Rick Bonus, *Locating Filipino Americans: Ethnicity and the Cultural Politics of Space* (Philadelphia: Temple University Press, 2000); Benjamin V. Carino, "The Philippines and Southeast Asia: Historical Roots and Contemporary Linkages," in *Pacific Bridges: The New Immigration from Asia and the Pacific Islands,* ed. James T. Fawcett and Benjamin V. Carino (Staten Island, NY: Center for Migration Studies, 1987).

23. Kingsley K. Lyu, "Korean Nationalist Activities in Hawaii and the Continental United States, 1900–1945," *Amerasia* 4 (1977): 23–89; Gary Y. Okihiro, *Margins and Mainstreams: Asians in American History and Culture* (Seattle: University of Washington Press, 1994); Glenn Omatsu, "The 'Four Prisons' and the Movements of Liberation: Asian-American Activism from the 1960s to the 1990s," in *The State of Asian America: Activism and Resistance in the 1990s,* ed. Karin Aguilar-San Juan (Boston: South End Press, 1994).

24. Anick Jesdanun, "Asian Pacific Americans among Top Net Users," *AsianWeek* 23, no. 20 (2002): 8.

25. Paul Y. Watanabe, *Ethnic Groups, Congress, and American Foreign Policy: The Politics of the Turkish Arms Embargo* (Westport, CT: Greenwood Press, 1984).

26. Charles McCurdy Mathias, Jr., "Ethnic Groups and Foreign Policy," *Foreign Affairs* 59 (1981): 998.

27. Samuel P. Huntington, "The Erosion of American National Interests," *Foreign Affairs* 76, no. 5 (1997): 29.

28. Angelo N. Ancheta, *Race, Rights and the Asian American Experience* (New Brunswick, NJ: Rutgers University Press, 1998); Frank Wu, *Yellow: Race in American beyond Black and White* (New York: Basic Books, 2001).

29. Arif Dirlik, "Asians on the Rim: Transnational Capital and Local Community in the Making of Contemporary Asian America," in *Across the Pacific: Asian-Americans and Globalization*, ed. Evelyn Hu-DeHart (Philadelphia: Temple University Press, 1999), 32.

30. Lee, *Orientals*, 152.

31. Joan M. Jensen, *Passage from India: Asian Indian Immigration in North America* (New Haven, CT: Yale University Press, 1988).

32. Lucie Cheng and Edna Bonacich, *Labor Immigration under Capitalism: Asian Workers in the United States before World War II* (Berkeley: University of California Press, 1984); James T. Fawcett and Benjamin V. Carino, eds., *Pacific Bridges: The New Immigration from Asia and the Pacific Islands* (Staten Island, NY: Center for Migration Studies, 1987); Evelyn Hu-DeHart, ed., *Across the Pacific: Asian-Americans and Globalization* (Philadelphia: Temple University Press, 1999); Shirley Hune, Stephen S. Fugita, and Amy Ling., eds., *Asian-Americans: Comparative and Global Perspectives* (Pullman: Washington State University Press, 1991); Okihiro, *Margins and Mainstreams*; Paul M. Ong, Edna Bonacich, and Lucie Cheng, eds., *The New Asian Immigration in Los Angeles and Global Restructuring* (Philadelphia: Temple University Press, 1994).

33. Dirlik, "Asians on the Rim," 30.

34. Ibid., 31.

35. Ibid., 36.

36. Him Mark Lai, "The Kuomintang in Chinese American Communities before World War II," in *Entry Denied: Exclusion and the Chinese Community in America, 1882–1943*, ed. Sucheng Chan (Philadelphia: Temple University Press, 1991), 199.

37. Yen Le Espiritu, *Asian-American Panethnicity: Bridging Institutions and Identities* (Philadelphia: Temple University Press, 1992), 60.

38. Ibid., 30.

39. Ibid., 140.

40. Nishi, "Asian-Americans at the Intersection of International and Domestic Tensions."

41. Hing, *Making and Remaking of Asian America*.

42. Palumbo-Liu, *Asian/American*, 310.

43. Bonus, *Locating Filipino Americans*, ix–x.

44. Hing, *Making and Remaking of Asian America*, 181.

45. Ibid., 182.

46. Wang, "Roots and Changing Identity of the Chinese in the United States," 192.

47. Chan, *Asian-Americans*, 187.

48. Bonus, *Locating Filipino Americans*, 28.

Chapter 8

Entangling Alliances: The Turkish-Israeli Lobbying Partnership and Its Unintended Consequences

Thomas Ambrosio[1]

> The Israeli lobby in the U.S. is far superior to all other ethnic lobbies put
> together. Whenever this lobby has worked for us, Turkey's interests have
> been perfectly protected against the fools in the U.S. The development
> of relations between Turkey and Israel and the formalization of their
> de facto alliance will place this lobby permanently on our side.

—Sükrü Elekdag, former Turkish ambassador to the United States[2]

In the mid-1990s, Israel and Turkey entered into a de facto alliance in order to further their security goals. Turkey gained access to Israeli technology, and its newfound relationship with the Jewish state helped to reinforce its own relationship with Israel's principal ally, the United States. Israel, too, hoped to benefit from closer ties with Ankara: Turkey's secular orientation and geographic contiguity to three enemies of Israel (Syria, Iraq, and Iran) made it a welcome ally in an often dangerous region. Although this relationship was important for geopolitics in the Middle East, it also had significant implications for interest group politics in the United States: pro-Israeli and pro-Turkish lobbies formed their own alliance on Capitol Hill, largely in support of the Turkish policy agenda and its close ally, Azerbaijan. This led to a number of uncomfortable situations that strained the Israeli lobby's relations with other ethnic groups, particularly the Armenians.[3]

This case is particularly interesting for a number of reasons. First, the Middle East's geopolitical significance is undeniable. The policies of Israel and Turkey and their respective relationships with the United States have important implications for the balance of power within the Middle East. Second, the Jewish-American lobby is the most powerful ethnic lobby in the United States and among the most powerful of all American interest groups. The policies it chooses to support and its relations with other lobbies impact both domestic political constellations and U.S. foreign policy abroad. Finally, the alliance between Jewish-American groups and the Turkish lobby clearly illustrates the connection between strategic interests and the interests of domestic lobbying groups. Ethnic interest groups are normally concerned with their homeland and ethnic kin, but they also have to consider the web of strategic relations that affect their homeland before taking a stand on certain issues. This connection gives credence to those who argue for a two-level (domestic and international) theoretical model of international relations or, quite possibly, for a "second image reversed" model—that is, international forces having a marked impact on domestic political alignments.[4]

This chapter examines the rise and repercussions of the Turkish-Israeli lobbying alliance during the latter half of the 1990s. In particular, it explores three connected questions. What is the relationship between the strategic interests of an ethnic group's homeland and its lobbying activities in the United States? How do ethnic lobbies interact with other such groups when the strategic interests of their respective homelands conflict? How does support for an ally within the domestic arena force an interest group to take positions on issues indirectly related to the overall basket of issues upon which it normally advocates for or against?

After providing a brief overview of the Israeli-Turkish strategic alliance, this chapter examines each of these questions in turn. First, Jewish-American interest groups as a whole actively supported the policy agenda of the Turkish lobby in an effort to bolster Israel's security interests. Second, the Jewish lobby's relationship with Turkey forced them to confront a historic ally: through its support for Azerbaijan, the Israeli lobby came into conflict with Armenian-Americans. Finally, Jewish support for Turkish interests led them to an issue that they would have rather not dealt with: the Armenian Genocide resolution. In essence, some Jewish-American organizations found themselves in the very uncomfortable position of de facto support for what their historical friends (and even some in the Jewish community) have labeled "genocide deniers."[5] The conclusion of this essay will make some observations about the importance of international-level factors on ethnic lobby politics and also offer some thoughts on the ongoing relations between Armenian-American and Jewish-American advocacy groups in light of the continuing (and strengthening) relationship between Israel and Turkey.

THE ISRAELI-TURKISH STRATEGIC ALLIANCE

The rapprochement between Israel and Turkey during the 1990s has had a profound effect on the strategic balance in the Middle East. Both Israel and Turkey are outsiders in this often hostile region dominated by Muslim-Arab states, and an alliance between them seems natural, especially given each state's close ties with the United States. A number of scholars have examined this budding relationship; this section serves as a summary designed to frame the relationship in a historical context and to identify the benefits each side hopes to accrue.[6]

The positive relationship between Turks and Jews goes back to the Spanish Inquisition, when Sultan Bayezid II of the Ottoman Empire offered sanctuary to many Jews expelled from Spain. When the Ottoman Empire collapsed and Mustafa Kemal Atatürk founded the secular and Western-oriented state of Turkey, he adopted a policy that opposed manifestations of anti-Semitism and allowed Jews to organize Jewish emigration to Palestine. Many of the Sephardic Jews from Turkey who live in Israel retain a strong identification with their former state and have vocally supported a pro-Ankara foreign policy.

Despite some ambiguity in Turkey's policy toward the 1947 United Nations General Assembly partition resolution that created the Jewish state, Ankara had recognized Israel by 1949 (the first Muslim state to do so) and established commercial ties. However, its diplomatic relations were limited to the level of legation, which meant that there was no formal exchange of ambassadors. This proscribed relationship was caused by Ankara's desire to convince Arab states to join the nascent Baghdad Pact during the first half of the 1950s. Once this failed, relations between Turkey and Israel blossomed in 1958 into what came to be known as the Peripheral Pact, which called for closer cooperation in the diplomatic, military, and intelligence spheres.

The Peripheral Pact was not fully implemented, and the relationship between Israel and Turkey was once again downgraded. Instead, Ankara adopted a policy of "benevolent neutrality," which attempted to maintain courteous, but not close, relations with both Arabs and Israelis. "As a Muslim country and a member of the Organization of the Islamic Conference, Turkey has always had to walk a tightrope between its interest in maintaining a relationship with Israel and its cultural, economic, historical, and emotional commitment to Islam."[7] However, in an attempt to bolster its influence in the United States during the mid-1980s, Ankara once again turned to Israel, and Turkish prime minister Turgut Özal "openly relied on the sympathy of the influential Jewish lobby to reach his aim."[8]

A sea change in Ankara's policy toward Israel came as a result of the aftermath of the Cold War and the Persian Gulf War. The collapse of the Warsaw Pact and the Soviet Union made Turkey's role in the North Atlantic Treaty Organization (NATO) less relevant, as the alliance's southern flank ceased to be a matter of critical concern for the West. Moreover, the political and social tensions between Turkey and the West, which were largely overlooked because of Turkey's strategic importance, now entered into the open as Ankara's record on human rights and democratization came under heightened scrutiny. Consequently, Ankara saw its relations with the West, and especially the United States, strained. Finally, the Persian Gulf War triggered a renewed Arab-Israeli peace process. Improved relations between Arab states and Israel made it easier for Ankara to have a close relationship with Tel Aviv[9] without jeopardizing its ties with Arab states.

In November 1993, Hikmet Çetin became the first Turkish foreign minister to visit Israel. After that, bilateral relations improved at a dizzying rate. The next year, Turkish prime minister Tansu Çiller visited Israel "with a full agenda, ranging from discussions on a free-trade agreement to joint projects in agriculture, defence-related industries, tourism, transport, telecommunications and water resources."[10] In February 1996, the two countries signed a military cooperation agreement, which provided for the exchange of military information, personnel, and technology. Moreover, intelligence ties have been strengthened, and a series of joint-training exercises have been held since the mid-1990s. This increased cooperation has not been limited to the military sphere: trade, industry, social, and educational relations were also intensified during the 1990s.

Despite perceptions in the Arab world that the recent impetus for the Israeli-Turkish alliance came from Tel Aviv,[11] Turkey has taken the initiative in courting Israel. Ankara sees a number of benefits arising out of its newfound alliance. The most important is that through Israel, and especially the pro-Israeli lobby in the United States, Turkey's influence in and ties to Washington will be strengthened: "For many countries, including Turkey, Israel is important as a conduit for access to the only remaining superpower. In short, the road to Washington leads through Jerusalem. This belief derives in part from the fact that Israel enjoys a privileged and intimate relationship with the United States, and in part from the myth of America's 'redoubtable' and 'omnipotent' Jewish lobby."[12] America's Turkish policy has long been assailed by the Greek and Armenian lobbies in Washington, and comparatively, the Turkish lobby is far weaker than its rivals. Although the strategic alliance between Turkey and Israel has military and security implications—such as sharing intelligence information, fighting terrorism, and purchasing high-tech military systems—from Turkey's perspective, the most important aspect is the lobbying alliance.

Although Turkey seems to benefit significantly from its alliance with Israel, the relationship is not one-sided. Despite Turkey's sometimes ambivalent policy toward Israel, Israel consistently sought better relations with Turkey ever since the Jewish state was established. Tel Aviv has long sought to overcome its geographic isolation by leapfrogging its immediate neighbors and seeking allies on the periphery of the Middle East. At various times during the Cold War, Turkey, Iran, and Ethiopia played this role. However, the Marxist revolution in Ethiopia (1974) and the fall of the Shah of Iran (1979) eliminated these two states as potential allies. Consequently, Israel focused on improving relations with Turkey. "The combination of Turkey's military power, its strategic location bordering Iran, Iraq, and Syria, and its close ideologically affinity with Israel [secular, Western-oriented, and largely democratic], make Turkey an invaluable ally in the region."[13] Turkey's close relationship with the United States (through its NATO membership) also serves to reinforce Tel Aviv's ties to Washington. Moreover, Turkey's historic and cultural connection with Central Asia may open the door for additional Israeli contacts with friendly Muslim states. For example, through Turkey, Israel's relationship with Azerbaijan has been very positive.[14]

In short, the Israeli-Turkish alliance has yielded benefits for both sides. As the next section illustrates, the Israeli lobby, in order to bolster the strategic relationship between Tel Aviv and Ankara, has found itself in a position of sometimes lobbying in favor of the Turkish policy agenda.

THE PRO-ISRAELI LOBBY AND TURKISH INTERESTS

The importance of Israel's strategic interests to the major Jewish-American organizations cannot be understated. The American Israel Public Affairs Committee (AIPAC), which has consistently ranked in the top five of *Fortune's* "power 25 list" of lobbies in the United States,[15] was established in the 1950s to further the U.S.-Israeli relationship and to help support policies that further Israeli security.[16] Other organizations, such as B'nai B'rith (BB), the American Jewish Congress (AJCongress), the American Jewish Committee (AJC), the National Conference on Soviet Jewry (NCSJ), and the Anti-Defamation League (ADL), have a wider mandate: supporting Jews and Jewish life throughout the world—including, but not limited to, Israel. All of these organizations support Israel's security interests and lend their support to efforts they see as furthering those interests.

Because of the Israel-Turkey partnership, Jewish-American organizations felt that it was important to support Turkey as well: given the growing alliance between Tel Aviv and Ankara, what was good for Turkey indirectly helped Israel. Jewish-American ties to Turkey and Turkish-Americans have run parallel to progress on the Israel-Turkey front. Consequently, the relationship between the two lobbies "has grown more intimate over the last couple of years."[17] As one observer put it, "We believe, and have been told by Israeli officials, that whatever we can do for Turkey helps the Turkey-Israel relationship."[18] Because of the alliance, the two communities increasingly have found a number of issues of common interest, such as American aid and arms sales to Turkey, economic bailouts of Turkey's struggling economy, the Silk Road Strategy Act, regional energy exports, and opposition to the passage of an Armenian Genocide resolution. Representatives from both communities are quite open about the relative weakness of the Turkish lobby in the United States (vis-à-vis its main rivals, the Armenian-Americans and Greek-Americans), which makes the support of the pro-Israeli lobby that much more important to furthering the Turkey-Israel relationship.[19]

This is not to say that the Jewish-American organizations have completely accepted the Turkish policy agenda: Turkey's poor human rights records, the ongoing conflict against its Kurdish population, and (as will be seen below) the question of the Armenian Genocide are all matters that make some in the Jewish-American community very uncomfortable. In fact, some Turkish policies have "created a bit of a challenge" for Jewish-American organizations.[20] Moreover, the historically close relationship between the Jewish-American community on the one hand and the Greek-American and Armenian-American communities on the other makes the alliance with Turkey that much more difficult. Nevertheless, there were a number of mitigating factors.

First, the policies of Ottoman Empire and Turkey toward its Jewish population have made many Jewish-Americans predisposed to have positive feelings toward Ankara. The five hundredth anniversary of the Jewish expulsion from Spain was commemorated by Turks and Jews alike in 1992 and helped to build goodwill between the communities. Once Jewish-American organizations began working with Turkish organizations, it was not difficult to build on this history and to transform it into a strategic relationship. Moreover, Turkey contains the largest Jewish population in the region outside of Israel. Thus, supporting Turkey indirectly helps Turkish-Jews.

Second, Jewish-American support for the 1999 Turkish earthquake relief operation helped build bridges between the two communities and resulted not only in the appreciation of Turks worldwide but also in an outpouring of sympathy for the beleaguered victims. For example, the AJC alone gave some $25,000 in aid immediately after the earthquake and raised upward of an additional $1 million in aid. According to AJC president Bruce Ramer, "Such moments challenge us to show the depth of our concern for our fellow human beings, whatever their race, religion or ethnicity.... They also permit us to demonstrate the true meaning of friendship. Turkey, a cherished friend of the United States, Israel, the American Jewish Committee and the Jewish people, is in desperate need."[21] Other Jewish-American organizations sent aid to Turkey as well.

Finally, Jewish-American support for Turkey was also seen as being within U.S. foreign policy interests: the long-standing, close relationship between Washington and Ankara plays an important role in America's security concept for the Middle East. Thus, by supporting Turkey, Jewish-American organizations not only supported Israel but also furthered U.S. interests in this volatile region. It is important to keep in mind that the Jewish-American positions on the Silk Road Strategy Act and the Armenian Genocide resolution (the two issues examined later in this chapter in which Jewish-Americans and Armenian-Americans clashed) were fully in line with the policies of both the Clinton and George W. Bush administrations.[22]

Across the board, representatives from both communities have characterized the relationship between them as very good and only getting stronger. There have been numerous meetings between organizations, community leaders, and government officials from both sides. For example, all of the major Jewish-American organizations have cosponsored forums with their Turkish counterparts in which the two sides get together to discuss common issues. Moreover, Jewish-American representatives have traveled extensively to Turkey to meet with Turkish officials, and Jewish-American organizations have organized similar trips for Turks meeting with Israeli officials in Israel. Access to Turkish officials is considered excellent, and the Turkish government has made a concerted effort to strengthen the connections between the Jewish-American community and Ankara.[23] Jewish-American organizations have also attempted to "help Turkey improve its image ... mostly through [giving] Turkish activists advice on how to deal with the media and with Congress."[24] Although Jewish-American organizations have at times assumed a public (or not so public) role in Congress on issues concerning Turkey, most of their help seems to come in the form of helping the pro-Turkey lobby to better position itself in Washington and to be more effective in championing its agenda. However, Jewish-American organizations have made it clear to their congressional allies that whatever is good for Turkey is also good for Israel and that they should support Ankara. Moreover, the connection between the Turkish community and the Jewish-American community has not remained solely at the level of elites: "What began as an approach between executives of Jewish [American] organizations ... has filtered town to the [local] level."[25]

Jewish-American support for Turkey was initially aimed at supporting the Ankara–Tel Aviv strategic relationship. The complexity of the Turkish-Israeli alliance—with its military, geopolitical, social, and economic manifestations—has, according to one observer, "led us to other issues."[26] The next two sections examine two of these issues in which Jewish-American support for Turkey unintentionally caused it to oppose the Armenian-American lobby. Although it is important not to exaggerate the "split" between the Jewish-American and Armenian-American communities,[27] support for Israeli security has created tensions between these two ethnic lobbies. In this case, the policy agenda on the international level came into direct conflict with relations within the domestic political arena.

THE ENEMY OF MY FRIEND'S FRIEND . . .

The growing affinity between pro-Israeli and pro-Turkish lobbies has inadvertently led to a worsening relationship between Jewish-American and Armenian-American organizations. For many years, the Armenian and Jewish lobbies were quite close because of their shared pro-Western outlook, the geographic isolation of their respective homelands (and in both cases, surrounded by Muslims), similar experiences as a diaspora, demographic similarities, and a shared history of being the victims of mass murder.[28] Moreover, the two communities worked tirelessly to win ratification of the Genocide Convention in the 1980s.[29] However, this close relationship began to fray as the Israeli-Turkish alliance began to develop. In order to understand the connection between the Jewish-Turkish relationship and the Jewish-Armenian relationship, it is necessary to first understand the Armenian-American lobby and its main issues.

The Armenian-American Lobby

The Armenian-American community mobilized during World War I in order to push the United States to stop the massacres against Armenians and to protect the nascent Republic of Armenia. However, it did not emerge as a significant political force until the late 1980s in response to the devastating earthquake in Armenia. The independence of Armenia in 1991 and the eruption of ethnic violence in the Armenian-populated region of Nagorno-Karabagh (located in Azerbaijan) heightened its level of political activism. Armenian-American lobbying efforts are largely directed by two, sometimes rival, organizations: the Armenian Assembly of America (Armenian Assembly) and the Armenian National Committee of America (ANCA).[30] Despite the sometimes caustic rhetoric between the two,[31] they have been able to work together to promote three key issues of concern to the Armenian-American community: U.S. economic aid to Armenia, support for the Armenians in Nagorno-Karabagh, and recognition of the Armenian Genocide of 1915–1923. Whereas the first is rather uncontroversial, the others are not.

The conflict between Armenians and Azeris over Karabagh began prior to the collapse of the Soviet Union.[32] Although Armenian forces occupied some 15 percent of Azerbaijan, the U.S. Congress imposed restrictions on nearly all American aid to Baku through the passage of Section 907 of the 1992 Freedom Support Act. That these restrictions were imposed at all was a testament to the strength of the Armenian-American lobby, which was able to frame the Karabagh conflict in such a way as to transform an Armenian irredentist project into what was widely perceived as an act of Azerbaijani aggression.[33] Azerbaijan became the only state of the former Soviet Union that was not permitted to receive American foreign aid. However, the Armenian-American lobby's success was due not only to their own strength but to the weakness of any opposing lobby.[34] One explanation for this was Baku's initial belief that it could quickly defeat the Karabagh-Armenians and therefore did not see the need for a lobby. Only in 1993, when the military balance had changed unquestionably in the Armenians' favor, did the Azeris begin to focus on establishing a lobbying infrastructure in the United States.[35]

The Turkish-Azeri-Jewish Strategic Triangle

A conflict in the Transcaucasus between Christian Armenians and Muslim Azeris would likely have been of little concern to Jewish-Americans or to the Israeli-Turkish alliance if it were not for the cultural and strategic ties between Turkey and Azerbaijan. The Turks and Azeris are similar in many ways: they share similarities in language, culture, and national identity.[36] In fact, post-Soviet Azerbaijan's first president, Ebulfeyz Elçibey, placed his country on a decidedly pro-Turkish path.[37] The successful 1993 coup against Elçibey by Heydar Aliyev represented a shift away from pan-Turkism, but Aliyev has flirted with Turkism off and on since coming to power.

Throughout the Nagorno-Karabagh conflict and afterward, relations between Turkey and Azerbaijan were close. Turkey saw Azerbaijan as the cornerstone of its policy during the early post-Soviet years of attempting to spread its influence by stressing its historical and linguistic ties to the Caucasus and Central Asia and to serve as a model of a Muslim, Western-oriented, secular, and capitalist democracy—Turkey was thought to be a "bridge" to Europe.[38] Azerbaijan saw Turkey as a source of aid as well as a window to the West. In January 1992, the two states signed a Friendship and Cooperation Treaty, and Turkey supplied Azerbaijan with significant humanitarian assistance. Moreover, Turkey dispatched military advisors and weapons to Azerbaijan.[39] It also supported the Azeri military effort in Nagorno-Karabagh by blockading Armenia and mobilizing its forces in eastern Anatolia to deal with, what they called, the Armenian "threat."[40] This relationship survived the fall of Elçibey as Aliyev attempted to strength his country's geopolitical position by entering into a rapprochement with Turkey in the mid-1990s.

Israel, too, has sought a closer relationship with Azerbaijan. Turkey's ties to Azerbaijan helped to foster a positive relationship between Tel Aviv and Baku: support for Turkey's main ally in the Caucasus meant that Israel was indirectly supporting Turkey. Moreover, Turkey has looked to Israel and the pro-Israeli lobby to aid Azerbaijan in its attempt to get Section 907 repealed. Ankara did not need to push the Israelis too hard: Azerbaijan's secular, Western orientation is exactly the type of state that Israel wants to support within the Muslim world. Moreover, Armenia's war against Azerbaijan and tensions with Turkey led it to seek allies in both Russia and Iran. Armenian-Iranian ties have soured the former's relations with the Jewish state because of Israel's extremely hostile relationship with the Islamic Republic of Iran.[41] Finally, Azerbaijan has treated its own Jewish population "very well" and is not tolerant of anti-Semitism; in fact, Hebrew was openly taught in Azerbaijan while it was still a Soviet republic.[42] According to Eytan Na'eh, Israeli Ambassador to Azerbaijan: "The tolerance of a country can be measured by its tolerance for its Jewish community. There is very high tolerance of Jews here, and no anti-Semitism. One could not wish for better treatment of Jews in a Moslem community than exists here is Azerbaijan."[43] In fact, Azerbaijan plans to open an embassy in Israel in 2002 and relations between the two countries are now very close.

The Silk Road Strategy Act

The developing ties between Azerbaijan and Israel have translated into Jewish-American support for legislation benefiting Baku. The Silk Road Strategy Act (SRSA) was introduced by Senator Sam Brownback (R-Kans.) in 1997 and aimed at guiding U.S. policy toward the Caucasus and Central Asia (the ancient 'Silk Road'), a region heretofore neglected by the Clinton administration. According to Brownback himself, "[The goals] of the bill include strengthening democratic government, resolving regional conflicts, promoting friendly relations with the United States, advancing market reforms, developing economic infrastructure between states in the region and supporting U.S. business interests and investments."[44] Among the most controversial aspects of the bill was its affect on Section 907: building on previous "carve outs" of Section 907 attached to the 1997 foreign aid bill, the SRSA "would effectively eliminate" these restrictions.[45]

The Armenian-American lobby came out strongly against the SRSA, arguing that repealing Section 907 would threaten the Nagorno-Karabagh peace process and "[reward] the corrupt and undemocratic government of Azerbaijan."[46] Armenian-American organizations have consistently argued that the SRSA would isolate Armenia by tilting U.S. aid and support toward Azerbaijan as well as doing nothing to pressure Baku to lift its embargo against Armenia and Karabagh. On the other hand, several major Jewish-American organizations took the opposite position on the SRSA.

Jewish-American support for the SRSA and the lifting of Section 907 aid restrictions stemmed from several sources. First, the general support exhibited by Israel for Azerbaijan was crucial. Despite a series of carve outs to Section 907 in 1997, this provision continued to restrict at least some U.S. aid to Azerbaijan, which reinforced Baku's international isolation and delegitimized its pro-Western orientation. This in turn threatened Azerbaijan's political stability, and an unstable Azerbaijan was seen by Israel as a threat to its own security: Tel Aviv feared the potential to "lose" Azerbaijan as it had "lost" Ethiopia and Iran during the Cold War. Thus, although the SRSA does not directly impact Israeli security, there was a strong perception of an indirect effect. Consequently, most Jewish-American organizations saw the SRSA issue to be well within their overall pro-Israeli agenda. Moreover, Azerbaijan's Jewish population was very supportive of the SRSA, and one observer called this support very "influential."[47]

Second, passage of the SRSA was seen as equally important to countering Iranian influence in the region. Azerbaijan stands in stark opposition to the Islamic Republic of Iran. Despite some attempts at reform by President Khatami, Iran remains one of Israel's most dangerous enemies. The transport of Azerbaijan's potentially significant oil reserves to the world market can either go north through Russia (which is seen as unacceptable because Moscow could use the oil exports to expand its influence and pressure Baku), south through Iran (which would provide Tehran with both money from transit rights and heightened influence in the Persian Gulf region and the southern tier of the former Soviet Union), or west, from Baku to the Turkish port of Ceyhan. According to most accounts, the pipeline running through Iran would be the cheapest and most effective export route but may be damaging to both Israeli and U.S. security interests. The third option, which is sometimes known as the Baku-Ceyhan Pipeline Initiative, was supported strongly by the Clinton administration and would avoid either Iranian or Russian control over the Caspian Sea oil.[48] Repealing Section 907 through passage of the SRSA was seen as a first step in establishing the Baku-Ceyhan route.[49]

Armenian-American organizations came out strongly against the Baku-Ceyhan route.[50] Azerbaijan would benefit from oil revenues, which, could, would be used to purchase military hardware in an effort to tip the strategic balance in the Nagorno-Karabagh war to their advantage. Moreover, the pipeline route would exclude Armenia, which is seen by Armenian-American organizations as a further attempt by Turkey and Azerbaijan to isolate Yerevan. However, similar to their support for the SRSA, Jewish-American organizations came out in favor of the Baku-Ceyhan route.

The ADL issued a press release that reported on a letter sent to President Clinton by the ADL's national chairman and national director. This letter called the Clinton policy "sound" and "forward-looking" and called for "vigorous U.S. efforts to advance the vital Baku-Ceyhan pipeline initiative."[51] In a joint letter to both the Senate Foreign Relations Committee and the House Appropriations Committee, five Jewish-American organizations—the AJC, BB, the AJCongress, the ADL, and the NCSJ—strongly urged the passage of the SRSA and the lifting of Section 907.[52] These organizations also had "discussions" with members of Congress, "some not so public, some in full view."[53] The largest pro-Israeli lobby, the AIPAC, did not publicly come out in favor of the SRSA or the repeal of Section 907, however. This had more to do with the AIPAC's mission, however, than with the policy itself: "We do not lobby Congress on issues that do not directly involve Israel," said Keith Weisman; the AIPAC's mandate is solely U.S.-Israeli relations, and the strategic alliance between Turkey and Israel is "not something we go to the Hill about."[54] Moreover, given the AIPAC's limited mandate, it has "to be more circumspect about relations with Turkey" and has to "play it much quieter."[55] Nevertheless, while most other Jewish-American organizations openly urged passage of the SRSA, the AIPAC gave its tacit support.

Armenian-American organizations criticized Jewish-American organizations for their support of the SRSA. Armenian Assembly Board of Directors chairman Van Krikorian stated that "Armenians continue to live with the constant threat of another genocide from Turkey and Azerbaijan, and we would naturally expect that Jewish-American organizations would be more sensitive to this concern."[56] The Armenian Assembly also sent an official letter to the Jewish-American organizations that had openly come out in support of the SRSA, urging them to change their position.[57] *The Armenian Reporter* provided the following analysis: "By intervening in favor of Azerbaijan, Israel has proven once again that when it comes to supporting a people, such as the Armenians, who have shared a similar fate and fortune at the hands of persecutors, national interests weigh supreme and there is no place in national policy for emotional considerations or compromise."[58] Moorad Mooradian observed that many members of the Armenian-American community have turned hostile toward the Jewish community:

Too often, Armenian communities are exposed to a subtle and, more often, not so subtle, "anti" virus concerning Israel. This virus is insidious and it hints of anti-Jewish undertones masked with facts about Israeli-Turkish cooperation. The remarks include sweeping statements by some commentators that lump people ethnically associated with Israel into the inane category of "enemy" by personalizing every issue that is not favorable to what they consider Armenia's best interest. ... [T]hey insist that Turkey is an enemy—now Israel and Turkey have affiliated, and Jews support Israel and its policies.[59]

Although Mooradian goes on to criticize these anti-Jewish feelings and clearly understands the intentions behind Israeli and the Jewish-American support for Turkey, he identifies an important trend in Armenian-American and Jewish-American relations: Israel's support for Turkey, although established for strategic reasons, has harmed relations between the two communities.

Jewish-American reaction to Armenian-American hostility ranged from surprise to understanding. According to Shai Franklin, "This was the first issue ... that really brought us into disagreement with the Armenian-American community."[60] In hindsight, Barry Jacobs admits, Jewish-American organizations were "maybe a little naive" and were "not aware of the commitment of the Armenians to [Section] 907": "When we came out publicly, ... we were not aware of what it would do with our relations with [the Armenian-Americans]."[61] The effect was to "put [the two communities] at odds" and to create an environment of "uneasiness."[62] Ross Vartian, the former executive director of the Armenian Assembly, stated that the differences created "a lot of consternation" on Capitol Hill.[63] Whereas some in the Armenian-American community believed that by siding with Azerbaijan on this issue, Jewish-Americans were taking the Azeri/Turkish side, Jewish-American groups asserted that their primary concern was to support Israeli strategic interests, not to appear anti-Armenian. Nevertheless, Jewish-American support for the SRSA "hasn't ... been an ingredient for advancing the relationship" between the two communities.[64]

Although the dispute over the SRSA strained relations between the two communities, the Armenian-American lobby was able to block the repeal of Section 907. That they could gain such an important victory on this highly emotional issue helped to alleviate tensions between the two groups. At the same time, it is important not to exaggerate Section 907's importance to the Jewish lobby: Section 907 was never seen as a first-tier issue for Jewish-Americans, and the eventual passage of a watered-down SRSA helped to promote Israeli strategic interests in the region at some level. However, the SRSA squabble was quickly followed by a much more significant fight over the passage of an Armenian Genocide resolution. Although the Jewish-American organizations did not openly oppose this measure, their silence spoke volumes to many Armenian-Americans.

THE ARMENIAN GENOCIDE RESOLUTION

The Nature of the Controversy

The deaths of upward of 1.5 million Armenians in the final years of the Ottoman Empire is a controversial and polarizing topic. Moreover, it is one that has been extremely uncomfortable for the Jewish-American community and many Israelis. The proper name for these events is even a matter of intense dispute. Armenian organizations unequivocally call it "genocide";[65] but Ottoman scholar Justin McCarthy criticized the Armenian version of the events in testimony before the House Subcommittee on International Operations and Human Rights,[66] and in his 24 April 2001 presidential message on the subject, President George W. Bush backed off of a campaign pledge to "properly recognize" the "genocidal campaign" perpetrated against Armenians and instead merely used the term "tragedy" to characterize the events.[67] Moreover, the debate over the Armenian Genocide question rages on the Internet.[68] A good part of the problem over the characterization of these events as "genocide" is due to the fact that the term has moral, political, historical, and legal uses and implications, not all of which agree with each other.[69] Although there is certainly a debate over the number of deaths, few sources provide an outright denial of the mass deaths suffered by the Armenian population of the Ottoman Empire.[70] Instead, the matter of dispute is whether these events constitute "genocide" as such.[71]

Armenian-American organizations have consistently supported the passage of a congressional Armenian Genocide resolution (AGR), which would officially recognize the events of 1915–1923 as genocide.[72] On the eighty-fifth anniversary of the events, the Armenian Assembly released a statement outlining its support for an AGR.[73] In this document and elsewhere, three reasons are typically given to justify the passage of such a resolution. First, the victims of genocide deserve to be recognized as such; any further denials or lack of recognition perpetuates the genocide itself and makes genocide deniers complicit in the crime. Second, recognition of the Armenian genocide, as one of a number of similar crimes against humanity, will (it is hoped) create an international climate that both makes it illegitimate for states to embark on such a project and forces the international community to actively intervene to prevent or stop genocide. Finally, the continued tensions between Armenia and both Turkey and Azerbaijan have led many Armenians to believe a "second genocide" to be imminent. Although the stalemate over Nagorno-Karabagh has lessened these fears somewhat, passage of an AGR would raise international consciousness of the Armenians' plight and make it more difficult for the Azeris and Turks to "think they can get away with it again."[74] The importance of the AGR for the Armenian-American community can scarcely be exaggerated: it is their most important issue after the survival of the Republic of Armenia and Nagorno-Karabagh.[75] Moreover, it is their most important resource for mobilizing members of their own community and sympathetic members of Congress.[76]

For its part, Turkey has rejected Armenian claims, arguing that calling the events of 1915–1923 genocide is biased, incomplete, and a misrepresentation of historical facts. According to this account, the Armenian deaths were the result of an armed rebellion against the Ottoman Empire by Armenians; civilian populations were merely "caught up in both an international war and an intercommunal struggle" and were not targeted by the Ottoman Empire or the nascent Republic of Turkey.[77] Not only did the events not constitute genocide, then, but the modern state of Turkey cannot be blamed for the actions of its predecessor. Other Turkish officials point to Armenian "political ambitions" aimed at isolating Turkey politically, deflecting blame from themselves for atrocities

committed by Armenians during the same time period and during the Karabagh
war of the 1990s, and "to prepare the moral ground for their political adven-
turism, including their claims of territory and 'reparations.'"[78] Although there
may exist some middle ground whereupon pro-Armenian and pro-Turkish
scholars can agree on a common set of facts, the polarization between the two
sides, the emotional nature of the debate, and the overt antagonism exhibited
by both sides toward their opponents likely preclude the waning of this fierce
dispute.

Unintended Involvement

Through their lobbying alliance with Turkey, Jewish-American organizations
were unwillingly thrown into the center of this debate. Officials from Jewish-
American organizations who were interviewed for this essay were unanimous
in stating that this was not a dispute they wished to be involved in and that at
every turn they attempted to limit their involvement. Moreover, none of those
interviewed denied that horrific atrocities occurred during the period in question. However, the perception among many Armenian-Americans at the time
was that the Jewish-Americans were taking the Turkish side against them. The
issue of genocide is obviously a difficult one for Jewish-Americans because the
term was first coined in reference to the wholesale slaughter of some six million
Jews by Nazi Germany. That the Jewish population of Europe was subjected to
genocide would seemingly lead to an emotional bond between Jewish-Americans
and Armenian-Americans.[79] Moreover, the historically close relationship between the two communities, when added to the fact that many of the staunchest
supporters of the AGR in Congress are Jewish,[80] makes differences over this
issue that much more difficult.

Jewish-American organizations have come at this issue from three directions.
First, for nearly all Jewish-Americans and Israelis, genocide is not an abstract
legal or moral concept. Rather, it is something that is very much a part of Jewish life and that was the impetus for the creation of a Jewish state. Moreover, it
is not merely a historical notion: Israel's geographic proximity to actual or potential enemies has created a "siege" mentality in which the potential exists for
"American Jews to see the Middle East through a lens of genocide."[81] Consequently, charges of genocide, even those directed against an ally such as Turkey,
are taken very seriously by most Israelis and Jewish-Americans. On the other
hand, there is often a tendency by many scholars of the Holocaust and layper-
sons to identify the Holocaust as a unique event that is not comparable to other
cases of mass slaughter.[82] For example, the Israeli ambassador to Turkey, Uri Bar-
Ner, stated, "We make a very clear distinction: the Holocaust is a unique tragedy
in man's recorded history and it can not be compared with anything else."[83] This
second issue (the perception of the Holocaust as unique) has at times conflicted
with the first issue (concern for genocide) because some in the Jewish commu-

nity believe that Armenian, or any other, attempts to equate their own suffering with the Holocaust is "to plunder the moral capital" of the Jewish people
and to "steal the Holocaust."[84] As a result, they are wary of other communities
attempting to claim the mantle of victims of genocide.

Finally, the strategic relationship between Turkey and Israel complicates attitudes toward the AGR. Passage of such a resolution would damage Turkey's
international image and could possibly provoke a backlash against Turkey's pro-
Western policies. This indirectly affects Israel's security interests. When Israeli
foreign minister Shimon Peres called Armenian claims "meaningless,"[85] he became the target of sharp criticism from numerous sources, including noted Holocaust and genocide scholar Israel Charny. Charny sent a letter to Peres strongly
criticizing him for putting Israel's strategic interests above the moral necessity
of acknowledging genocide:

It seems that because of your wishes to advance very important relations with Turkey,
you have been prepared to circumvent the subject of the Armenian genocide in
1915–1920. ... [I]t may be that in your broad perspective of the needs of the state of
Israel, it is your obligation to circumvent and desist from bringing up the subject with
Turkey, but, as a Jew and an Israeli, I am ashamed of the extent to which you have now
entered into the range of actual denial of the Armenian genocide, comparable to denials of the Holocaust.[86]

Earlier, in May 1999, Hebrew University held a series of forums on the Armenian Genocide in which top Holocaust scholars attacked the Israeli government's
position.[87] A public petition, which was reprinted in the *Jerusalem Post* and *New
York Times*, was signed by 126 Holocaust scholars who affirmed the "incon-
testable historical fact" of the Armenian Genocide.[88]

Nevertheless, Turkey has taken a hard line on the genocide recognition issue,
even going as far as threatening that U.S.-Turkey ties would be "seriously
harmed" if Bush used the term *genocide*.[89] It is safe to assume that Israeli-Turkey
ties would likewise run the risk of being damaged if Israel moved toward recognition; at the very least, this is the perspective in Tel Aviv. Israel did not act on
a direct call from the Armenian foreign minister to recognize the Armenian
Genocide.[90] In May 2000, Israeli foreign ministry officials were quick to meet
with Turkish officials to repudiate the comments of Yossi Sarid—the Israeli minister of education who said in a speech that the Armenian Genocide should be
taught in Israeli public schools—and to assure Ankara that there would be no
change in official Israeli policy.[91] The Israeli foreign minister was reported to
have said that the issue "may negatively reflect upon the military alliance between Tel Aviv and Ankara."[92] Earlier, Israel's choice for ambassador to Turkey,
Ehud Toledano, was withdrawn at Turkey's behest for fear of upsetting Ankara—
it appears that Toledano made some comments during a radio interview over a
decade earlier that were considered by the Turkish government as being too pro-
Armenian.[93] Even as early as the 1980s, the genocide issue was of concern to the
Israeli government: in 1982 the foreign ministry attempted to force the cancel-

lation of the first International Conference on the Holocaust and Genocide because it dealt with Armenian issues;[94] and reportedly, the Israeli Embassy in Washington "actively lobbied" to block an Armenian Genocide resolution in 1989.[95]

Jewish-American organizations have generally followed the Israeli policy on the Armenian Genocide resolution issue.[96] Keith Weisman, at AIPAC, noted that this was the "most sensitive issue" in the triangle of Jewish-American, Armenian-American, and Turkish relations; the Jewish-American community "doesn't want to deal with this issue" because "we find it difficult to say to the Armenians that we had a genocide and you didn't."[97] Others commented that, "We didn't enter into this decision lightly" because of the "shared history in the United States between the two communities."[98] Nevertheless, although "we did not want to get involved" in the issue, "higher authorities," including those in Israel, asked us to "quietly" oppose the AGR "behind the scenes."[99] Although there was some dissent over the Jewish-American stance at the community level and among genocide scholars, the "only divide [at the level of the advocacy organizations] was over to go public or not."[100] The policy adopted by some organizations was to refuse to publicly oppose the AGR but also not to provide any support for its passage. "We did not play a public, physical role"; instead, it was "more a matter of not doing something rather than doing something."[101] By remaining silent, however, these organizations made it clear that they did not wish to see the AGR passed.

The reasons for Jewish-American disapproval of the AGR stem from the same sources as Israel's opposition to official recognition of the Armenian Genocide. In interviews with representatives from the major Jewish-American organizations, the difficult nature of genocide as a concept for all Jews at times clashed with the sense of the Holocaust as unique; comparisons between the Holocaust and the events of 1915–1923 were either seen as historically questionable or even opportunistic. The importance of Turkish-Israeli relations, however, consistently took center stage: especially when "the situation in the Middle East is at a very difficult time, ... it is not beneficial" to bring up the issue; "Israel, right now, lives in a very dangerous neighborhood," and it is important not to be seen as "pushing the Turks away."[102] In short, this is "not a time to criticize ... Israel's most important ally" in the region.[103] Interviewees consistently returned to the tension between the moral/humanitarian concerns of recognition and the strategic interests of Israel. Nevertheless, the Israeli-Turkish alliance was the deciding factor guiding Jewish-American policies.

The way in which the Armenian-American lobby went about attempting to raise the issue—through a congressional resolution—was also seen as counterproductive: the issue "should be left to historians rather than politicians,"[104] and is "not a matter for Congress."[105] "We didn't feel that it was the appropriate avenue to take," Jason Epstein said. "It wasn't helpful to make it a provocative issue."[106] Rather than seeking legislation that would invariably hurt U.S.-Turkish relations and possibly Turkey's Western orientation, the perception among some was that the issue was "essentially a political tool being used by some to embarrass the Turks."[107]

At the same time, Jewish-American organizations were not completely happy with the way in which the Turkish government and Turkish-American organizations have dealt with the issue. "We are very uncomfortable with what the Turks say and what they do on the issue," Keith Weisman argued; they "cannot win the way that they are fighting it."[108] In fact, Jewish-American organizations have tried to urge their Turkish counterparts to be more receptive to an open examination of the historical facts. Moreover, Turkey needs to be more understanding of Armenian feelings on the issue, rather than discarding them out of hand. There is a common opinion that Ankara's obstinate refusal to seek common ground with the Armenians does not make it any easier for Turkey's Jewish friends.

According to the NCSJ's Web site, "Some Armenians believe that Jews have not been active enough in protesting the Armenian genocide."[109] There certainly seems to be a strong sense of disappointment with Jewish-American organizations for not backing the Armenians when it comes to the genocide issue; given their similar histories and historically good relations, there is even a sense of betrayal among a minority in the Armenian-American community. At the same time, there is some understanding among Armenian-Americans of the strategic issues involved.[110] However, relations between the Armenian-American and Jewish-American communities have "become somewhat strained."[111] Although open hostility between the two lobbies has not erupted, the relationship between the two communities has been damaged. However, the genocide issue has not affected relations between Jewish-American organizations and their Armenian-American counterparts equally: whereas dealings with the Armenian Assembly remain strained but cordial (and on some issues productive), there has been more of a rupture with the hardline ANCA, to the point where it is reportedly difficult for Jewish-American organizations to have constructive discussions with that organization. As the AGR controversy endures, and as the Turkish-Israeli alliance continues to strengthen, the strains between the two communities may get worse: "The genocide issue threatens to become a larger issue if communication between the two groups does not take place. ... [It] can be the real tinderbox."[112]

CONCLUSIONS

Ethnic interest groups are primarily concerned with the well-being of their ethnic kin and the interests of their historic homeland. The Jewish-American "defense organizations"—such as the ADL, AJCongress, BB, and AJC—focus their attention on the treatment of Jews worldwide, whereas the AIPAC lobbies almost exclusively on behalf of U.S.-Israeli ties. As this chapter has illustrated, these mandates can become more expansive if the web of strategic relationships are taken into account: in order to bolster Israel's most important alliance in the region, Jewish-American groups found themselves taking positions on policies that only indirectly impact their ethnic kin and homeland. The SRSA was important to Turkey because of Ankara's close relationship to Azerbaijan. Although other factors were certainly at work—such as the desire to further Israel's own relationship with Baku and to block Iranian influence in the region—the Turkish connection made it important to Jewish-Americans. Turkish opposition to the passage of the AGR was a factor leading many Jewish-American organizations to get involved in this issue, despite their strong reservations. Nevertheless, it became one of concern to Jewish-American organizations because of the potential repercussions of the AGR's passage—such as an anti-West backlash in Turkey—which could hurt Israeli security.

The stance of Jewish-American organizations on the SRSA and the AGR were based almost entirely on furthering the security interests of Israel and the well-being of Jews in the former Soviet Union. Moreover, the Clinton and George W. Bush administrations supported the SRSA and opposed the AGR; thus, the Jewish-American positions on these issues were well in line with Washington's policies. Nevertheless, these positions unintentionally led Jewish-American organizations into conflict with the Armenian-American community. Although many Armenian-Americans understand the reasoning behind the Jewish-American stance, it clearly put a strain on the relationship between the two communities.

The fight over the SRSA, which the Armenian-Americans largely won, was the first time the two communities clashed on an issue of significant importance to one of them. For Jewish-Americans, the issue was second-tier at best, but for Armenian-Americans, the SRSA was seen as impacting the very survival of the Armenian state and the Armenian-populated enclave of Nagorno-Karabagh: Azerbaijan's oil revenues could tip the balance of power in favor of Baku and reverse Armenian gains in their decade-long dispute. More damaging to the relationship between the two communities was the Jewish-American silence on (or even mild opposition to) the AGR—an issue that is obviously very emotionally important to Armenian-Americans. This policy stance was extremely disappointing to many Armenian-Americans who believed that the two communities' similar history of mass murder established a bond that would normally lead Jewish-Americans to support their counterparts in the Armenian-American community. The defeat of the 2000 AGR means that the controversy over its passage—and the potential conflict with the Jewish-American community—will continue.

Relations between the Jewish-American and Armenian-American communities, though strained, have not ruptured. Many congressional supporters of Israeli/Jewish concerns are also supporters of Armenian issues: often, humanitarian concerns and constituency demographics naturally push certain members of Congress toward support for both communities. Although this makes it difficult for some members Congress, it also prevents the political battles from becoming too acrimonious. Also, individuals and organizations from both communities continue to share an overall positive relationship, such as in the Los Angeles area. Partly, this is the result of the decentralized nature of the Jewish-American community: local organizations tend not to deal with the larger, strategic issues that have caused so many problems between their national counterparts.[113] Moreover, at the local level, the two communities tend to deal with similar issues and have similar needs: "I cannot foresee a situation in the next fifty-plus years where the Jewish-American organizations and Armenian-American organizations will not be able to get along [at the local level]," because of the strategic issues.[114]

Moreover, Jewish-American groups continue to send delegations to Armenia and continue to meet with some Armenian-American organizations. For example, an exchange of letters over Jewish-American support for lifting Section 907 resulted in a meeting between representatives of the Armenian Assembly and the six major Jewish organizations. According to the Armenian Assembly press release: "The two groups concluded the meeting with a better understanding of the other's position. They adopted a policy of 'prior consultation,' promising to engage each other in dialogue as issues arise in order to promote cooperation between the two communities."[115] In addition, a delegation from the AJC met with leaders from Armenia and Karabagh.[116] Similar meetings were also held with other Jewish-American organizations.

Although Jewish-American organizations have made a concerted effort to work with Armenian-Americans and Armenia (and vice versa), there are still important strategic issues at stake. Support for Turkey and Azerbaijan, while only indirectly helping Israel, is still an important issue for many Jewish-American organizations and an irritant to many Armenian-Americans. It is therefore important not to ignore the degree to which being on opposite sides of two issues of extreme emotional importance to Armenian-Americans has created problems for relations between the two lobbies. As one observer summed up the impact of the Israeli-Turkish alliance, it has "alienated us from Armenian-American communities."[117] That this was not intentional from either side is of little comfort when strategic interests clash with domestic political relations.

A number of lessons can be learned from this case. First, the international level matters when examining the role of ethnic interest groups in U.S. foreign policy. The positions that they take are not necessarily determined solely by the immediate, direct interests of their ethnic kin or homeland. Instead, the intricate web of strategic relationships must also be considered. Second, a potential problem arises for ethnic interest groups once they take a broader view of the interests and security of their homeland: ethnic interest groups could unintentionally clash over issues that are not of direct concern to their identity group. In this case, the relationship was only strained; however, more open disputes between groups with no direct areas of conflict could erupt, making ethnic politics more difficult for the communities involved and members of Congress who become caught in the middle of constituencies that, under normal circumstances, would naturally support (or at least be neutral toward) each other. Finally, it is important not to exaggerate the potential for conflict: even when interests clash because of the desire of one group to support the strategic relationships of its homeland, the issue will rarely be of such concern to the group in question that it would be willing to risk an open confrontation with another group for which the issue is of first-tier importance. Unless there is a direct reason to clash—such as Albanian-Americans and Serb-Americans or Arab-Americans and Jewish-Americans—it is in the interests of all ethnic lobbies to keep relations with their counterparts in other communities cordial. In addition to the fact that many of these groups live in the same communities, one never knows when the support of another group may become useful. Nevertheless, the potential negative consequences of the interaction between strategic interests and an ethnic lobby's policy stances will continue to be of significance as U.S. foreign policy remains fluid and the power of ethnic lobbies grows.

NOTES

1. The author would like to thank all of those who provided telephone interviews for this essay, including Tahir Tagi-Zadeh at the Azerbaijani embassy, who is not listed below. Any mistakes are entirely the fault of the author.

2. Wolfango Piccoli, "Alliance Theory: The Case of Turkey and Israel," *Copenhagen Peace Research Institute*, August 1999, <https://wwwc.cc.columbia.edu/sec/dlc/ciao/wps/pic01/pic01.html> (accessed June 2001).

3. Some may object to the use of the word *lobby* given its sometimes negative connotation. The following definition of lobby guided the analysis of this essay: "an organization or a group of persons that seeks to influence government officials in line with a specific agenda." This definition does not contain any moral judgment of the agenda itself. Moreover, this chapter acknowledges that no community is a monolithic bloc and that differences within a community do exist.

4. The two-level model of international relations has been most forcefully argued by Robert Putnam, who put forth an overarching framework for explaining multiple-level foreign policy processes. Putnam's argument is that one cannot fully understand a state's foreign policy without examining domestic-level forces, and vice versa. Robert D. Putnam, "Diplomacy and Domestic Politics: The Logic of Two-Level Games," *International Organization* 42, no. 3 (1988): 427–59. The notion of "second image reversed" seeks to understand the impact of international forces on domestic politics and structure. Peter Gourevitch, "The Second Image Reversed: The International Sources of Domestic Politics," *International Organization* 32, no. 4 (1978): 881–912.

5. Leora Eren Frucht, "A Tragedy Offstage No More," *Jerusalem Post*, 12 May 2000, 7B.

6. For a more detailed examination of the Israeli-Turkish strategic relationship, see: Piccoli, "Alliance Theory"; Anat Lewin, "Turkey and Israel: Reciprocal and Mutual Imagery in the Media, 1994–1999," *Journal of International Affairs* 54, no. 1 (2000): 239–61; Meliha Altunisik, "The Turkish-Israeli Rapprochement in the Post-Cold War Era," *Middle Eastern Studies* 36, no. 2 (2000): 172; George E. Gruen, "Dynamic Progress in Turkish-Israeli Relations," *Israel Affairs* 1, no. 4 (1995): 40–70; Suha Bolukbasi, "Behind the Turk-

ish Israeli Alliance: A Turkish View," *Journal of Palestine Studies* 29, no. 1 (1999): 21–35; M. Hakan Yavuz, "Turkish-Israeli Relations through the Lens of the Turkish Identity Debate," *Journal of Palestine Studies* (Autumn 1997): 22–37; Raphael Israeli, "The Turkish-Israeli Odd Couple," *Orbis* 45, no. 1 (2001): 65–79; Efraim Inbar, "Regional Implications of the Israeli-Turkish Strategic Partnership," *Middle East Review of International Relations* 5, no. 2 (2001): 48–65. Also see the Jewish Institute for National Security Affairs' collection of articles on the subject, <http://www.jinsa.org>.

7. Israeli, "The Turkish-Israeli Odd Couple," 69.

8. Piccoli, "Alliance Theory."

9. Although Israel proclaimed Jerusalem as its capital in 1950, the United States, like nearly all other countries, had maintained its embassy in Tel Aviv. Consequently, the use of Tel Aviv in this chapter merely follows U.S. policy and is not meant to suggest any personal position on the Israeli capital.

10. Gruen, "Dynamic Progress in Turkish-Israeli Relations," 40.

11. "Netanyahu Advocates Strategic Alliance with Turkey," *Xinhua News Agency*, 2 May 1997.

12. Israeli, "The Turkish-Israeli Odd Couple," 74.

13. Piccoli, "Alliance Theory."

14. Hershel Shanks and Suzanne F. Singer, "Oil and Jews on the Silk Road," *Moment* 23, no. 5 (1998): 38.

15. "The Influence Merchants," *Fortune*, 7 December 1998, 134.

16. According to its official agenda, the AIPAC does not see a difference between advancing U.S. interests and supporting Israel's security interests. See <http://www.aipac.org /documents/whoweare.html#agenda>.

17. Jess Hordes (government and national affairs director of the ADL), telephone interview by author, June 2001.

18. Keith Weisman (analyst for the AIPAC), telephone interview by author, June 2001.

19. Guler Koknar (executive director of the Assembly of Turkish American Associations), telephone interview by author, June 2001; Jason Epstein, of BB, telephone interview by author, June 2001.

20. Barry Jacobs (assistant director for international affairs for the AJC), telephone interview by author, June 2001.

21. American Jewish Committee, "American Jewish Committee Launches Turkish Relief Fund," <http://www.ajc.org/pr/turkrelieffund.htm> (accessed June 2001).

22. Successive American administrations have seen the U.S.-Turkish alliance as extremely important. Moreover, in an effort to block Russian and Iranian influence in the southern tier of the former Soviet Union (and to expand its own influence), the United States has supported the Silk Road Strategy Act and has sought a closer relationship with Azerbaijan; at the same time, however, it provides Armenia with approximately $100 million in aid per year.

23. Koknar, interview.

24. Weisman, interview.

25. Epstein, interview.

26. Jacobs, interview.

27. David B. Ottaway and Dan Morgan, "Jewish-Armenian Split Spreads to the Hill," *Washington Post*, 9 February 1999, A15. Several interviewees have commented that Ottaway and Morgan overstated the issue somewhat.

28. Ibid.

29. Hordes, interview.

30. Razmik Panossian, "Between Ambivalence and Intrusion: Politics and Identity in Armenia-Diaspora Relations," *Diaspora* 7, no. 2 (1998): 148–97.

31. Murat Acemoglu, "Unity: A Mirage or Reality?" *Armenian Reporter* 29, no. 22 (1996): 26.

32. For an overview of the conflict, see Michael P. Croissant, *The Armenia-Azerbaijan Conflict* (New York: Praeger, 1998).

33. Thomas Ambrosio, "Congressional Perceptions of Ethnic Cleansing: Reactions to the Nagorno-Karabagh War and the Influence of Ethnic Interest Groups," *The Review of International Affairs* (forthcoming).

34. Dick Kirschten, "Greetings, Comrades!" *National Journal* 25, no. 37 (1993): 2188.

35. James Morrison, "Up against the Lobby," *Washington Times*, 22 August 1995.

36. It is important, however, not to exaggerate the similarities between the two ethnic groups. For some works on Azeri nationalism, see F. Malekafzali, "Primordial, Instrumental Identities and the Formation of Ethnic Collective Movements: The Case of Azeri Nationalism," *Canadian Review of Studies in Nationalism* 19, no. 1–2 (1992): 31.

37. Büsra Ersanli Behar, "Turkism in Turkey and Azerbaijan in the 1990s," *Eurasian Studies* 3, no. 3 (1996): 2–21.

38. Shireen Hunter, "Bridge or Frontier? Turkey's Post–Cold War Geopolitical Posture," *International Spectator* 34, no. 1 (1999), <https://wwwc.cc.columbia.edu/sec/dlc/ciao/olj/iai/iai_99hus01.html> (accessed June 2001).

39. "Azerbaijan and Turkey to Cooperate in Military Training," *British Broadcasting Corporation—Summary of World Broadcasts*, 3 February 1992, SU/1294/A4/1.

40. Amberin Zaman, "Turks Square Up to Armenian 'Threat,'" *Daily Telegraph*, 8 April 1993, 14.

41. See, for example, BB's press release, B'nai B'rith Center for Public Policy, "Tell Your Senators to Vote for the Silk Road Strategy," <http://www.bnaibrith.org/cpp/randa/silkroad699.html> (accessed June 2001).

42. National Conference on Soviet Jewry, "Azerbaijan Country Page," <http://www.ncsj.org/Azerbaijan.shtml> (accessed June 2001).

43. "Israeli Ambassador Lauds Treatment of Jews in Azerbaijan," *International Reports.net* <http://www.internationalspecialreports.com/ciscentralasia/01/azerbaijan/israeliambassador.html> (accessed June 2002).

44. "Brownback Introduces Major Legislation Calling for New U.S. Policy in Central Asia," 10 March 1999, <http://www.senate.gov/~brownback/pressapp/record.cfm?id=175950> (accessed June 2001).

45. Commission on Security and Cooperation in Europe, *Report on Armenia's Presidential Election*, June 1998, 98-J-892-16 (Washington DC: Congressional Information Service, 1998).

46. Armenian National Committee of America, "The Ban on U.S. Aid to Azerbaijan," Winter 2001, <http://www.anca.org/anca/pospapers.asp?ppid=6> (accessed June 2001). Also see Armenian Assembly of America, "Silk Road Strategy Act of 1999 (S. 579)," <http://www.aaainc.org/armenia-nkr/silkroad.htm> (accessed June 2001).

47. Jacobs, interview. This view was confirmed in interviews with Epstein and Shai Franklin (director of governmental relations of the NCSJ), telephone interview by author, June 2001.

48. Jofi Joseph, "Pipeline Diplomacy: The Clinton Administration's Fight for Baku-Ceyhan," WWS Case Study 1/99 (Woodrow Wilson School for Public Affairs, Princeton

University), <http://www.wws.princeton.edu/~cases/papers/pipeline.html> (accessed June 2001).

49. See the comments by S. Frederick Starr before the House Subcommittee on Asia and the Pacific, *U.S. Interests in the Central Asian Republics*, 105th Cong., 2d sess., 12 February 1998. Also see Marc Grossman before the Senate Subcommittee on International Economic Policy, *U.S. Policy on the Caspian*, 105th Cong., 2d sess., 9 July 1998.

50. See Bryan Ardouny's testimony before the Foreign Operations Subcommittee of the Hose Appropriations Committee, 106th Cong., 1st sess., 4 March 1999 and the Foreign Operations Subcommittee of the House Appropriations Committee, 106th Cong., 2d sess., 31 March 2000.

51. Anti-Defamation League, "ADL Urges Vigorous U.S. Action to Promote Caspian Oil Pipeline through Turkey," 16 October 1998, <http://www.adl.org/presrele/mise%5F00/3254_00.asp> (accessed June 2001).

52. The letter was dated 1 September 1998 and was reproduced as "Jewish-American Organizations Urge Repeal of Section 907," in *Armenian Reporter* 31, no. 50 (1998): 18.

53. Epstein, interview.

54. Weisman, interview.

55. Ibid.

56. Armenian Assembly of America, "Armenian Assembly and Jewish Organization Leaders Meet," 14 January 1999, <http://www.aaainc.org/press/archive99/1-14-99.htm> (accessed June 2001).

57. "Armenian Assembly Responds to Letter of Jewish-American Organizations Calling for Repeal of Section 907," *Armenian Reporter* 31, no. 50 (1998): 18.

58. "Jewish Support of Azerbaijan," *Armenian Reporter* 31, no. 39 (1997): 2.

59. Moorad Mooradian, "Be 'Pro,' Not 'Anti,'" *Armenian Reporter* 32, no. 46 (1999): 3.

60. Franklin, interview.

61. Jacobs, interview.

62. Epstein, interview.

63. Ottaway and Morgan, "Jewish-Armenian Split Spreads to the Hill."

64. Franklin, interview.

65. Armenian Assembly of America, "Affirmation of the Armenian Genocide," <http://www.aaainc.org/genocideintro.htm> (accessed June 2001); Armenian National Committee of America, "Armenian Genocide Commemoration," <http://www.anca.org/anca/pospapers.asp?ppid=1> (accessed June 2001).

66. See Justin McCarthy's testimony before the House Subcommittee on International Operations, *Hearing on H. Res. 398, The United States Training on and Commemoration of the Armenian Genocide Resolution*, 106th Cong., 2d sess., 14 September 2000 <http://www.house.gov/international_relations/hr/armenmcc.htm> (accessed June 2001). Professor McCarthy has been criticized by Armenian-American organizations for his views: see Murat Acemoglu, "Scholarship and Its Demands: Opening Dialogue on the Armenian Genocide Denial," *Armenian Reporter* 31, no. 46 (1998): 7.

67. Armenian National Committee of America, "President Bush Breaks Pledge to Recognize Armenian Genocide," <http://www.anca.org/anca/pressrel.asp?prid=73&pressregion=anca> (accessed June 2001).

68. Arpie Nakashian, "Armenian Genocide Debate Goes on the Web," *Asbury Park (New Jersey) Press*, 3 August 1997, 6.

69. Christian P. Scherrer, "Comparative Genocide Research," *Journal of Genocide Research* 1, no. 1 (1999): 13–24.

70. It is clear, however, that the Turkish government has spent considerable sums of money to promote its version of events in American academia. Roger Smith, Eric Markusen, and Robert Jay Lifton, "Professional Ethics and the Denial of Armenian Genocide," *Holocaust and Genocide Studies* 9, no. 1 (1995): 1–22.

71. I am not a scholar of the period in question and therefore feel uncomfortable with taking sides in this dispute—although I certainly recognize both the importance of the debate to Armenians worldwide and the evidence in favor of the use of the term *genocide* in reference to these events. However, the point of this section is not to argue in favor of one term or another but rather to illustrate the intersection between the Israeli-Turkish alliance and the Jewish-American stance on the Armenian Genocide resolution.

72. One recent version of this bill was introduced in November 1999 (H. Res. 398).

73. Armenian Assembly of America, "Armenian Assembly of America Statement on the April 24, 1999 Commemoration of the Armenian Genocide," <http://www.aaainc .org/record/genocide_statement.htm> (accessed June 2001).

74. Salpi Haroutinian Ghazarian, "Selective Remembrance: The Changing Politics of Genocide Recognition," *Armenian International Magazine* 5, no. 4 (1994): 16.

75. It is interesting to note that on both the Armenian Assembly's and ANCA's Web pages, recognition of the Armenian Genocide is listed at the top of the page on their "key issues" and "position papers," respectively.

76. See Rachel Anderson Paul, "Grassroots Mobilization and Diaspora Politics: Armenian Interest Groups and the Role of Collective Memory," *Nationalism and Ethnic Politics* 6, no. 1 (2000): 24–47; and Thomas Ambrosio, "Congressional Perceptions of Ethnic Cleansing," A Century of Killing: Genocide and Ethnic Cleansing in the 20th Century (University of South Dakota), October 2000.

77. Republic of Turkey, Ministry of Foreign Affairs, "The Armenian Allegation of Genocide: The Issue and the Facts," <http://www.mfa.gov.tr/grupa/ad/adf/massacre .wash.be.ing.htm> (accessed June 2001).

78. Nuzhet Kandemir, "Letter from Ambassador Kandemir," 21 April 1995, <http://www.turkey.org/politics/p_armn07.htm> (accessed June 2001).

79. "Prof. James Russell of Harvard Examines Connections between Armenians and Jews," *Armenian Reporter* 33, no. 8 (1999): 12.

80. For example, Representatives Stephen Rothman and Tom Lantos were some of the most vocal Jewish members of Congress in favor of the AGR.

81. Franklin, interview.

82. See Alan S. Rosenbaum, ed., *Is the Holocaust Unique?* (Boulder, CO.: Westview Press, 1996); Katherine Bischoping and Andrea Kalmin, "Public Opinion about Comparisons to the Holocaust," *Public Opinion Quarterly* 63, no. 4 (1999): 485–507; and Lilian Friedberg, "Dare to Compare," *American Indian Quarterly* 24, no. 3 (2000): 353–80.

83. Quoted in Selcuk Gultasli, "Holocaust Is Unique, Can't Be Compared to Anything," *Turkish Daily News,* 9 February 2001.

84. Edward Alexander, quoted in David E. Stannard, "The Dangers of Calling the Holocaust Unique," *Chronicle of Higher Education* 42, no. 47 (1996): B1. It should be noted that Alexander is among the most radical proponents of Holocaust uniqueness.

85. "Peres: Armenian Allegations Are Meaningless," *Turkish Daily News,* 10 April 2001.

86. Quoted in Robert Fisk, "Peres Stands Accused over Denial of 'Meaningless' Armenian Holocaust," *The Independent* (London), 18 April 2001, 13.

87. Marilyn Henry, "A Genocide Denied," *Jerusalem Post,* 28 May 1999, 10.

88. Reproduced by Armenian National Institute, "Statement by 126 Holocaust Scholars," 8 June 2000, <http://www.armenian-genocide.org/affirmation/petitions /21-attach2.htm> (accessed June 2001).

89. *Sabah* (Istanbul), 24 April 2001, 19, reproduced as "Genocide Warning," *World News Connection*, FBIS-WEU-2001-0425.

90. Marilyn Henry, "Armenia Asks Israel to Recognize Turkish Genocide," *Jerusalem Post*, 22 April 1999, 3.

91. *Anatolia* (Ankara), 2 May 2000, reproduced as "Turkey: No Change in Israeli Policy on Armenian Genocide," *World News Connection*, FBIS-WEU-2000-0502.

92. *Snark* (Yerevan), 25 April 2000, reproduced by *World News Connection* as "Armenia: Snark on Israeli MP's Proposal on Genocide Issue," FBIS-SOV-2000-0425.

93. "New Ambassador Selected," *Financial Times* (London), 20 February 1998, 4.

94. Marilyn Henry, "A Genocide Denied," *Jerusalem Post*, 28 May 1999, 10.

95. Leora Eren Frucht, "A Tragedy Offstage No More," *Jerusalem Post*, 12 May 2000, 7B.

96. The sole exception has been the NCSJ, which used the term *genocide* in its country report for Armenia. National Conference on Soviet Jewry, "Armenia Country Page." This was so important that the Armenian Assembly drew special attention to it in its "Assembly Thanks Jewish Organization for Acknowledging the Armenian Genocide," *Assembly This Week*, 22 June 2001.

97. Weisman, interview.

98. Epstein, interview.

99. Jacobs, interview; Weisman, interview. Also see Zvi Bar'el, "Armenian History Will Have to Wait," *Armenian Reporter* 34, no. 10 (2000): 19.

100. Jacobs, interview.

101. Hordes, interview.

102. Epstein, interview.

103. Jacobs, interview.

104. Weisman, interview.

105. Jacobs, interview.

106. Epstein, interview.

107. Hordes, interview.

108. Weisman, interview.

109. National Conference on Soviet Jewry, "Armenia Country Page."

110. According to Mooradian, "Israel differs from Turkey and Azerbaijan in one respect. Its government will not arbitrarily condemn the defenders of the Armenian Genocide unless there is a connection with Israeli realpolitik goals." Moorad Mooradian, "The Continuing Genocide," *Armenian Reporter* 31, no. 30 (1998): 3. Also see Murat Acemoglu, "Turkey Warns Israel: Don't Talk to PKK," *Armenian Reporter* 32, no. 22 (1999): 3.

111. Epstein, interview.

112. Ibid.

113. Weisman, interview.

114. Epstein, interview.

115. Armenian Assembly of America, "Armenian Assembly and Jewish Organization Leaders Meet."

116. Armenian Assembly of America, "American Jewish Committee Meets Armenia And Karabagh Leaders," *Armenia This Week*, 9 July 1999, <http://www.aaainc.org /armenia_week/archive99/7–9-99.htm> (accessed June 2001).

117. Jacobs, interview.

Chapter 9

Peace as a Three-Level Game: The Role of Diasporas in Conflict Resolution

Yossi Shain and Tamara Cofman Wittes[1]

Many violent conflicts in the world today center around the definition of ethnic and national communities according to the territories they hold and the populations they include. Some of these identity conflicts not only involve issues of sovereign boundaries and security within a specific territory but also impact on the lives and well-being of other communities—in particular, kin communities outside the state—that share ethnic ties with the people engaged in the conflict. The resolution of violent conflicts that revolve around identity issues often requires addressing an audience beyond the boundaries of the state and the arena of the conflict: the audience of diaspora communities in far-off lands. This has been the case for the Jewish and Armenian diasporas, in the United States and elsewhere, which participate, directly and indirectly, in their homelands' conflicts and must therefore be taken into account by governments in building state policies that shape the prospects for conflict resolution.

The Armenian-American diaspora consists of nearly one million people, the Jewish-American diaspora about six million. They are generally acknowledged to be the two most effective ethnic groups at advocating their issues in the U.S. political system. Armenia and Israel, undoubtedly in part as a result, are the largest per capita recipients of U.S. foreign aid.[2] Moreover, the Arab-Israeli conflict and the war over Nagorno-Karabagh both engage world attention because of their implications for key issues of concern to the United States and others: regional stability in the Middle East and the Caucasus, access to oil resources, protection of human rights, and the dangers of weapons proliferation and spiraling regional conflict that could draw in neighboring states. The ways in which diaspora involvement in these cases influences the prospects for peace are therefore of direct concern to the United States and other states that invest time and money in peacekeeping, diplomatic initiatives, and economic development in these important regions.

As this chapter will show, the diaspora role in homeland conflict resolution can be large and powerful enough that homeland leaders ignore diaspora preferences at their own peril. Moreover, we argue that diasporas are endemic to the international system, with a capacity for independent political action that is assertively employed. In confronting the kin state's conflict, the diaspora attempts to promote its own view of its ethnic community's identity and interests, a view that is not always congruent with the view of the homeland authorities. This is particularly, but not uniquely, evident in the Armenian and Jewish diasporas. Their behavior and its effects on Armenian-Azerbaijani and Palestinian-Israeli peace efforts show that conflict resolution in communal conflicts often is not just a two-level but a three-level game of peacemaking, with the diaspora becoming a key constituency of concern for homeland leaders, for their homeland's adversaries, for the governments of their host states, and, through their international diplomatic activities, for other states as well.[3]

Our analysis into diasporas and conflict resolution does not concentrate on refugees and exiles, who represent, in a sense, personified consequences of a territorial conflict. Neither are we concerned with "stateless" diasporas, irredentist and secessionist groups that reside in a "near abroad" and wish to reconfigure the boundaries of existing states to include their current homes within their desired homelands. Such communities, as for example many postcommunist minorities in Eastern Europe, tend to view themselves (or are viewed by their kin states), as "kidnap victims" and thus have an inherent and direct stake in a particular outcome to their homeland conflict.[4] Our focus, instead, is on far-removed diasporas that are well established and well organized in their countries of domicile and who have normalized and embraced life outside their ancestral homeland. These groups are removed from the arena of the conflict and are generally not making territorial or communal claims on their own behalf. Their implication in the conflict is mainly indirect and reflects the increasingly important phenomenon of *transnational communal politics*. This politics is as defined by the states in which these communities reside as it is by the ethnicity of the group in question.

The notion that communal conflicts in far-off regions are subject to a force we call transnational communal politics requires elaboration. This chapter will outline the theoretical perspective that informs this view, a perspective that is rooted in the constructivist insight that the identities and interests of states are both flexible and mutually constitutive. The essay will develop several propositions about the identities and interests that engage diasporas in homeland communal conflicts and will illuminate these propositions with examples drawn from case studies of Armenian-Americans' and Jewish-Americans' attitudes and activism surrounding the Nagorno-Karabagh and Palestinian-Israeli conflicts in the 1990s.

Through discussion of these two diasporas, we will explore how diaspora communities interact with their homeland states, their host states, and third parties to affect the process of and prospects for conflict resolution. The chapter will propose and illustrate four factors that affect diaspora communities' attitudes toward and activism on peace efforts in their homeland regions: concerns over identity maintenance, contestation for leadership of the transnational community, social or political status in the host state, and organizational or bureaucratic interests. We conclude with some suggestions for a research agenda to further elucidate the diaspora role in international conflict resolution.

DIASPORA INFLUENCE ON HOMELAND CONFLICTS: A THREE-LEVEL GAME

Peace agreements tie together not only governments but also societies that may be severely divided and deeply suspicious of one another. Successful conflict resolution demands that political leaders build and sustain a national coalition to support the peace process through the implementation phase, which is often drawn out and fraught with crises and occasional violence.[5] Although not often recognized, diaspora communities are an important part of this public coalition; failure to include diaspora interests and identity concerns in the political equation can be a dangerous move for homeland leaders interested in pursuing a peace deal. We are not addressing the eventual outcome of peace diplomacy but rather the evolution of support and opposition within the process itself. Indeed, both Israeli and Armenian leaders who pursued peace with their enemies were supported by diasporic peace lobbies or were accused by opponents within their own ethnic community of betraying the national cause. Diasporic Armenian and Jewish diaspora groups have organized their communities to show both mass support and mass opposition to government policies. They have taken their viewpoints into the arena of homeland politics, using monetary contributions, affiliated political parties, and transnational communal organizations to sway public opinion and influence domestic political developments. Moreover, diasporic elements have both influenced and bypassed their homeland's sovereign bilateral international relations through privately funded activities and by lobbying governments in their host states and elsewhere. In the United States, the Armenian-American lobbying groups successfully passed a congressional ban on U.S. aid to Azerbaijan (known as Section 907 of the Freedom Support Act) that has withstood many years of White House efforts to have it overturned. Likewise, Jewish-American lobbying organizations have pressed for the United States to move its embassy in Israel from Tel Aviv and Jerusalem, against the wishes of the U.S. administration and often those of the Israeli government as well. In a more congenial vein, the American Jewish Committee and B'nai B'rith both devoted impressive lobbying efforts to encourage newly independent post-Soviet states to establish diplomatic relations with Israel.[6]

Because the diasporas we have examined demonstrate an impressive capacity for independent action with important international ramifications, we argue that peacemaking must be viewed as a political activity that engages more parties than the usual "domestic" and "diplomatic" categories. The notion that international negotiations are a "two-level game," rather than merely a government-to-government interaction, was originally developed by Robert Putnam in the late 1980s and has been investigated further in a number of arenas including economic affairs and security policy. Putnam describes a state's leader as playing at two game tables at once in an international negotiation, working to satisfy both his domestic political constituencies and also his negotiating counterpart's minimum demands on the road to a successful agreement.[7]

Our analysis of the Armenian and Jewish cases suggests that when active diasporas exist (as they do in many other conflicts, including those between Ethiopia and Eritrea, Indian Sikhs and Hindus, Kurds and Turkey, and Irish Catholics and Protestants), these diasporas cannot be viewed simply as a domestic constituency within their host state but must also be viewed as independent actors in the conflict resolution process. The Armenian and Jewish diasporas in America have influenced their homelands' peace policies in important ways through lobbying U.S. foreign policymakers, through intervening monetarily and rhetorically in Israeli and Armenian politics, and through international diplomatic activities that affected Armenia's and Israel's relationships with other sovereign states. These diasporas appear to have made peace negotiations into a three-level game for their homelands' leaders, and those leaders have suffered when they have tried to treat the process as only having two levels. As we have noted, host states and other third parties recognize and try to influence the independent role of diasporas as political actors in homeland conflicts.

Jeffrey Knopf has already noted the necessity of expanding the two-level game concept when analyzing bilateral security negotiations, such as the U.S.-Soviet Intermediate Range Nuclear Forces (INF) Treaty talks. He develops the two-level game framework into a "three-and-three" framework, encompassing transgovernmental, transnational, and cross-level interactions between combinations of government leaders and domestic constituencies. His analysis shows that using three levels rather than two enables the analyst to explain outcomes not predicted by unitary-actor approaches to international relations.[8]

Building on these insights, this chapter argues that Knopf's "transboundary connections" are particularly relevant to the analysis of ethnic conflicts, where relevant constituencies naturally extend beyond state borders. These peoples include domestic publics within the "homeland" state as well as their diasporic kin in "host states" around the world. These diasporas act as more than domestic constituencies within their countries of domicile, constituencies that Knopf notes enhance their domestic effectiveness through transboundary connections. They also function as an important "domestic" constituency for homeland political leaders and moreover, as transstate players, acting on behalf of their entire people in interactions with third-party states and international organizations. Thus, we suggest, analyses of peacemaking in ethnic conflicts must include diasporas as a third-level actor in their own right.

NATIONAL SECURITY: THE IMPACT ON INSIDERS AND OUTSIDERS

The connection between a sense of endangerment to the homeland and the sense of diasporic peril may be definite or more psychological. The diasporic connection with events at home may be largely social and psychological, through their identification with their homeland's aspirations and struggles. Israel's successive struggles with its Arab neighbors heightened the attachment of diasporic Jews to the homeland as they "became increasingly bound up in the Jewish state's travails as well as its successes."[9] Homeland conflicts can also affect diasporas more directly: economically, socially (in terms of their self-image and how their host society views them), and even through physical threats directed against them by the group in conflict with their homeland kin.[10] Indeed, whether "stateless"—aspiring to establish an independent sovereign state in a claimed homeland—or "state-based," with kin communities already forming a majority in their own established nation-state, diasporas are affected by homeland conflicts even if they live far from the arena of violence.[11]

The ties and the psychological identification of diaspora communities with their kin states, along with the more concrete effects of a homeland conflict on their own lives, lead diasporas to perceive high stakes in homeland conflicts and to try to play an active role in such conflicts' resolution or continuation. The type and degree of their activities are determined by conditions in their countries of domicile—their political and social status, their host society's and government's views of the conflict—and above all, by the political and social character of their kin state.

Diasporic support of the homeland during violent conflicts can be important to the homeland's well-being. Diasporas may provide a lifeline of resources and weapons, serve as a source of recruits, act as a propaganda platform, and be enlisted to lobby and influence host governments and other international players. In the latest war between Eritrea and Ethiopia, the Eritrean and Ethiopian diasporas in the United States together contributed hundreds of millions of dollars toward weapons purchases by their homeland countries. But much of this support was colored by how the two diasporas viewed their respective homeland states and their national interests. Thus, many members of the large and diverse Ethiopian diaspora withheld support from the new (Tigrian) regime, which they considered to be a usurper of Amhara national identity.[12] "The energy and organization of the Eritrean diaspora, however, was simply overpowering.... With none of the credibility baggage of the Tigrian regime in Ethiopia, Eritrea called upon its wealthy and energetic ... Diaspora.... The fundraising efforts of President Issaias Afeworki in the United States have reached legendary status among those who follow the conflict."[13]

Just as they play important roles in supporting violent conflicts involving their homeland states, far-off diasporas may play a critical role in conflict resolution. Diasporas may support or oppose a peace proposal involving their homeland states and in doing so may affect the outcome of the negotiations. They often have strong preferences regarding conflict outcomes, and they can and do act on those preferences by influencing domestic homeland politics and the foreign policies of their host countries, as well as through independent international action. Throughout the 1990s, many leaders of the Jewish-American community have acted both as a peace lobby or as players against peace diplomacy. In the Armenian case, diaspora money was instrumental in mobilizing Armenian public opinion against President Levon Ter-Petrossian and his peace efforts with Azerbaijan and Turkey, ultimately forcing his resignation. In Israel, the religious-nationalist campaign against Prime Minister Yitzhak Rabin was largely financed by diaspora sources. In 2000 Prime Minister Ehud Barak of Israel lost diaspora support over his agreement to an American peace proposal that would have yielded Israeli sovereignty over religiously significant areas of Jerusalem to the Palestinians.[14] During the peace process, American Jews also acted as unofficial emissaries in the efforts to open new diplomatic channels to countries that had no diplomatic relations with Israel, lift the Arab boycott, reward Arab and Islamic states that normalized relations with the Jewish state, and encourage others to do the same.[15] These missions were not always undertaken with the prior approval of the Israeli government at the time; indeed, at times both the Jewish and the Armenian diasporas have undertaken international political initiatives that conflicted with the desires of their homeland governments.[16]

Diasporic activities may also help to set the ideological parameters of a homeland conflict and the requirements for a termination of hostilities.[17] Diasporic Armenians in the United States and in France, for example, are responsible for instilling into the current Armenian-Azerbaijani conflict an echo of the Armenian Genocide of 1915, in which over half the Armenian population of Turkey was massacred by Young Turk officers. The genocide, which became the central "chosen trauma" of the Armenian nation and embodied in the diaspora,[18] was invoked when Turkey extended its support to Azerbaijan, another Turkic country. Richard G. Hovannisian has argued that Turkish moves to support Azerbaijan in the Karabagh conflict was seen by the diaspora "as the logical continuation of a long-term policy to keep Armenia helpless and vulnerable. . . . [A]t a convenient moment it can, perhaps, seize upon an excuse to eliminate the little that was left of the historic Armenian territories."[19] One analyst notes that "[m]any Armenians do not distinguish between Azeris and Turks and fear encirclement by Turkish/Islamic expansionism."[20]

Host states, particularly Western democracies, take into account the interests and political power of diaspora communities in formulating policies toward homeland conflicts.[21] For example, regardless of France's official reluctance to consider itself a host country for immigrants or a breeding ground for ethnic identity, it cannot escape the American-type manifestation of diasporic politics. When in January 2001, President Jacque Chirac hosted President Robert Kocharian of Armenia and President Heydar Aliyev of Azerbaijan in Paris in an attempt to settle the conflict over Nagorno-Karabagh, the *New York Times* reported that "with municipal elections approaching in France, Mr. Chirac would like to have a settlement to offer the 400,000 ethnic Armenians in France."[22] The United States' keen interest in the conflicts in Northern Ireland, Cyprus, between Armenia and Azerbaijan, and between Israel and its Arab neighbors are all heavily influenced by the noticeable strength of those well-organized ethnic diasporas in American politics.[23] As one Washington lobbyist noted, "In the Near East, Greece is small and Turkey is big—in Congress it's the opposite."[24] Because of U.S. leadership in encouraging conflict resolution in these and other regions, homeland governments rely on the aid of diaspora communities to influence U.S. foreign policy in congenial directions. American decision makers, for their part, try to commission diaspora leaders to promote U.S. interests in the homeland and U.S. preferences for the way in which the homeland's violent conflicts are resolved.

Even the adversaries of kin states recognize and try to confront or work with diasporic forces involved in the homeland conflict. After the defeat of the Labor government in Israel's 1996 elections, the Palestine Liberation Organization (PLO) reached out to liberal Jews in America to try to sustain the progress of Palestinian autonomy in the West Bank and Gaza. Azerbaijani officials, for their part, name the Armenian-American lobby in Washington as the primary obstacle to peace in the Caucasus and to their developing relations with the United States.[25] Azerbaijan has even worked to cultivate the Jewish organizations in Washington as allies to counterbalance Armenian lobbying efforts. The Turkish mission in Washington also devotes immense resources to combating the Armenian diaspora's lobbying efforts.[26]

TWO DIASPORAS AND THEIR HOMELANDS' CONFLICTS: AN OVERVIEW

In many respects, the Armenian- and Jewish-American diasporas are the carriers of national mythologies that do not always coincide with the central national narratives of their kin states' governments or their people. The Armenian genocide is central to diaspora identity, but less so to the homeland community, which for the most part escaped the trauma of the event. Diaspora hard-liners are said to care less about the homeland's present and future than about the past's dead. Notably, no diaspora Armenians in the West are from Karabagh; but the issue matters to them in light of their historical memory of losing lands and lives to Turkish nationalists.[27] Certainly, the genocide issue has complicated Armenian-Turkish relations in ways detrimental to both states, as we will discuss. Elements in Israel and the Jewish diaspora have often clashed over the role of religion in public life and over the application of religious values to questions of Israeli security and the state's conduct in international relations.[28] In the last decade, as both Israel and Armenia have engaged in negotiations with their adversaries, the gaps between diasporic and homeland identities and interests have come to the fore.

Over a four-year peace process with Azerbaijan (a cease-fire was established in 1994) Armenia's first president, Levon Ter-Petrossian, earned the ire of the diasporic community for his attempts to reconcile with Turkey and resolve a war with Turkic Azerbaijan, in part by means of downplaying the genocide issue. Gerard Libardian, an Armenian-American who served as senior foreign policy advisor to President Ter-Petrossian from 1991 to 1997, argued that the president set out to establish "normal relations with Turkey without preconditions.... [T]he politicization of the Genocide had served, wittingly or unwittingly, to create the mentality and psychology that Turkey, through its nonrecognition of the Genocide, is likely to repeat it, that Turkey is the eternal enemy. If Turkey is the eternal enemy, then Russia is the eternally necessary friend. And this then creates pressures on your policy of independence."[29] Ter-Petrossian refused to recognize the self-declared independence of Nagorno-Karabagh, rejected calls for its annexation, and insisted that the conflict was between the Armenians of Karabagh and the government of Azerbaijan. However, his position was weakened when Turkey refused to establish diplomatic relations with Armenia until Yerevan withdrew its forces from the territories occupied in Azerbaijan and agreed to Azerbaijani sovereignty over Nagorno-Karabagh. The diasporic-led Dashnak Party—a transnational, pan-Armenian organization that viewed itself as the guardian of Armenian nationalism—took the opportunity to deliver a coup de grace, and Ter-Petrossian was ultimately forced to resign on 3 February 1998 after the Dashnak funded newspapers and other organs to galvanize domestic Armenian opinion against his handling of the Karabagh negotiations and label them as treasonous.

After Ter-Petrossian's ouster, newly installed President Robert Kocharian made the pursuit of genocide recognition an integral part of Armenia's foreign policy agenda. According to Ronald Suny:

Almost immediately the new government reverted to a more traditional nationalism, one more congenial to the diaspora and in line with the hard-line position adopted by the Karabagh government. Armenia ... reemphasized the genocide issues, always a source of pain and emotion for Armenians and a powerful wedge between Armenia and Turkey. As a consequence, a profoundly risky attempt to reorient the national discourse ultimately failed before intractable obstacles both domestic and foreign.... The power and coherence of the Armenian national identity, the popular projection of the images of genocide onto the Karabagh conflict, and the closing off of the Turkish option all contributed to the fall of a once-popular national leader whose move beyond the limit of Armenian identity choices and national discourse did not bring the expected political payoff (i.e., stability, economic well-being, integration in the region, etc.).[30]

For its part, the government of Yitzhak Rabin in Israel, although enjoying support for the Oslo peace accord among most American Jews, also became the target of venomous opposition from specific sectors of the diaspora. In addition to outright hostility directed at government officials (eggs were thrown at the Israeli ambassador when he spoke in one Brooklyn synagogue), American diaspora groups that opposed the peace process financed a public relations campaign against the accords, gave financial support to the Jewish settler movement in the occupied territories, and established American affiliates of key right-wing Israeli parties to financially support their political campaigns against Rabin and his Labor Party successors, Shimon Peres and Ehud Barak. After the Oslo Accords were signed, American Jews who opposed them joined with Israeli Likud members to obstruct U.S. improved relations with the PLO. Over the objections of the Clinton administration and despite lobbying by Israeli diplomats, anti-Oslo Jewish organizations were able to convince the U.S. Congress to enact the Middle East Peace Facilitation Act in such a way as to limit America's participation in the donor efforts.[31] The sharp divide within Israel over the peace process was also exacerbated by diaspora activists, even to the point of American ultra-orthodox rabbis issuing rulings that sanctioned Israeli soldiers' insubordination and the assassination of Prime Minister Rabin.

Despite the parallels just noted between these two diaspora-homeland relationships, there are important differences. In the case of Israel and American Jews, from the time of Israeli independence, the country, its leaders, and the Jewish diaspora all considered the homeland community as the vanguard of the Jewish nation, and its authorities were viewed as having the moral legitimacy both to make life-and-death decisions for the state and also to speak on behalf of the nation as a whole. Thus, Jewish-American voices did not dispute Israel's right to negotiate for national reparations from Germany for the Holocaust.[32] On the other hand, the diasporic Armenian community was itself the vanguard of the nation during the long period of communist rule in the homeland. Indeed, the Dashnak Party led the nation's drive for self-determination for over a hundred years after the organization's founding in 1890.[33] After independence in 1991, the new state was too weak politically, economically, and culturally to assert effectively its own leadership of the transnational community. As Israel's democracy flourished, ingathered other Jewish communities, and triumphed over its enemies, its strength in the homeland-diaspora relationship grew. By contrast, Armenia's endemic corruption and its culture of violence only weakened the state's claims to speak in the name of the diaspora and the nation as a whole. In this case, the homeland is very dependent on diaspora assistance to sustain itself. It is thus no surprise that when President Kocharian declared in a recent interview, "Armenia will not present any legal claim [for territory or compensation] after Turkey admits having committed genocide," his Turkish interviewer expressed incredulity. Indeed, there is a real question as to whether his claim is sustainable in light of the diaspora's power in Armenian politics.[34]

DIASPORAS IN INTERNATIONAL RELATIONS

Diasporas are an inherent part of the imperfection of the nation-state. Almost no states match perfectly territory with populations, whether they define themselves in civic-nationalist or ethno-nationalist terms. Diasporas are thus an endemic feature of the international system, and transnational ethnic ties are an inevitable part of international relations.[35]

A community's view of itself as a nation is not static but shifts with time and circumstance.[36] The "national interest" as a concept that drives state policies shifts along with national identity. As Peter Katzenstein has pointed out, "[D]efinitions of identity that distinguish between self and other imply definitions of threat and interest that have strong effects on national security policies."[37] Ronald Suny has written that "'[n]ational histories' may be investigated, not so much to discover the 'real' story behind the Serb-Albanian conflict in Kosovo or the Armenian-Azerbaijani hostility in Karabagh ... but rather ... to assess [how] particular conceptualizations of nationhood contribute to notions of national interest and threats to national security."[38] Gil Merom has shown how the historical mythology of the Jewish people as preordained to "dwell apart" (*am levadad yishkon*) coupled with the Holocaust creed of "Never Again" have shaped Israel's sense of "national security exceptionalism."[39]

Diaspora communities identify themselves, and are identified by others, as part of the national community. The tie between homeland and diaspora as constituting one nation is especially close for relatively weak, new, or reconstituted states such as those in the former Yugoslavia and the former Soviet Union. For these states, the national identity was often "held in trust" by the diaspora during the years of communist domination. This was the central political role of the Armenian diaspora throughout the Soviet era. Indeed, Soviet domination and its suppression of nationalities made many diasporic communities the custodians of their "captive nations." When these states were reconstituted in 1991, diasporic activists expected their homelands' new governments to take the diasporas' vision of the nation and its history into account. When these diasporas also established political and financial clout abroad or inside their country of origin, their voice became more immediately effective.

In the late 1980s, the Armenian diaspora began to mobilize major aid efforts to the homeland after an immensely destructive earthquake. After the demise of the Soviet Union and the onset of the Karabagh struggle, diaspora activists were in a strong position to make their preferences felt in homeland politics. Ter-Petrossian was the first to assert the state's interest over the interests of the nation as a whole. His view of "political realism" fell victim to the homeland-diaspora power struggle as Armenia's domestic politics became dominated by views more congruent with the nationalist factions of the diaspora. Recognizing this power shift, in his inaugural address on 8 April 1998, Armenian president Robert Kocharian made close diaspora involvement in homeland affairs a central part of his vision for Armenia's future development:

Our generation is here to shoulder one more responsibility of the unification of efforts of all Armenians, and ensuring the Armenian Diaspora's active participation in the social, political and economic life of our republic. A constitutional solution to the issue of dual citizenship will also contribute to this issue. Armenia should be a holy mother-land for all Armenians, and its victory should be their victory, its future their future. We have to realize that a nation, acknowledging the value of its combined forces, can never be defeated.[40]

Thus, for Ter-Petrossian, the diaspora was an integral part of the nation he led, and he wished to ensure that diasporic activism was in total harmony with Ar-menian state policy. By contrast, Kocharian, understanding the need for dias-poric support, gave heavy weight to diasporic preferences in the *creation* of state policy. Most significant was Kocharian's affirmation that the genocide was a cause of the entire nation and not only of the diaspora.[41] The renewed empha-sis on the genocide and confrontation with Turkey revealed diaspora preferences: keeping their most important issue close to the heart of homeland politics was worth the cost of an Armenian state that was economically and diplomatically isolated, weakened, and dependent on Russia.[42]

Of course, the very notion of a unified people that stretches across frontiers is complicated because in international relations, a state can in principle represent only the people living within its boundaries. But in reality, neither the diaspora nor the homeland community ultimately dominates in constituting and com-municating national identity. Indeed, a certain degree of flexibility can be pre-served because of the distance between homeland and diaspora: each can, to a de-gree, put its own "spin" on the national narrative and live out their shared identity in its own way. The degree to which the one influences the other is associated with the relative strength that the homeland and the diaspora can exercise vis-à-vis one another through monetary flows, cultural productions, community leadership, and the like. Sufficient areas of overlap exist that homeland-diaspora ties can be quite close despite differences of emphasis in the national narrative. This is evident, for example, in the vibrancy and pride of American Judaism, whereas the traditional Zionist-Israeli version of the Jewish historical narrative insists that only in the Jewish state can Judaism survive, sheltered from the on-slaught of anti-Semitism that endangers Jews in the rest of the world.[43]

But this live-and-let-live situation fails in the case of a homeland engaged in a violent conflict over identity issues. Although national identity can be nego-tiated between homeland and diaspora, the structure of modern international relations gives the prerogative of constituting, elaborating, and implementing the national interest to the government of the homeland state. Diasporas may be considered by kin states as part of their national-security equation under the premise of mutual responsibility. They may even be recruited as active partici-pants in the homeland's conflict. Israel, for example, considers itself responsible for the well-being of all Jews around the world.[44] At the same time, it regards the Jewish diaspora, and especially American Jewry, as "one of Israel's strategic assets."[45] Such a homeland attitude can also create diaspora resentment, as when Armenian-American scholar Khachig Tölölyan complained that in Armenia, "they want service and money from diasporans, not thoughts or opinions."[46]

Indeed, homeland governments may construct the national interest with the explicit intent of protecting the whole kin community, both diaspora and homeland. Israel for many years and the newly established state of Armenia more recently have made such claims.[47] In practice, however, struggles often erupt between homeland and diaspora over the definition of the nation or the kin community and of the homeland versus "the people's" interest. And the homeland's claim to defend the diaspora or even to speak on its behalf may be rejected as interference that endangers its status in the "host land."[48]

CONFLICT RESOLUTION AND NATIONAL IDENTITIES

The national interests articulated by the homeland government with respect to how or whether to resolve a violent conflict with a neighboring state or internal ethnic minority can impact significantly on the identity of the transnational community. Disputes erupt between diasporic elements and homeland authorities over the definition of the people and especially over the emphasis placed in the national narrative on certain historical and modern conflicts. The homeland government's attitude toward an ongoing conflict and the conflict's implications for the communal life and identity of the diaspora abroad become particular points of potential tension.

For example, consider a state that gives up its claim to a piece of historically significant territory in order to achieve peaceful relations with a neighboring state. Diaspora and homeland citizens often have different attitudes toward the implications such policies have for ethnic and national identity. For many homeland citizens, territory serves multiple functions: it provides sustenance, living space, and security, as well as a geographical focus for national identity. If giving up a certain territory, even one of significant symbolic value, would increase security and living conditions, a homeland citizen might find the trade-off worthwhile. By contrast, for the diaspora, the security of the homeland is of course important as well; but the territory's identity function is paramount. Its practical value (and indeed, the practical value of peace with a former rival) is not directly relevant to the diaspora's daily experience. In such situations, altering the geographic configuration of the homeland state for the sake of peace may be far more disturbing to diaspora elements than to segments of the homeland community.

In precisely this vein, a rupture opened in 1999–2000 between many American Jews and Israeli Prime Minister Ehud Barak over his acceptance of a U.S. peace plan that called for giving the Palestinians sovereignty over the Temple Mount. Several Israeli analysts of the Jewish-American diaspora expressed their concern "that a hand-over of the Temple Mount and parts of Jerusalem threatens to undermine the Jewish identity of American Jews and tear away at the already delicate fabric of their relationship with Israel."[49] According to one Israeli newspaper report:

A full page advertisement was published in Israel's leading newspapers, in The New York Times and in major Jewish-American publications. Signed by 32 prominent American Jewish leaders, the ad declares that "Israel must not surrender Judaism's holiest site, the Temple Mount." It quotes Malcolm Hoenlein, executive vice chairman of the Conference of Presidents of Major American Jewish Organizations, who was moved by the issue to deviate from the organization's traditional support for the positions of any Israeli government. "In future years, all of us will have to answer to all our children and grandchildren when they ask us why we did not do more to protect their heritage and safeguard Har Habayit [the Temple Mount]," Hoenlein is quoted as saying in a recent address. "Our essence as a people is embedded in the bedrock of this mountain.... The solemn pledge by Jews throughout the ages, 'If I forget thee, O Jerusalem ... ' must not be allowed to ring hollow now."

Similar sentiments were expressed by Hoenlein, who stated in an interview with the Jewish Telegraphic Agency that "Israel has a right to make decisions that affect its security. All Jews have a right to discuss it, but it's up to the government of Israel. The Temple Mount is a different issue. It belongs to all Jews, it is the inheritance of all Jews, and all Jews have a vested interest in it."[50] As one Israeli activist responded to such sentiments: "Israel is a make-believe land for American Jews. It's a symbol. They don't live here, they don't drive on the roads, or send their sons to the army.... I don't make light of Jerusalem and the Temple Mount. But it's nice to live in New York, Philadelphia, and L.A. and to know that the Temple Mount is in our hands. But what is really to see up there? Mosques. And for what price?"[51] The different priorities, functions, and meanings assigned to the homeland territory by the diaspora versus the homeland citizenry can lead to tremendous tensions over peace policies.[52]

When the conflict is hot and the homeland is under severe threat, diaspora concerns about the homeland's existential survival are often paramount, and divergent opinions may be subsumed under a broader show of support. But when the possibility of peace arises, homeland-diaspora debates and power struggles reemerge. This can also happen in reverse order. In the summer of 2000, as the Camp David peace summit took place, American Jews demonstrated publicly both for and against the peace process. But once violent clashes began between Israelis and Palestinians in September 2000, Jewish organizations organized solidarity missions to Israel and other events to demonstrate their unified support for the state under siege. Explained one Jewish-American Democratic political consultant, "Jews can call themselves liberal, conservative, Reconstructionist, Reform, it doesn't matter. When Israel is in danger, a different alarm system goes off."[53] When peace negotiations are a live option, differences in the diaspora's and the homeland's conceptions of the nation imply different conceptions of the national interest and thus distinct views on policy toward the ongoing conflict. Depending on their available political and financial resources, diaspora activities can, in this situation, have a strong influence on the outcome of any peace initiative.

The homeland government (or other political elements, including the opposition) may have an ambivalent view of how much to take diaspora concerns into account in formulating domestic and international policies, particularly those that relate to ongoing conflicts. To a large degree, homeland leaders and publics feel that their direct stake in the outcome of their conflict with their neighbors should trump any diaspora preferences. On the other hand, they often have come to rely on the diaspora's political clout and financial assistance, at home and internationally. As one Israeli columnist noted, "'The children of Diaspora Jews will not have to fight if war breaks out here' is a view that doesn't hold much water since Israelis do expect American Jews to intervene on Israel's behalf in their own political system."[54]

The homeland-diaspora nexus is such that on some occasions, the diaspora may feel threatened by homeland decisions; in other situations, the homeland may feel that diaspora preferences threaten national goals. In 1992, for example, a Labor-led Israeli government took office shortly after the American Israel Public Affairs Committee (AIPAC) had gone to the mat with the Bush administration to support settlement-building activities in the West Bank and Gaza. The new prime minister, Yitzhak Rabin, flew almost immediately to the United States to confront the AIPAC board, telling them that he rejected their traditionally heavy involvement in Israel's bilateral relations with the U.S. government and that he would prefer to handle those relations himself.[55]

In the homeland-diaspora tug-of-war to define the national and the people's interest, many voices inside and outside the state feed off of one another. Indeed, an increasingly important aspect of kinship politics is the transnational community organization. The diaspora-led Armenian Dashnak is an early example: it once served as the leadership organization of Armenians worldwide and quickly established itself as a political party within Armenia when the new state was formed. The Young Israel movement is a more recent example. A grouping of nationalist Orthodox synagogues in North America and Israel and a spin-off of the American organization the National Council of Young Israel, it serves (among other purposes) as a means of mobilizing religious nationalist opinion both in the diaspora and in Israel against territorial concessions to the Palestinians.

Nevertheless, the motivation and interests in the two centers of domicile are, for many segments of the community, fundamentally different in light of their different circumstances. For example, being removed from the arena of violence, those diaspora segments that are fully integrated into their host societies may feel more desire to settle a long-standing violent dispute than the homeland government, especially if the homeland's policies conflict with values adopted by the diaspora in their country of domicile, and particularly if their host state is pressing for a settlement. Reform Jews in the United States, for example, promoted a Palestinian-Israeli rapprochement in part because they viewed the Israeli occupation of the West Bank and Gaza as belying the liberal political principles that underlay their identity as Jewish-Americans and which, they argued, were the foundation of Israel's natural and close alliance with the United States. By contrast, religious Zionists in the United States, whose identity as an ethnic group in American society is much less important to them than their religious identity, opposed the peace accords because they required Israel to relinquish land that the religious community considered part of the biblical patrimony and necessary for Israel to fulfill the function they envisioned for it: the harbinger of the Redemption.

Diasporic members who are the product of some long-standing historical conflict might identify the current conflict with the historical conflict that caused their dispersion, as many Armenian-Americans have tied the Nagorno-Karabagh conflict to the early twentieth-century genocide. This dynamic is not exclusive to the two cases under study here. One scholar of the Chinese diaspora notes that they

> tend to embrace a pure cause. They treat today as if it were still an evil yesterday with which one could not compromise....[They also] tend to not hear the nuanced complexities and possibilities of change for the better in the situation back home. They dwell in the past [and are] ... too locked inside hates and angers of the past. Complete victory, the annihilation of the adversary, not peaceful diversity or democracy, is too much the cause of the diaspora.[56]

The domestic political system of the host state affects the degree to which this can be taken as a general statement, however. Ethnic diasporas in the United States have often absorbed a great deal of America's multicultural ethos and liberal social values, and indeed they sometimes try to export those values back to their homeland. This tends to make diasporas favor peace efforts when the U.S. government does so.[57] The largest and most mainstream Armenian organization, the Armenian Assembly of America, is far more supportive of conflict resolution in Karabagh, for example, than is the extremist Dashnak.[58]

WHAT AFFECTS DIASPORA ATTITUDES TOWARD CONFLICT RESOLUTION IN THE HOMELAND?

A diaspora community's interests in and attitudes toward potential peace deals involving its kin state stem from the interrelated concerns of identity and interest. Four main concerns can be identified that influence diasporic postures toward conflict resolution efforts in their homeland:

· a concern to maintain their ethnic identity as they conceive of it;

· a competition with the homeland for leadership of the transnational community;

· organizational or bureaucratic interests stemming from diasporic organizations; and

· the diaspora's other political interests and goals in its host state.

Concern to Maintain Identity

As noted previously, the ethnic identity of a diaspora group is made up of elements that are shared with the homeland as well as other elements that are unique to the diaspora and derive from its separate experiences. The diaspora's identity is also affected by the degree to which its leaders are actively engaged in domestic affairs in the homeland. The homeland itself is a key component of the diaspora's identity, providing a territorial, cultural, and social focus for the ethnic identity of the diaspora community. In the homeland, the community's language is the language of daily interaction, and all the symbols of sovereignty—currency, stamps, military, flag, and the like—are ingredients that reinforce the identity of the diaspora kin in ways similar to their functions in cultivating and sustaining the national identity of the homeland's citizens. The homeland's function as a territorial, tangible focus of diasporic identity means that the "wholeness" of the homeland's territory is a key marker of the nation's well-being (it serves the same role, as well as other, more practical roles, for the homeland community). Thus, a territorial conflict between the homeland and a neighboring state or internal separatist movement generally becomes a major ingredient in diasporic identity.

The threat to the community's survival that the conflict represents can serve as an important mobilizing force for diasporic communities, enabling them to build institutions, raise funds, and promote activism among community members who might otherwise allow their ethnic identity to fade to the level of mere "folkways." This is especially true for diasporas who are part of the rich and accommodating tapestry of American multiculturalism. Zvi Gitelman has argued that the open nature of American society has led diaspora Jewry, similar to many other ethnic Americans, to lose much of the "content" of their ethno-cultural and religious identity and create instead a "a highly individualized ethnic [Jewish] identity." This dynamic "further erodes commonality of experience, the 'mutual understandings and interpretations' that are the substance of 'thin' Jewish content."[59] In such an environment, a visit to the homeland is often seen as the "silver bullet that can magically transform a spoiled suburban teenager into a committed Jew in a few short weeks."[60] The fate of the homeland's violent conflict can thus play an important role in the diaspora community's ability to maintain and nourish its own ethnic identity.

Peace itself can threaten diasporic identity because the threat to the homeland is a powerful tool to mobilize diaspora community members to fund diaspora organizations and engage in political activity in the host state. After the signing of the Oslo Agreement in September 1993, Arthur Hertzberg wrote that with peace in the Middle East, Israel would no longer remain Jewish-America's "secular religion," and the diaspora would have to reshape its identity and institutions to meet domestic American challenges.[61] Indeed, after Oslo, many Jewish-American organizations began to ask what their source of political recruitment would be in the era of peace and what would compel them to remain Jews if the danger to Israel receded.[62] It was in this context that some sounded the alarm that "the declining needs of Israel will contribute to the steady decline of Jewish giving, weakening American Jewish institutions and accelerating the rate of [Jewish] assimilation."[63]

Moreover, if a homeland government chooses to pursue reconciliation with a historical enemy, diaspora communities may feel that their identity as historical victims of that enemy is under threat. To the extent that an Armenian rapprochement with Turkey requires de-emphasizing the genocide issue, for example, it threatens the identity of diaspora Armenians, for whom, as has been noted, the genocide is a central feature of their national narrative. As Khachig Tölölyan and Krikor Beledian write, "The diaspora ... has the Genocide as its point of departure. It clings to the memory of the Catastrophe; the more distant the memory becomes, the more the diaspora seems to write about it."[64] If the Armenian state, the international embodiment of Armenianness, decides to put the Genocide lower down on its list of national priorities, it is by implication devaluing diaspora Armenians as part of the transnational Armenian community.

In other cases, however, a peace deal may be congruent with the diaspora's ethnic-American identity. Some Armenian-American community leaders, for example, concerned that the ongoing Nagorno-Karabagh conflict is sustaining corrupt and antidemocratic political tendencies in Yerevan, are now pressing harder for Armenia to clean up its affairs.[65]

Contestation with the Homeland over National Leadership

In transnational ethnic communities, we have noted, the very notion of the national interest is often contested: diasporas may believe that national politics should take their preferences and situation into account, while homeland elites may wish to vest national politics entirely within the institutions of the nation-state. The leadership of the diasporic Armenian Dashnak Party rejects any distinction between "native Armenians" and "diasporans" in involvement in Armenia's politics as "insulting," whereas the former Armenian president Ter-Petrossian saw Armenia and the diaspora as "two different polities."[66] The Dashnak Party and the Armenian government in this period struggled mightily over who represented Armenian interests in settling the conflict in Nagorno-Karabagh.

The diaspora community's activism can be valuable for the homeland in its conflict with a neighbor. Armenian-American political clout was essential to instituting and maintaining a ban on U.S. aid to Azerbaijan over the objections of major American oil firms and the U.S. State Department.[67] Likewise, Jewish lobbying helped establish that compliance by American companies with the Arab boycott of Israel was illegal in the United States. But when the homeland government decides to pursue reconciliation with a historical rival, diaspora activism can be perceived as interference in the homeland's developing sovereign relations with other nations, including the United States. For example, in response to efforts by the Armenian diaspora in the fall of 2000 to push a U.S. congressional resolution condemning the genocide, Turkey closed its borders to Armenian nationals. Thus, homeland citizens bore the brunt of Turkish anger at a diaspora political initiative that was only weakly supported by the homeland government.

Indeed, the Armenian-American diaspora is perhaps the example par excellence of homeland-diaspora rivalries over leadership and national interest because of the diaspora's overwhelming role in sustaining Armenian national identity during the years of Soviet rule. As noted before, for a long time, the Armenian national cause was upheld by the diaspora, specifically by the Dashnak Party, which served as a sort of "government-of-exiles."[68] The degree of diaspora dominance extended even to the Armenian Church because the Armenian Church in the Soviet Union had been co-opted by the Soviet government. The Armenian diaspora, especially its highly mobilized U.S.-based community, has always been dedicated to homeland affairs, often serving as a critical lifeline for Armenian security and welfare needs. By the mid-1990s, "contributions to Armenian relief from the Armenian [diaspora] community amounted to $50 million to $75 million a year."[69] Razmik Panossian has written that since the time of Armenia's independence from Soviet rule in 1991, "sending financial and material aid to Armenia has become [the] operative paradigm of homeland-diaspora relations."[70] The Armenian government of President Ter-Petrossian sought to control the diaspora fund-raising efforts under a government-controlled Armenia Fund—allegedly to "keep politics out" of the process of the building of the country but actually to neutralize the influence of traditional diaspora parties on it. While the more moderate diaspora parties generally lent unqualified support to the Armenian government, the Dashnak bloc, the Armenian Revolutionary Federation (ARF), assumed an opposition role.[71] The Dashnak, with its pan-Armenian orientation and long-established prominence in carrying the torch of Armenian nationalism, challenged the home regime's monopoly in defining Armenia's national interests vis-à-vis Nagorno-Karabagh and relations with Turkey, its religious and cultural practices, its national mythology (particularly with regard to the Armenian genocide), and even the very notion of "Armenianness." These disputes led to the withdrawal of the century-old Dashnak organization from the Armenia Fund and intensified the dissension in homeland-diaspora relations.[72] Similarly, in Israel's early years, Ben-Gurion sought to curtail the influence of Zionist funds from overseas on policymaking.[73]

The emergence of the independent state of Armenia itself challenged the status of the diaspora within the transnational Armenian community, and the new state brought a new set of interests to the discussion of Armenian national interest. The diaspora leadership has little reason to consider repairing relations with Turkey, for example, but the weak Armenian state has strong incentive to do so. Turkey has been forced by circumstance to recognize the harm diasporic activism can wreak on its bilateral relations with Armenia, the United States, France, and other states where diaspora activists have managed to put the genocide issue on the national political agenda. These diaspora efforts were not coordinated with the government in Yerevan and were to a degree imposed upon it. Yet the Turkish government held Armenia's present leadership responsible for the ongoing recognition campaign. At the same time, Turkey has been trying to use direct negotiations with the Armenian state government over the genocide issue as a way of defanging the Armenian diaspora's capacity for independent action. Turkey announced in January 2001 that it had "opened a direct diplomatic channel" with Yerevan to discuss the genocide issue.[74] The U.S. government has also found diaspora activism to be a confounding factor in its foreign policy. When the U.S. House of Representatives neared passage of a nonbinding resolution recognizing the Armenian Genocide, Turkey had threatened to halt American military flights from the Incirlik air base that were used to enforce the northern no-fly zone over Iraq. The House leadership pulled the resolution only after then President Bill Clinton intervened with a letter to members of Congress. Likewise, the French National Assembly unanimously passed a law recognizing the massacres as a genocide in January 2001. Turkey has since curtailed its relations with France, a fellow North Atlantic Treaty Organization member and a prominent member of the European Union, which Turkey hopes to join.

In a similar and ironic fashion, the Azerbaijani and Turkish governments have both improved ties with Israel in part as a way of compensating for their lack of a strong American diaspora.[75] By cozying up to Israel, they have tried to win the support of Jewish diaspora organizations on Capitol Hill and fracture the Jewish groups' previously close ties with their Armenian counterparts. Explained the Azerbaijani ambassador to Washington: "We understood that we needed to make friends in this country. We knew how strong Jewish groups are. They have asked us about the condition of Jews in our country. I helped them to go to Azerbaijan and open Jewish schools. They came back with [a] good understanding [of the conflict]."[76] Thus, the son of the Azerbaijani president announced in 1999, "We now have a lobby in the United States and that is the Jewish community."[77]

In the case of the Armenian genocide issue, competing interests (the homeland's political interests and the diaspora's identity interests) over the homeland's conflicts with historical rivals have become a focal point for competing claims to leadership of the transnational Armenian community. This case also illustrates well the independent capacity for action enjoyed by diaspora activists in international affairs, and the consequently serious fashion with which they are treated by governments beyond their homeland.

Organizational and Bureaucratic Interests in Homeland Conflicts

In addition to those concerns about homeland conflicts that derive directly from the impact of those conflicts on the diaspora's identity, diasporas may have organizational or political interests that are affected by the homeland conflict and its potential resolution. Settlement of a homeland conflict may threaten long-cherished political institutions in the diaspora community. If the Arab-Israeli conflict is resolved peacefully, for example, the AIPAC is likely to see its mission greatly diminished, along with its membership, its funding, and its level of attention from elected officials in Washington.[78] As one senior diaspora activist explained, "We are an organization that receives [many] millions of dollars a year. We must continue to create issues to satisfy our donors and convince them of our importance. Thus, even when there is peace, we will still be finding issues to deal with."[79]

Moreover, for communities that were deeply involved in homeland struggles, resolution of the conflict may lead to a loss of status in both the homeland and the host states, as the diaspora's support becomes less crucial for the homeland leadership, and the host state's foreign policy establishment turns its attention elsewhere. The importance of diaspora political activism to both homeland and host governments can also elevate diaspora leaders to new heights of political prestige. For example, the American Jewish Committee plays an active role at the United Nations, holding dozens of meetings every year with sovereign state missions in New York in an effort to promote support for Israel and protection for smaller diaspora Jewish communities in other countries.[80] In the American context, diaspora community leaders gain status within the community and within the broader American polity through such political connections; there is a sort of secondary value attached to activism on behalf of community interests.

The diaspora's support and influence may also be called upon both by the homeland government and by the host state's government as each seeks to influence the other's policies in a congenial direction. Once a conflict is settled, the high-level meetings and phone calls may recede, and diasporic community leaders find that their internal communal prestige and their external levers of influence both degrade as a result. In addition, the struggle between different diasporic camps over homeland peace policies may become an extension of their broader competition for position and power among their ethnic constituents and within host state politics. Within the Jewish-American and Armenian communities, multiple organizations compete for time and attention on Capitol Hill and other corridors of power. They likewise try to link themselves to political allies in the homeland so as to increase their prestige there.

Concerns about Political and Social Status in the Host Society

In many cases, the policies of homeland authorities with respect to their ongoing violent conflicts may also impinge on diaspora communities' political or social status in their host society. When kin states violate norms that are valued by the host state (such as, for Americans, democracy or human rights), diasporas are often implicated or held accountable morally and politically. The U.S. government and perhaps even the U.S. public may expect diaspora leaders to persuade or pressure their homeland government to alter its policies in a more congenial direction. Israel's democratic system of government has certainly made proud ethnic identification and activism easier for American Jews. To the extent that the young state of Armenia fails to combat corruption and consolidate its democracy, this makes diaspora lobbying work more difficult and threatens the strength and degree of U.S. support for Armenia. It also limits the degree of financial support the American diaspora is willing to provide. As reported by the *Washington Post,* "During a visit to Washington [in June 2000], President Kocherian pleaded with leaders of the diaspora to invest more money in Armenia. But, according to participants in the meeting, he got a cool reception. There was a general sense that the country needs to put its own economic house in order before appealing for more funds from outside."[81]

The homeland's policies toward its violent conflict can also impinge on the diaspora's ability to achieve cherished political goals. This is especially true when the homeland government rejects U.S. policy preferences in dealing with the conflict or a potential peace process. The violence sponsored by the Palestinian nationalist movement over many years, and Arab states' endorsement of that violence, severely hampered the ability of Arab-Americans generally (and Palestinian-Americans more particularly) to integrate themselves into American electoral politics. In 1999, a prominent Arab-American was removed from a government-convened panel examining U.S. counterterrorism policy because of (perhaps prejudicially rooted) concerns about his attitude toward Arab terrorism against Israeli and American targets.[82] Thus, homeland policies can affect the status of diasporic communities in America.

Finally, homeland conflicts and peace efforts can confront diaspora leaders with a dilemma of dual loyalties and torn allegiances. For example, when the Bush administration in 1991 threatened to withhold loan guarantees to Israel unless Israel agreed not to spend the money in the occupied West Bank and Gaza, Jewish-American advocacy organizations were forced to choose between their good relations with the U.S. foreign policy establishment and their loyal support of Israeli policies in its conflict with the Palestinians. Most chose to support Israeli policy at the cost of incurring the wrath of their American partners. But after the bilateral U.S.-Israeli confrontation was resolved and the loan guarantees were put into place, many of those same organizations joined the effort to pressure the Israeli government to adopt a different attitude toward settlement activity in the West Bank and Gaza.

CONCLUSION

The foregoing analysis of the Armenian and Jewish cases suggests, although it cannot demonstrate conclusively, the existence of an important third level, in addition to the international and the domestic levels, in the negotiation and res-olution of ethnic conflicts. This level is composed of kin communities that cross state boundaries and that act independently within their states of domicile, within their ethnic homeland, and internationally in relations with third-party states and international organizations. As the Armenian and Jewish cases show, this third level can have a significant impact on the sovereign decision making of states with respect to questions of peace and war.

Studying the role of diasporas in homeland conflicts is important for reasons beyond the need to encompass empirical complexities in any analysis of conflict resolution. Exploring further the contest between homeland and diaspora over national identity and national interest, and how that context influences poten-tial peace deals, enables scholars to better integrate identity issues, including transnational communal politics, as a variable into the study of international re-lations. First, it illuminates a shadowy facet of conflict resolution: that the com-munities wrapped up in an ethno-national conflict often extend far beyond the arena of fighting. Second, it highlights the elastic nature of national interest as defined by constituencies inside and outside the state. Third, it will improve the understanding of how international and domestic level forces combine to pro-duce U.S. foreign policy.

These elements are usually neglected in traditional international relations scholarship, which bases its understanding of state behavior on limited as-sumptions about a state's identity and interests. Realist theorists argue that states are interested primarily in security and therefore search for power, whereas liberal theorists argue that states are concerned also with gains in wealth and other goods. As an increasing proportion of violence within and be-tween states has centered around issues of communal identity rather than power and wealth, international relations scholars have tried to struggle with the nature of national identity and how it shapes states' understanding of their interests. Although constructivist theoretical developments are most hospitable to this type of analysis, they are not necessarily the only path to understand-ing how identity affects interests. This chapter has emphasized simply the ne-cessity of developing such an understanding, through recognizing that national communities transcend state boundaries; identity-focused conflicts within and between states thus engage the attention and interests of kin communities that may reside far from the battlefield. In confronting the kin state's conflict, the diaspora attempts to promote its own view of its ethnic community's identity and interests, a view that is not always congruent with the view of the home-land authorities. This is particularly, but not uniquely, evident in the Armenian and Jewish diasporas.

The importance of the diaspora in such conflicts shows that neither the vision of identity as fixed and dependent on material factors nor the vision of identity as entirely subjective, contingent, and shifting are wholly accurate. The national groups under study here do shift their self-conceptions, and by consequence their politics, over time in response to geographic separation, life in different types of societies, and other separate experiences. However, at the same time, they retain certain objective components of a coherent national identity: shared history, folkways such as food and music, and most important, the objective reality of a territorial homeland. The homeland serves as the physical embodiment of the shared national identity, and its political and territorial fate has profound implications for the subjective identity of the diaspora and the transnational community. Thus, both subjective and objective factors combine to shape national identity and transnational communal politics. We hope that the foregoing analysis will inspire further work on similar topics that will spur theoretical development to integrate cultural identity as a variable within international relations.

NOTES

1. The authors are grateful to Khachig Tölölyan for his generous contributions of ideas and information while this project was in formation.

2. See Michael Dobbs, "Foreign Aid Shrinks but Not for All," *Washington Post*, 24 January 2001, 1.

3. The role of diasporas most frequently cited in the news media is their financial role in sustaining a conflict by funding either armed insurrectionist groups or government efforts to eradicate them. A recent study by scholars at the World Bank shows that "by far the strongest effect of war on the risk of subsequent war works through diasporas. After five years of post-conflict peace, the risk of renewed conflict is around six times higher in the societies with the largest diasporas in America than those without American diasporas. Presumably this effect works through the financial contributions of diasporas to rebel organizations." These are certainly dramatic findings. Yet as our research shows, the diaspora's involvement in homeland conflicts can be much more complex and engage many traditional tools of interstate politics in addition to money. For more on the financial contributions of diasporas to homeland conflict, see Paul Collier and Anke Hoeffler, "Greed and Grievance in Civil War," The World Bank, Policy Research Working Papers, May 2000.

4. Michael Mandelbaum, ed., *The New European Diasporas: National Minorities and Conflict in Eastern Europe* (New York: Council on Foreign Relations, 2000).

5. This aspect of conflict resolution, known as "public diplomacy," is examined with respect to the Israeli-Palestinian conflict by Tamara Cofman Wittes, *Symbols and Security in Ethnic Conflict: Confidence-Building in the Palestinian-Israeli Peace Process, 1993–1995* (Ph.D. diss., Georgetown University, 2000).

6. Rabbi Andrew Baker and Barry Jacobs, American Jewish Committee, interview by Yossi Shain, Washington DC, 21 December 2000.

7. Robert D. Putnam, "Diplomacy and Domestic Politics: The Logic of Two-Level Games," *International Organization* 42 (Summer 1988): 427–60.

8. Jeffrey W. Knopf, "Beyond Two-Level Games: Domestic-International Interaction in the Intermediate-Range Nuclear Forces Negotiations," *International Organization* 47 (Autumn 1993): 599–628. Lee Ann Patterson expanded Putnam's model into a "three-level analysis" when she studied agricultural policy reform in the European Union. See

"Agricultural Policy Reform in the European Community: A Three-Level Game Analysis," *International Organization* 51 (Winter 1997): 135–65.

9. Bernard Waserstein, *Vanishing Diaspora: The Jews in Europe since 1945* (London: Penguin Books, 1996), 91.

10. For example, an Argentine Jewish community center was bombed in 1994 by Islamist terrorists who opposed Israeli policies.

11. Some prestate diasporas may play a critical role in the struggle for the creation of a new ethnocentric state in the traditional homeland. This has been the case of diasporic Sikhs who have led the struggle for an independent Khalistan in India, or the diasporic Tamils who are the core supporters of the separatist Liberation Tigers of Tamil Eelam. Gabriel Sheffer has argued that with the establishment of independent states in their claimed homelands, stateless diasporas are likely to shift their methods of activism from an aggressive posture, which often includes being a source for military recruits or terrorists, to more "innocuous exchanges" involving cash transfers, tourism, and other nonlethal activities that help in consolidating their kin states. Gabriel Sheffer, "Ethno-National Diasporas and Security," *Survival* 36, no. 1 (1994): 64.

12. U.S. Ambassador Richard Bogosian, "Conflict in the Horn of Africa: Middle Eastern and African Perspectives" (remarks at The Middle East Institute, Washington DC, 17 January 2001).

13. Jesse Driscoll, "The Economics of Insanity: Funding the Ethiopia-Eritrea War" (Georgetown University, photocopy, 2000), 6–7.

14. The consensus among American Jewry against the concession on Jerusalem appears quite broad; nonetheless, the ongoing Palestinian-Israeli violence and the Israeli election campaign have tempered criticism; many diaspora leaders were aghast when the chairman of the Conference of Presidents of Major American Jewish Organizations, Ron Lauder, addressed an antigovernment rally in Jerusalem with strong words against the concessions. Thus, the sense of an immediate security threat strengthens the imperative for expressions of unity with the homeland government even when it is clear that the diaspora strongly disagrees. Elihu Salpeter, "Israel Has a Right to Know on Whose Behalf Ron Lauder Will Speak from Now On," *Ha'aretz Daily—English Internet Edition*, 17 January 2001, <http://www.haaretz.co.il/eng> (accessed 17 January 2001). See also "US Reform Leader Slams Ron Lauder for Addressing Jerusalem Rally," *Ha'aretz Breaking News*, 9 January 2001, <http://www2.haaretz.co.il/breaking-news/jewishnews /346612.stm> (accessed 9 January 2001).

15. See Janine Zacharia, "The Unofficial Ambassadors of the Jewish State," *Jerusalem Post*, 2 April 2000, 1.

16. The clearest examples in the Jewish case are the attempts of diaspora organizations to tend to the welfare of small and vulnerable Jewish diasporas in other countries and their lobbying the U.S. government to move its embassy from Tel Aviv to Jerusalem. In the Armenian case, the homeland government does not officially oppose diaspora efforts to win international recognition of the Armenian Genocide but often finds that these efforts complicate its bilateral relations.

17. Indeed, war and peace are deeply influenced by historical images of hostility and friendliness among nations. As Kenneth Boulding has observed, in conflict resolution the most critical images "are those which the nation has of itself and of those other bodies in the system which constitute its international environment. ... Whether transmitted orally and informally through the family or more formally through schooling and the written

word, the national image is essentially a historical image—that is, an image which extends through time." See Kenneth Boulding, "National Images and International Systems," in *Approaches to Peace: A Reader in Peace Studies*, ed. David P. Barash (Oxford: Oxford University Press, 2000), 46–47. Diasporic communities often personify the national community even after the reestablishment of an independent nation-state. They may embody the experience of calamity and suffering stemming from dispossession and the loss of the homeland, as well as the ideals of recovery and restoration. Armenians and Jews have often been identified as the archetypal diasporaic communities, or "mobilized diasporas," to use John Armstrong's expression. Their chronicles and legends continue to play an important role in the life and politics of their independent homelands. Anthony D. Smith, "Zionism and Diaspora Nationalism," *Israel Affairs* 2, no. 2 (1995): 1–19.

18. On the concept of an ethnonational group's "chosen trauma" and its effects on conflict resolution, see Vamik Volkan, *Bloodlines: From Ethnic Pride to Ethnic Terrorism* (New York: Farrar, Straus and Giroux, 1997).

19. See Richard G. Hovannisian's lectures: "On Historical Memory and Armenian Foreign Policy," Haigazian University, Beirut, Lebanon, 31 July 2000, <http://www .haigazian.edu.lb/announce/pressrelease.htm> (accessed January 2002).

20. Carol Migdalovitz, "Armenia-Azerbaijan Conflict," *CRS Issue Brief for Congress*, #92109 (1 October 1999), 10, <http://www.fas.org/man/crs/92-109.htm> (accessed January 2002).

21. Even in Germany, where ethnic lobbies do not play a large role in politics, the government's controversial decision to recognize Croatia was influenced by the large Croatian presence in the country.

22. Douglas Frantz, "Armenia and Azerbaijan Signal Progress in Talks on Enclave," *New York Times*, 20 February 2001, A3.

23. Other countries also note the impressive influence of ethnic lobbies on U.S. foreign policy priorities. See Yossi Shain, "For Ethnic Americans, the Old Country Calls," *Foreign Service Journal*, October 2000, 17–24.

24. Anonymous Jewish-American lobbyist, interview by Yossi Shain, Washington DC, 15 October 1999.

25. Hafiz M. Pashayev (Azerbaijani ambassador to the United States), interview by Yossi Shain, Washington, DC, October 21, 1999.

26. Inan Ozyildiz (counselor, Turkish Embassy, Washington, DC), interview by Yossi Shain, Washington DC, November 4, 1999.

27. This point was made by Khachig Tölölyan in a letter to Yossi Shain, 4 October 1999.

28. See Harvey Sicherman, "Judaism and the World: The Holy and the Profane," *Orbis* (Spring 1998): 195–216.

29. Armenian Forum, "The New Thinking Revisited," <http://www.gomidas.org /forum/af2c.htm> (accessed January 2002).

30. Ronald Suny, "Provisional Stabilities: The Politics of Identities in Post-Soviet Eurasia," *International Security* 24, no. 3 (1999–2000), 139–78.

31. Thomas Friedman described these actions as attempts to subvert the Israeli democratic process by Jewish-American groups that "could only thrive if they have an enemy, someone to fight. They have no positive vision to offer American Jews on the central question of American Jewish identity or the fate of Israel-Diaspora relations in this new era." Thomas L. Friedman, "Mischief Makers," *New York Times*, 5 April 1995, A25.

32. David Vital, "Diplomacy in the Jewish Interest," Occasional Paper no. 1, Nahum Goldman Chair in Diplomacy, Tel Aviv University, Tel Aviv, 1993, 8.

33. Aviel Roshwald, *Ethnic Nationalism and the Fall of Empires: Central Europe, Russia, and the Middle East, 1914–1923* (New York: Routledge, 2001), 52–53.

34. See "Kocharian Discusses Territorial Claims in Interview with Turkish TV," CNN-TR, 2 February 2001.

35. See Yossi Shain and Martin Sherman, "Dynamics of Disintegration: Diaspora Secession and the Paradox of Nation-States," *Nations and Nationalism* 4, no. 3 (1998): 321–46.

36. See Benedict Anderson, *Imagined Communities: Reflections on the Origin and Spread of Nationalism* (London: Verso, 1983); Anthony Smith, *National Identity* (Reno: University of Nevada Press, 1991).

37. Peter J. Katzenstein, ed., *The Culture of National Security: Norms and Identity in World Politics* (New York: Columbia University Press, 1996), 19.

38. Suny, "Provisional Stabilities," 147. For a study of how Israeli and Palestinian national identity affect those communities' threat perception, see Wittes, *Symbols and Security in Ethnic Conflict.*

39. Gil Merom, "Israel's National Security and the Myth of Exceptionalism," *Political Science Quarterly* 114, no. 3 (1999): 412–13.

40. "Kocherian Inaugural Address Calls For Strengthening Ties with Armenian Diaspora," Media Advisory, Armenian National Committee of America, Washington DC, 9 April 1998, <http://www.anca.org/press/press98/04–09.html> (accessed January 2001).

41. Kocharian demonstrated his commitment to the issue in September 2000 at the United Nations Millennium Summit, when he condemned Turkey's denial of the genocide in his speech. See Hovann Simonian, "The Armenian Diaspora Gets Its Second Wind, as Relations with the Homeland Improve over the Genocide Issue," *Transition Online-TOL,* January 18, 2001, <http://www.tol.cz>.

42. Ibid.

43. When in September 2000, the newly elected Israeli president spoke before a large gathering of Jewish educators from Israel and the diaspora, he announced that Jewish education and identity outside Israel "could at best last two or three generations." These words angered diaspora leaders, who decried his ignorance about Jewish diasporic life, and even Israeli commentators attacked the president for his "foolish outbursts." The New York–based Jewish weekly *The Forward* wrote in a lead editorial that President Moshe Katzav's speech was scandalous. When pressured by the media, the president amended his statement and declared that he believed that diaspora Jews "have the right to live abroad." A leading Israeli journalist observed that "what the Jews of the Diaspora were willing to hear (even as they clenched their teeth) from someone like [Israel's founding prime minister David] Ben-Gurion 40 years ago, they are not prepared to put up with from someone like President Katzav." Eliahu Salpeter, "Unfortunate Utterances on the Diaspora," *Ha'aretz Daily—English Internet Edition,* 20 September 2000. Also see Gil Hoffman, "Katzav: More Cash Needed for Western Aliya," *Jerusalem Post,* 15 September 2000.

44. For the case of Israel, see Alan Dowty, "Israeli Foreign Policy and the Jewish Question," *Middle East Review of International Affairs* 3, no. 1 (1999): 8, <http://meria.idc.ac.il/journal/1999/issue1/dowty.pdf> (accessed January 2001).

45. Yair Sheleg, "The Diaspora as a Strategic Asset," *Ha'aretz Daily—English Internet Edition,* 9 January 2001, <http://www.haaretz.co.il/eng>.

46. Khachig Tölölyan and Krikor Beledian, interview, *Armenian Forum: Fresh Perspectives on Armenia-Diaspora Relations,* <http://www.gomidas.org/forum/af3c.htm> (accessed January 2002).

47. In his first public speech as head of the Mossad, Ephraim Halevy stated that one of the reasons for the existence of a strong Jewish state is to provide a source of strength to the diaspora: "Whether we like it or not, the security of Israel impacts and influences the fate of Jews abroad. … What happens in Jerusalem, Tel Aviv and Haifa has an impact on the plight of Jews in New York, London, and Moscow. I believe that when an [Israeli] fighter sets out on a mission he isn't endangering his life not only to protect the borders of the state and universal values. He is doing so with the very deep awareness and desire to protect the existence of the Jewish nation." Ephraim Halevy, "The Zionist Ethos and the Security of Israel," speech reported in *Yediot Aharonot*, 22 December 2000.

48. This point is, of course, most acute for those kin communities that do live in the "near abroad" or in countries that have hostile relations with the homeland.

49. Tamar Hausman, "Sacrifice of Temple Mt. 'Risks Ties to U.S. Jews,'" *Ha'aretz Daily—English Internet Edition*, Anglo-File section, 5 January 2001, <http://www.haaretz.co.il/eng> (accessed January 2001).

50. Yair Sheleg, "World Jewry Thinks Jerusalem and Temple Mount Is an Issue for All Jews—Not Just Barak—to Decide," *Ha'aretz Daily—English Internet Edition*, 1 January 2001, <http://www.haaretz.co.il/eng> (accessed January 2001).

51. Rabbi David Clayman, quoted in Hausman, "Sacrifice of Temple Mt."

52. It is important to remember that on issues of national mythology, neither the homeland nor the diaspora communities are monolithic. According to Stephan Astourian, "It is difficult to talk of the diaspora as a united entity. [In the case of Armenia] the following generalizations can be made. The ARF [Armenian Revolutionary Federation] was rabidly opposed to any and all of the tentative peace deals. The Ramgavar party had split into at least two groups. Those in Armenia opposed the final peace deal. Those in the U.S. were more ambiguous.… The Hunchakian party was also divided into three groups.… Those in Armenia were in fact a dummy organization totally controlled by Ter-Petrossian. They supported the peace deals. The attitude of the other ones, who are in general of very little influence in Armenian life, is unclear.… The Armenian Assembly … did not take a stance on that issue. Beyond these organizations, there was a group of diaspora Armenians under the influence of, or in agreement with, the views propounded in the columns of the Armenian International Magazine published in Glendale. They tended to support the peace deal in the name of realism, pragmatism, moderation, etc.…[T]hese individuals [generally] consist of Armenians disaffected with the established organizations, some professionals, some half-assimilated Armenians, and some anti-ARF people." Stephan Astourian, personal communication with Yossi Shain, 25 January 2001. For more on diaspora Armenian views, see Edmond Y. Azadian, *History on the Move: Views, Interviews and Essays on Armenian Issues* (Detroit, MI: distributed by Wayne State University Press, 1999).

53. Hank Sheinkopf, quoted in Rachel Donadio, "GOP Woos Arabs and Hawks; Dems on Mideast Defensive," *Ha'aretz Daily—English Internet Edition*, 26 October 2000, <http://www.haaretz.co.il/eng>.

54. Salpeter, "Israel Has a Right to Know."

55. See Matthew Frankel, "The $10 Billion Question: AIPAC and Loan Guarantees to Israel," *Fletcher Forum* (Winter/Spring 1995): 169.

56. See Edward Friedman, "The Diaspora and Why Taiwan's Future Matters So" (paper prepared for a conference on the Taiwan Question, University of Californian-Berkeley, 28–29 September 1996), 12.

57. By contrast, if the U.S. government supports one side in the conflict exclusively, it often cultivates the diaspora community to support its policy. This was the case with the Cuban-American diaspora, as described in Yossi Shain, *Marketing the American Creed Abroad: Diasporas in the U.S. and Their Homelands* (Cambridge, England: Cambridge University Press, 1999).

58. Ross Vartian (executive director of the Armenian Assembly of America), interview by Yossi Shain, Washington, DC, 8 March 2000.

59. Zvi Gitelman, "The Decline of the Diaspora Jewish Nation: Boundaries, Content, and Jewish Identity," *Jewish Social Studies* 4 (Winter 1998): 128.

60. Ibid., 122.

61. Arthur Hertzberg, "Less Religious on Israeli Matters," *Ha'aretz* (Hebrew Edition), 10 October 1993, B2.

62. Amy Dockers Marcus, "Burden of Peace: American Jews Grapple with an Identity Crisis as Peril to Israel Ebbs," *Wall Street Journal*, 14 September 1994, 1, 6.

63. J. J. Goldberg, *Jewish Power: Inside the American Jewish Establishment* (Reading MA: Addison-Wesley, 1996), 359.

64. Tölölyan and Beledian, *Armenian Forum: Fresh Perspectives on Armenia-Diaspora Relations.*

65. Michael Dobbs, "Armenia Pins Economic Hopes on Peace," *Washington Post*, 6 September 2000, A13, A16.

66. Razmik Panossian, "Between Ambivalence and Intrusion: Armenia-Diaspora Relations," *Diaspora* 7, no. 2 (1998): 171.

67. Migdalovitz, "Armenia-Azerbaijan Conflict," 13.

68. Khachig Tölölyan, "Exile Governments in the Armenian Polity," in *Governments-in-Exile in Contemporary World Politics*, ed. Yossi Shain (New York: Routledge, 1991), 166–87.

69. Samuel P. Huntington, *The Clash of Civilizations and the Remaking of World Order* (New York: Simon and Schuster, 1996), 280.

70. Panossian, "Between Ambivalence and Intrusion," 175. (Italics removed from original.)

71. R. H. Dekmejian and Angelos Themelis, "Ethnic Lobbies in U.S. Foreign Policy: A Comparative Analysis of the Jewish, Greek, Armenian and Turkish Lobbies," Occasional Research Paper no. 13, Institution of International Relations, Athens, Greece, 1997, 31.

72. Panossian, "Between Ambivalence and Intrusion," 177; Levon Hm. Abrahamian, "Armenian Homeland and Diaspora: Divergence and Encounter" (1999, photocopy).

73. David Schoenbaum, *The United States and the State of Israel* (New York: Oxford University Press, 1993), 63.

74. Armenian Assembly of America, "Armenia This Week," 12 January 2001, <http://www.aaainc.org/press.htm>.

75. See Ambrosio's contribution (chapter 8) to this volume.

76. Pashayev, interview.

77. David B. Ottaway and Dan Morgan, "Jewish-Armenian Split Spreads on the Hill," *Washington Post*, 9 February 1999, A15.

78. Marcus, "Burden of Peace."

79. Anonymous Jewish-American activist, interview by Yossi Shain, Washington, DC, 21 December 2000.

80. Internal Jewish organization document on file with authors.

81. Michael Dobbs, "Armenia Pins Economic Hopes on Peace," *Washington Post*, 6 September 2000, A13.

82. Caryle Murphy and Juliet Eilperin, "Muslim Won't Serve on Terrorism Panel," *Washington Post*, 10 July 1999, A6.

Chapter 10

Legitimate Influence or Parochial Capture? Conclusions on Ethnic Identity Groups and the Formulation of U.S. Foreign Policy

Thomas Ambrosio

In many ways ... the participation of ethnic diasporas in shaping U.S. foreign policy is a truly positive phenomenon.

—Yossi Shain[1]

At present, the negative consequences of ethnic involvement may well outweigh the undoubted benefits this activism at times confers on America in world affairs.

—Tony Smith[2]

The role of ethnic identity groups in the formulation of U.S. foreign policy appears to be a durable characteristic of the foreign policy process. Prior to the rise of a "multicultural foreign policy"—in which non–Anglo-Saxon groups became increasingly prevalent and powerful—U.S. foreign policy had long had an ethnic component. McCartney's chapter (chapter 2), for example, shows how American national identity was closely connected to the dual principles of Anglo-Saxon superiority and democratic political values. America's entry onto the world stage during the Spanish-American War was driven in large part by the ethnic-ideological identity of Americans. Furthermore, Catherine Scott's chapter (chapter 3) identifies "whiteness" as a basic principle shaping U.S. policy toward South African apartheid. Together, these two chapters illustrate that the "ethnic influence" on U.S. foreign policy began much earlier than many commentators would admit.[3] The principal cause of this misunderstanding is what Walker Connor, an outstanding observer of nationalism, called the "terminological chaos" that continues to infect much of political science and sociology—in particular, ignoring the distinctions between nations (political-cultural entities) and states (political-territorial entities) and employing the term *ethnic group* to refer almost exclusively to minorities within the United States or cultural groups outside of the United

States.[4] Associating *ethnic groups* solely with non–Anglo-Saxon minorities ignores the fact that American national identity has never lacked an ethnic component.[5] On the other hand, increased immigration and the rise of multiculturalism have added significantly more ethnic voices to the foreign policy process.

The revival of the old debate about the proper role for ethnic groups in the U.S. foreign policy process could be seen as an attempt by entrenched interests to preserve their own influence in the face of heightened competition, both in terms of the number of groups and their relative strength. Although these entrenched interests are not necessarily ethnic, there appears to be a sense in which the traditionally dominant ethnicity (i.e., white, Anglo-Saxon) considers itself threatened by the political rise of "new" ethnic groups, which may not have America's best interests at heart.[6] However, it is important not to take this distinction between "old" versus "new" ethnic groups too far. Even those who consider domestic multiculturalism and diversity something truly beneficial to the American body politic may still reject these principles when applied to America's foreign affairs. As Senator Charles McCurdy Mathias (R-Md.) put it in his seminal *Foreign Affairs* article: "[T]he diversity that enriches our domestic life remains a recurrent cause of difficulties in our foreign relations."[7]

As multiculturalism and diversity continue to strengthen, the debate between those who believe that U.S. foreign policy has been captured by ethnic parochialism and those who believe that ethnic interest groups have a legitimate role to play in the foreign policy process will continue apace and will likely grow in the foreseeable future. The remainder of this chapter presents a summary of the arguments of both sides and evaluates them in light of the case studies and the tragic events of 11 September 2001.

LEGITIMATE INFLUENCE

Ethnic influence on U.S. foreign policy is a reality, and ethnic identity groups compete for influence with a plethora of other special interest groups and institutional interests. At a base level, those arguing in favor of a "multicultural foreign policy" see little wrong with ethnic groups having a voice in the foreign policy process. They tend to discount the negative consequences of such influence and believe that a more diverse foreign policy actually enriches America both at home and abroad.

Six common arguments have emerged in favor of the "ethnic voices" position:

· A multicultural foreign policy is a reflection of our liberal democratic ethos.
· It respects the diversity of the United States.
· It serves as a correction for historically "white" foreign policies.
· It helps to resist the trend toward isolationism.
· It spreads democratic principles throughout the world.
· Ethnic identity groups can reinforce U.S. interests.

Liberal Democratic Values

As part of a liberal democratic state that is nominally responsive to the people, interest groups have long been an accepted part of American politics. That some groups mobilize along ethnic lines should be neither surprising nor threatening. Ethnic identity groups have legitimate interests and a right to have their voices heard. To shut certain groups out of the process merely because they are based on cultural, rather than economic or social, interests is unfair and fundamentally undemocratic. It is true that interest groups have been historically less active on foreign policy issues and that those with ties to foreign interests have been viewed with suspicion by many Americans. However, there appears to be a "new mantra" in American society in which "All politics is global!"[8] This has provided greater room for interest groups to play a part in the foreign policy process. Thus, ethnic influence on U.S. foreign policy is merely a reflection of American politics as usual. Moreover, a multicultural foreign policy is seen as good for American democracy itself: "[T]he new foreign policy role of ethnic groups is likely to reflect positively in American civic culture by reinforcing the values of democracy and pluralism at home."[9]

Diversity

As Nathan Glazer exclaimed, "We Are All Multiculturalists Now."[10] The changes in American national identity that have characterized the last half century have fundamentally altered the legitimacy of ethnic identity groups in the United States. No longer is America identified solely with the Anglo-Saxon or white identity—the American myth of the "melting pot," which assumed that individual ethnic groups would assimilate into an overarching "American" identity, has been transformed into an "American mosaic" in which "colorful individual pieces are fitted together to make a single picture."[11] Ethnic identity groups have emerged as vocal, politically relevant, and legitimate parts of the American polity. Even those groups that used to be covered solely under the rubric of "white" have begun to express their individual and unique identities. In order to reflect the American commitment to diversity, ethnic identity groups should have a role in the political process, either foreign or domestic. Moreover, one could make an argument that an active role for ethnic identity groups in the American political system may actually prevent the much-feared Balkanization of the American polity: as ethnic groups become part of the political process, they will be forced to find common ground with other ethnic groups and express a commitment to liberalism in order to remain legitimate players in the political process.[12]

Multicultural Foreign Policy as a Corrective

Some scholars have argued that U.S. foreign policy, far from being nonethnic in the past, was inherently based on ethnic principles: namely, whiteness.[13] According to this line of reasoning, ethnic identities have always played a role in the formulation and implementation of U.S. foreign policy. As additional "ethnic voices" emerge in the foreign policy process, U.S. policy will become more balanced and more accurately reflect the diversity of the country.[14]

Resisting Isolationism

U.S. internationalism during World War II and the Cold War was a divergence from the tendency toward the isolationism that had driven U.S. foreign policy since its founding. With the end of the forty-five-year struggle against the Soviet Union and a growing sense of Cold War fatigue, the potential existed for America to reorient its energies toward problems at home. Candidate Bill Clinton's unofficial slogan during the 1992 presidential campaign—"It's the Economy, Stupid!"—reflected the newfound primacy of the country's domestic agenda over international concerns.[15] However, the tendency toward isolationism has been restricted somewhat by a multicultural foreign policy.[16] Given their strong ties overseas, ethnic identity groups continue to stress the importance of foreign policy issues and of an active and internationally engaged United States. For example, African-Americans, although for a long time "noninterventionist,"[17] have emerged in the post–Cold War period as "one of the leading forces behind U.S. interventionism" in places like Haiti and Africa.[18] Moreover, Armenian-Americans and Croatian-Americans pushed the United States to become active in places like Nagorno-Karabagh and the former Yugoslavia, respectively. Although some may criticize an active role for the United States in world affairs,[19] most politicians, scholars, and commentators have rejected "neo-isolationism" as detrimental to U.S. interests.[20] Ethnic identity groups simply reinforce that rejection.

Agents of Democracy

Yossi Shain is perhaps the most prominent advocate of the idea that ethnic identity groups actively support democratization throughout the world. These groups are, in effect, "'commissioned' by American decision makers to export and safeguard American values abroad and are expected to become the moral conscience of new democracies or newly established states in their homelands."[21] Personal visits to the homeland and regular interactions with those who still reside there have served both of these ends. Moreover, the United States at times has become the primary base for political exiles who seek to overthrow authoritarian regimes at home. For example, East European ethnic groups, anti-Castro Cuban-Americans, and pro-Aristide Haitian-Americans actively supported the democratization of their respective homelands. Because all post–Cold War administrations have identified the spread of democracy as a core American national interest,[22] Shain's thesis points to a crucial role for ethnic identity groups in the promotion, rather than the detraction, of American national interests.

Reinforcing U.S. Interests

Ethnic identity groups can play an active role in reinforcing "objective" U.S. interests by augmenting U.S. policy and strengthening America's commitment to its allies. For example, the American-Israeli Public Affairs Committee (AIPAC), the largest and most powerful Jewish-American lobby and among the most powerful lobbies in the country, works to maintain and deepen America's alliance with Israel, which successive administrations have claimed to be an enduring U.S. interest.[23] For example, the U.S. State Department's "Background Note" on Israel states that America's "[c]ommitment to Israel's security and well being has been a cornerstone of U.S. policy in the Middle East since Israel's creation in 1948. . . . Israel and the United States are bound closely by historic and cultural ties as well as by mutual interests."[24] Likewise, during the Cold War, East European ethnic lobbies reinforced U.S. opposition to Soviet expansion in Europe.[25] During the Clinton administration, Irish-Americans were instrumental in pushing President Clinton toward active engagement in the Northern Ireland dispute, which had dogged U.S.-British-Irish relations for decades.[26] Rather than standing in opposition to America's "objective" national interests, ethnic identity groups go out of their way to connect their own interests to the broader national interest of the country. As the chairman of the AIPAC acknowledged: "[U]nless you can always translate [your proposals] in terms of what's in America's interest, you're lost."[27]

PAROCHIAL CAPTURE

Although it is clear that ethnic identity groups have played and continue to play a role in the U.S. foreign policy process, some raise the question of whether this should be the case. Those who argue against the legitimacy of a multicultural foreign policy often start with the premise that there exist "objective" U.S. national interests that may (or may not) differ from the interests of substate political actors (ethnic, business, or otherwise). Thus, a tension potentially exists between "national" and "special" interests. According to this argument, ethnic identity groups may harm the United States if these groups distract America from the pursuit of its national interests or induce it to pursue a foreign policy contrary to its national interests. In the worst-case scenario, ethnic groups can effectively hijack the foreign policy process and use the strength of the United States for their parochial interests.

Seven common arguments have emerged in favor of the "parochial capture" position:

· Ethnic interest groups often put their own interests ahead of "American" interests.
· They undercut the foundations of American democracy.
· They may be agents of foreign (and possibly hostile) governments.

· They promote an incoherent foreign policy.
· They resist/prevent necessary changes in U.S. foreign policy.
· Certain ethnic interest groups are simply too powerful.
· They may get the United States involved in conflicts where no American interest is threatened.

Parochial Interests versus National Interests

Samuel Huntington correctly observes that in the post–Cold War international system, uncertainty regarding U.S. national interests is widespread and understandable.[28] America is facing an environment that is racially different from the one that existed for more than four decades during the Cold War. However, Huntington alerts the reader to a more serious cause of confusion: the breakdown of American identity following the rise of multiculturalism. Without a coherent national identity, the state finds it very difficult to determine what its interests are. Ethnic interest groups, according to Huntington, reject the idea of a common American culture and refuse to concern themselves with the common good. Instead, they are primarily concerned with their parochial (ethnic) interests and the interests of their ethnic kin abroad. Unlike commercial interests, which do promote benefits for Americans (even if the circle of beneficiaries is small), "Ethnic groups promote the interests of people and entities outside the United States."[29] While at times these parochial interests coincide with American interests, Huntington warns his readers that this coincidence is more accident than intention: ethnic interest groups attempt to "influence the actions and policies of their host country and co-opt its resources and influence to serve the interests of their homeland," even if such policies are contrary to American security and national interests.[30]

Undercutting Democratic Citizenship Principles

Tony Smith takes a similar tack as Huntington, but with a different emphasis. Although the distinction between parochial and national interests is important in Smith's analysis, his primary concern is the impact of ethnic identity groups on the "enduring problem for democratic citizenship: how to balance the rights and interests of the organized few against the rights and interests of the often inattentive many."[31] Smith believes that the principles of democratic citizenship, which serve as the very foundation for the American political system, produce both privileges and obligations to individuals and substate actors. If a country is to sustain its political system, it must instill its citizens with a moral and ethical imperative to place a high premium on the common good. Unfortunately, according to Smith, ethnic identity groups often stand in opposition to the common good because they are primarily concerned with the well-being of their ethnic kin: "American power in world affairs is not something to be divided up among ethnic constituencies to be used as they will; in matter of foreign policy, the greater community should be consulted and its interests protected, while the nation's representatives should determine policy based on some idea of the common good."[32] If ethnic identity groups are allowed to accumulate too much power, the very foundations of the American political system may be threatened by substate actors as loyalty in "America" is replaced by loyalty to one's ethnic group.[33]

Agents of a Foreign Government

Both Huntington and Smith cite worries that ethnic lobbies might ultimately be in the employ of foreign governments, providing foreign states with direct access into the American political system under the guise of multiculturalism.[34] Although both are careful to avoid the negative connotations surrounding the terms *divided loyalty* or *fifth column*, the implications are clear. Connections between the diaspora and the homeland operate both ways: just as an ethnic group has influence in the homeland, the homeland has influence over the diaspora, which in turn seeks to influence Washington. This state of affairs may be dangerous if a diaspora is manipulated (or willing) to push for an American policy toward its homeland that undercuts U.S. power. For example, China could one day become a powerful enemy of the United States, but Chinese-Americans have consistently pushed for trade packages that benefit China and will ultimately strengthen it vis-à-vis the United States.[35] This argument takes the contrast between parochial and national interests one step further: ethnic interest groups may be directly working for a foreign, and possibly hostile, power.

Incoherent Foreign Policy

The dramatic decrease in the insulation of the U.S. foreign policy decision-making structure has led to an equally dramatic increase in the number and significance of domestic influences on the foreign policy process. As James Schlesinger has pointed out, "Never before in history has a dominant power been a democracy so sensitive to the claims of multiple domestic pressure groups."[36] This means that U.S. foreign policy is constantly pushed and pulled by multiple forces, some of which are dominant at certain times while others are weaker. This constantly shifting set of domestic political constellations has led to serious problems for U.S. foreign policy: in order for the United States to remain the world's leader, it must have a coherent, predictable, and consistent foreign policy; instead, other countries find it increasingly difficult to "judge what we will do or what we will say on the basis of the touchstone of national interest, permanent or transitory" since such "interests" are constantly changing.[37] Ultimately, this will harm American national interests because it will become more and more difficult to build international coalitions to achieve foreign policy goals. In short, Schlesinger asks, why should countries take risks or incur costs for American policies that may change at a moment's notice?

Static Foreign Policy

The opposite problem may be just as damaging to America's long-term security interests: the political influence of certain ethnic lobbies may become so entrenched that they prevent necessary changes in U.S. foreign policy. In other words, the United States is unable to adjust its foreign policy to changes in its external environment because certain ethnic groups support the status quo and resist any policy revisions. For example, many critics of U.S. foreign policy toward Cuba have commented that the role of the Cuban-American lobby—possibly the second- or third-strongest ethnic lobby in the United States—has ultimately harmed the American interest in spreading democracy to Cuba.[38] Moreover, the Helms-Burton Act, which penalizes foreign companies that do business with Havana, has angered many of America's European allies whose companies are punished for their dealings with Cuba. Others argue that irrespective of U.S. interests, economic sanctions against Cuba, in the form of a trade embargo, are relics of the Cold War fight against communism. And although Cuba remains formally communist, Castro's regime is no longer a serious threat. However, these sanctions remain in place (albeit in a modified and weakened form) largely because of the Cuban-American lobby.

Another example can be seen in U.S. policy toward the Caucasus. The strength of the Armenian-American lobby has prevented the Clinton and George W. Bush administrations from fully eliminating Section 907 of the 1992 Freedom Support Act, which bans U.S. foreign aid to Azerbaijan and which was placed on Baku during the Nagorno-Karabagh conflict. Both administrations have argued that Section 907 has hampered American geopolitical interests, energy security, and commercial opportunities.[39] Nevertheless, Section 907 persists as an impediment to U.S. national interests as defined by successive presidents.

Imbalances among Ethnic Lobbies

Ethnic interest groups not only attempt to influence American foreign policy, but they also attempt to block the influence of rival ethnic lobbies. Although one could "rely on the Madisonian formula of setting social interest groups against one another as countervailing powers,"[40] it is possible that one ethnic lobby might be so strong that there is no effective opposition to its influence. This could lead to a problem connected to the previous section: particular ethnic interest groups may entrench themselves so deeply into the political process that they become permanently dominant. Not only does this prevent substantive change in U.S. foreign policy, but it effectively prevents other ethnic interest groups from having their say. For example, there is little contest between the Jewish-American and the Arab-American lobby: Mitchell Bard's statement from 1988 is just as true today, "[I]f we examine the agenda of the [National Association of Arab-Americans], it is clear the Arab lobby has lost on every issue relating to Israel."[41]

Moreover, simply having a prior institutional presence in Washington provides one ethnic interest group with disproportionate influence in the foreign policy process. For example, Armenian-Americans were able to get Section 907 of the Freedom Support Act passed largely because the Azeris had virtually no presence in Washington.[42] "Even if the [ethnic interest] groups were balanced—if Turkish-Americans equaled Greek-Americans or Arab-Americans equaled Jewish-Americans," as Senator Mathias explained, "the result would not necessarily be a sound, cohesive foreign policy."[43] But without such balance, U.S. foreign policy could effectively be captured by a particular ethnic group to the exclusion of others.

Entangling Alliances

Referencing the increasing role of ethnic lobbies in American politics, *The Economist* quoted Herman Melville: "You cannot spill a drop of American blood without spilling the blood of the whole world." To this they responded: "A modern Melville might add that, thanks to its ethnic diversity, you cannot spill a drop of foreign blood without spilling the blood of an American family. Watch the news in any great American city and you get the impression that the world stops at the city limits. Walk into any ethnic enclave, however, and you find people obsessed by politics 'back home.'"[44] Ethnic interests groups, by their very nature, want the United States to support *their* ethnic kin abroad over any possible rivals. Given that the United States is home to ethnic identity groups with cultural and/or political ties throughout the world, if these groups were permitted to significantly influence U.S. foreign policy, then Washington might find itself involved in conflicts in which the United States has no national interest or is forced to take particular sides in a conflict irrespective of U.S. interests. Again, the case of the Azeri-Armenian dispute is instructive: largely because of the influence of the Armenian-American lobby, the United States has effectively taken sides against Azerbaijan in the Nagorno-Karabagh conflict, despite the obvious strategic benefits to be gained from an alliance with Baku. Similarly, the Jewish-American lobby could be seen as preventing the United States from effectively pressuring both sides in the Israeli-Palestinian dispute to achieve peace in the region. Although both lobbies point to "objective" national interests to explain America's alliance choices, it is clear that ethnic interest groups had a role in influencing, and reinforcing, this choice. In his farewell address, President Washington warned the American people to avoid permanent alliances in Europe, and Thomas Jefferson, in his first inaugural address, similarly warned against "entangling alliances." A multicultural foreign policy effectively prohibits neutrality even if neutrality is in American interests.

EVALUATING THE ARGUMENTS

Both the "ethnic voices" and the "parochial capture" arguments identify some of the promise and problems associated with the influence of ethnic identity groups on U.S. foreign policy. Those against this ethnic influence, such as Schlesinger, Huntington, and Smith, begin with the premise that there exists a set of "objective" U.S. national interests that can be contrasted with the more parochial interests of ethnic identity groups. This proposition informs much of their subsequent arguments: the United States, because of the influence of ethnic lobbies, may pursue certain policies that are ultimately damaging to its national interests. Of course, scholars such as Catherine Scott (chapter 3 in this volume) would argue that even an "objective" account of American national interests is inherently ethnic because of the importance of race and racial concepts in the formulation of U.S. national interests. Others, namely the constructivists, contend that all interests are inherently subjective and thus, any objective account is impossible.[45] Both of these responses—racial essentialist and constructivist—would undercut the very foundation of the parochial capture argument. Nevertheless, one need not throw up one's hands and discard the entire concept of national interests altogether. Most racial essentialists do not contend that all U.S. interests are racial, but rather that under certain circumstances, they can be strongly influenced by notions of race. Moreover, even if one accepts the notion that national interests are constructed—and this remains a matter of contention in the international relations theory literature[46]—one can still make a distinction between the set of national interests constructed through the process of foreign policy formulation (the ultimate output at a given point in time) and substate interests (the individual parts that helped to influence the ultimate output). Thus, we return to a distinction between national and parochial interests that is at some level real, but less diametrically opposed as some would suggest.

Smith's primary argument, which is fundamentally based on the principle of democratic citizenship, is correct in asserting that if ethnic interest groups, like all substate interest groups, wish to be part of a broader community, they have a political, and indeed an ethical, obligation to support the common good. This suggests a permissible range of influence in the process that leads to the determination of the common good. At one end of this spectrum would be cases in which ethnic interest groups are completely prohibited from the foreign policy process; at the other extreme, ethnic identity groups would be allowed to define the country's policies toward their respective homelands exclusively. Neither of these are acceptable. In the first case, it is fundamentally undemocratic to arbi-

trarily exclude certain groups from legitimate expressions of political preference. Moreover, it would be nearly impossible: ethnic identity groups have
ingeniously found ways around bans on ethnic mobilization in places like
prewar Bosnia-Herzegovina and postcommunist Bulgaria. In addition, many
interest groups that support a specific ethnic agenda may argue that they are not
ethnic-specific. For example, the AIPAC is not officially "ethnic" in nature—unlike, say, the American Jewish Congress, the American Jewish Committee, and
the National Conference on Soviet Jewry. How is one to determine which interest groups are and are not ethnic? Moreover, what if a specific policy is supported by both ethnic and nonethnic interests groups? Should not the policies,
rather than the groups making them, be the focus of policymakers?

On the other hand, allowing ethnic identity groups to be the sole determinant of U.S. foreign policy is just as problematic. It is fundamentally undemocratic because it allows a small minority to determine policy for the vast majority (just as it is fundamentally undemocratic to allow any small interest group
to determine U.S. foreign policy). It is also unwise because the process itself tends
to moderate policies; that is, extremism will be more likely if the process is cir-
cumvented. Finally, it is a recipe for conflict: if a policy needs to be determined
toward a specific region where ethnic groups are in conflict, how do we determine which diaspora should effectively make U.S. foreign policy? For example,
in terms of the Israeli-Palestinian conflict, should Jewish-Americans or Arab-
Americans decide? Obviously, this would not work.

It should not be surprising that neither extreme amounts to what can rea-
sonably be called sound foreign policy. In fact, none of the authors included in
this book, or even the proponents of the two camps presented in this chapter,
would wholeheartedly embrace either extreme. Instead, a more sympathetic perspective of both arguments would result in differences over the *range* of legitimate ethnic influence, not over the influence itself (although, for some, the
range could be quite limited or quite broad). Indeed, the debate over the legitimate range of influence by special interest groups can be a healthy part of the
political process. However, such a debate must always be focused on the end goal
of defining, protecting, and advancing the interests of the broader community.
It is possible that the debate over the legitimate range of ethnic influence may
instigate a desire by politicians, scholars, and public figures to more clearly define U.S. national interests. Ultimately, this would make U.S. foreign policy more
coherent and would provide America's grand strategy with greater internal con-
sistency, even if ethnic identity groups have a role in the process.

When discussing the policies advocated by any interest group, reference
should be consistently made to U.S. national interests. For example, if we agree
that the spread of democracy is a critical American national interest, then ethnic identity groups who support democratization have greater legitimacy than
those who shield dictatorships in their homeland. Likewise, those ethnic identity groups who reinforce America's alliances will have greater legitimacy than
those who support America's enemies. If ethnic identity groups, through their

influence, prohibit the United States from adjusting to new international circumstances, then it is not the status quo itself that is illegitimate, but rather the degree to which the status quo is harmful to broader U.S. foreign policy goals. Thus, it should not be the groups influencing the debate themselves that are the target for criticism or praise, but whether they are advancing U.S. interests. Ignoring the broader community's interests is just as dangerous as ostracizing certain groups from the foreign policy process merely because they are based on ethnic identities.

SEPTEMBER 11

The tragic events of what is now simply called "September 11" have galvanized and united the American community like no time since Pearl Harbor. Although there are certainly significant differences between the two events—most important, that a stateless terrorist organization, rather than a state, attacked the United States—there are similarities as well. The most important is the development of a new "national mission," this time, to destroy international terrorism. It is unclear the degree to which this mission will be fulfilled or the breadth of the operation.[47] Nevertheless, current evidence indicates that there will likely be three significant effects on the relationship between ethnic identity groups and U.S. foreign policy:

· Heightened executive branch control over foreign policy;
· A clearer sense of national interests;
· The impact on Muslim-Americans.

Recentralized Foreign Policy

Following September 11, the Bush administration assumed decisive control over U.S. foreign policy, with some describing a return to an "imperial presidency."[48] Although the administration itself is divided between those who wish for a broader war (led by Defense Secretary Rumsfeld and his deputy, Paul Wolfowitz) and those who are more conservative (led by Secretary of State Powell), there was a remarkable amount of public unity as 2001 ended.[49] Moreover, the nature of the threat requires an increased role for secretive covert operations, which, for obvious reasons, allows for greatly reduced oversight and external influence.[50]

With the United States in an international crisis, both the public and Congress are granting the presidency a tremendous amount of leeway in international affairs. Ordinarily, interest groups in general, and ethnic interest groups in particular, find it much easier to influence U.S. foreign policy when Congress has a larger role in the process. However, the centralization of the foreign policy process in the White House has eroded many of the factors (outlined in this volume's introduction) that have resulted in increased access and influence for ethnic identity groups—namely, increased congressional oversight, a more open foreign policy process, and renewed focus on domestic concerns. Although ethnic lobbies will not be completely shut out of the process, the scope of their influence has been curtailed.

Clearer National Interests

Although the war against terrorism will likely be as amorphous as its target, and such a war has little historical precedent, the newfound unity on the American homefront has been felt, at least at some level, within the foreign policy establishment. Although decision makers and observers may certainly disagree over the "next target" in the war,[51] there is considerable consensus regarding the basic premise of the conflict—that international terrorism must be eliminated. Ethnic identity groups who find themselves connected (either through ethnic kinship or homeland) to something involving international terrorism (either as victim, perpetrator, or even bystander) will have significantly less room to promote an "independent" foreign policy. For example, the Armenian-American lobby has lost considerable support for maintaining sanctions against Azerbaijan given Baku's support for the war on terrorism: "[Secretary of State] Powell urged Congress to lift the sanctions, pointing to Azerbaijan's help in the antiterrorism campaign, including granting the United States overflight rights, the use of its air bases and intelligence support.... Sen. John Kerry, D-Mass., a Foreign Relations Committee member who had written the original restrictions, acknowledged he had little choice but to accept the change."[52] In short, the international fluidity that characterized the decade before September 11 has been significantly curtailed.

Moreover, a far greater emphasis is now being placed on expressions of patriotism. Although the American body politic will likely remain committed to multiculturalism, there may be less tolerance of division on foreign policy issues and more important, less tolerance for endorsement of foreign policies that appear to support interests overseas. In times of crisis, people tend to rally around the flag. If particular groups are seen as undercutting American interests or unity, there may be a negative reaction from the general public and politicians.

Muslim-Americans

In terms of influencing foreign policy, no group will be more deeply affected by September 11 than Muslim-Americans, who are still in the process of developing an effective lobbying structure. The relationship between terrorism and America's Muslim population is complex. The United States government and many Muslims (in America and elsewhere) have argued that the terrorists are decidedly "un-Islamic"—because Islam prohibits the taking of innocent life, terrorists are by definition an abomination to the Muslim faith. In the first weeks after the terrorist attacks, U.S. officials and civic leaders, led by President Bush, went out of their way to disassociate Muslim-Americans with Bin Laden and the al-Qaeda terrorist network.

Nevertheless, the connection between terrorism and the Muslim world will make attempts by Muslim-Americans to influence U.S. foreign policy even more difficult. The major international terrorist groups principally justify their violence on the basis of Islam and are primarily based in Islamic countries. Consequently, the domestic reaction to terrorist acts and the U.S. fight against terrorism will naturally be of concern to Muslim-Americans. Moreover, some of the items on the terrorists' agenda—namely, championing a Palestinian homeland, ending sanctions against Iraq, and preventing the use of force by the United States against Muslim countries—are also supported by many Muslim-Americans, thus further putting them in a delicate position. This will be especially challenging if certain Muslim groups or states are labeled as "terrorist." For example, support for the Palestinian Authority and Yasser Arafat becomes more difficult as attacks continue to be committed against Israel, and calls for lifting sanctions against Iraq are hampered by Saddam Hussein's support for international terrorism and his desire for weapons of mass destruction. Opponents of Arafat and Hussein have learned quickly to label their foes as terrorists: Israeli prime minister Ariel Sharon has repeatedly called Arafat "our bin Laden,"[53] and many are trying to push Baghdad as "phase two" in the war against terrorism.[54] In short, the Muslim-American agenda has been severely compromised by the events of September 11 even as Americans across the political spectrum avoid scapegoating at home.

CONCLUSIONS

The debate over the proper role of ethnic identity groups in the U.S. foreign policy process will undoubtedly continue well into the upcoming decades. As American national interests and America's international grand strategy evolve during the early years of the twenty-first century, ethnic identity groups will play a role in the formulation and implementation of U.S. foreign policy. That most ethnic lobbies realize that they need to frame their parochial interests in terms of furthering the broader national interest should mollify complaints about "ethnic capture" of the foreign policy process. Although in some cases ethnic identity groups may have a disproportionate level of influence over specific policies, it is important not to exaggerate their power. Only in very rare circumstances is the influence of a particular ethnic lobby the sole factor in determining policy. Instead, ethnic identity groups merely play an important, and indeed legitimate, role in the overall foreign policy process. To stand Senator Mathias on his head, the diversity that enriches our domestic life may, under certain circumstances, likewise enrich our foreign relations.

NOTES

1. Yossi Shain, "Multicultural Foreign Policy," *Foreign Policy* 100 (1995): 87.

2. Tony Smith, *Foreign Attachments* (Cambridge, MA: Harvard University Press, 2000), 2.

3. Paul Glastris, Kevin Whitelaw, Bruce Auster, and Barbra Murray, "Multicultural Foreign Policy in Washington," *U.S. News and World Report,* 21 July 1997, 30–35.

4. Walker Connor, *Ethnonationalism: The Quest for Understanding* (Princeton, NJ: Princeton University Press, 1994), 28–66, 89–117.

5. Alexander DeConde, *Ethnicity, Race, and American Foreign Policy* (Boston: North-eastern University Press, 1992).

6. Mathias's article follows this line in his contrast between assimilated and unas-similated ethnic groups. Charles McCurdy Mathias, Jr., "Ethnic Groups and Foreign Pol-icy," *Foreign Affairs* 59 (Summer 1981): 979–80.

7. Ibid., 981.

8. "All Politics Is Global," *Wall Street Journal,* 25 November 1992, A12, cited in Eric M. Uslander, "All Politics Are Global: Interest Groups and the Making of Foreign Pol-icy," in *Interest Group Politics,* 4th ed., ed. Allan J. Cigler and Burdett A. Loomis (Wash-ington, DC: Congressional Quarterly Press, 1995), 370.

9. Shain, "Multicultural Foreign Policy," 87.

10. Nathan Glazer, *We Are All Multiculturalists Now* (Cambridge, MA: Harvard Uni-versity Press, 1997).

11. Joan Morrison and Charlotte Fox Zabusky, quoted in William Keough, "The View from the Melting Pot," *Christian Science Monitor,* 1 October 1980, 17.

12. Shain, "Multicultural Foreign Policy," 86.

13. See McCartney (chapter 2) and Scott (chapter 3) in this volume. Also see many of the pieces in this volume's Selected Bibliography under "White Identity" and "African-Americans."

14. See Charles P. Henry, "Introduction: Black Global Politics in a Post–Cold War World," in *Foreign Policy and the Black (Inter)national Interest,* ed. Charles P. Henry (Albany: State University of New York Press, 2000), 1–16.

15. James Risen and Jonathan Peterson, "Economy Elbows Other Issues Aside," *Los Angeles Times,* 2 November 1992, A14.

16. It should be noted, however, that there is little public support for a return to full isolationism. Moreover, America continues to have enduring foreign interests that re-quire at least some level of internationalism, and events overseas may force it to assume an unwanted role internationally. Thus, it is important not to exaggerate the tendency for post–Cold War isolationism. Ole R. Holsti, "Public Opinion and U.S. Foreign Policy after the Cold War," in *After the End,* ed. James M. Scott (Durham, NC: Duke Univer-sity Press, 1998), 138–69.

17. Kenneth Longmyer, "Black American Demands," *Foreign Policy* 60 (Fall 1985): 3–17.

18. Shain, "Multicultural Foreign Policy," 74.

19. Richard N. Haass summarizes the arguments of the neo-isolationists in *The Re-luctant Sheriff* (New York: Council on Foreign Relations, 1997), 55–60.

20. For example, during the 2000 presidential campaign, only Reform Party candidate Patrick Buchanan actively supported isolationism.

21. Shain, "Multicultural Foreign Policy," 87. Also see his longer treatment in Yossi Shain, *Marketing the American Creed Abroad: Diasporas in the U.S. and Their Home-lands* (Cambridge, England: Cambridge University Press, 1999).

22. For example, in "A National Security Strategy for a New Century" (Washington, DC: The White House, December 1999), the Clinton administration consistently referred to democratization as advancing American security and prosperity.

23. American Israel Public Affairs Committee, "U.S.-Israel Partnership," <http://www.aipac.org/usispartnership.PDF> (accessed November 2001).

24. U.S. Department of State, "Background Note: Israel," <http://www.state.gov/r/pa/bgn/index.cfm?docid=3581> (accessed November 2001).

25. Stephen A. Garrett, "Eastern European Ethnic Groups and American Foreign Policy," *Political Science Quarterly* 93, no. 2 (1978): 301–23.

26. Joseph O'Grady, "An Irish Policy Born in the U.S.A.: Clinton's Break with the Past," *Foreign Affairs* 75, no. 3 (1996): 2–8.

27. Quoted in "Lobbying and the Middle East," *Congressional Quarterly*, 22 August 1981, 1529.

28. Samuel P. Huntington, "The Erosion of American National Interests," *Foreign Affairs* (September/October 1997): 28–49.

29. Ibid., 38.

30. Ibid., 39.

31. Smith, *Foreign Attachments*, 2.

32. Ibid., 10.

33. Arthur M. Schlesinger, Jr., *The Disuniting of America: Reflections on a Multicultural Society* (New York: Norton, 1992).

34. Huntington, "Erosion of American National Interests," 39; Smith, *Foreign Attachments*, 34.

35. Robert Dreyfuss, "The New China Lobby," *The American Prospect* (January–February 1997): 30–38; Xiao-Huang Yin and Zhiyong Lan, "Chinese Americans: A Rising Factor in U.S.-China Relations," *Journal of American-East Asian Relations* 6, no. 1 (1997): 35–58.

36. James Schlesinger, "Hyphenating Foreign Policy," *National Interest* 62 (Winter 2000/2001): 112. Also see James Schlesinger, "Fragmentation and Hubris: A Shaky Basis for American Leadership," *National Interest* 49 (Fall 1997): 3–10.

37. Schlesinger, "Hyphenating Foreign Policy," 112.

38. James M. Wall, "U.S. Cuba Policy Is Obsolete," *The Christian Century* 111, no. 25 (1994): 803–4; Walt Vanderbush and Patrick J. Haney, "Policy toward Cuba in the Clinton Administration," *Political Science Quarterly* 114, no. 3 (1999): 387.

39. See, for example, Subcommittee on Asia and the Pacific of the House International Relations Committee, *U.S. Interest in Central Asia*, 105th Cong., 2d sess., 12 February 1998.

40. Smith, *Foreign Attachments*, 83.

41. Mitchell Bard, "The Influence of Ethnic Interest Groups on American Middle East Policy," in *The Domestic Sources of American Foreign Policy*, ed. Charles W. Kegley, Jr., and Eugene R. Wittkopf (New York: St. Martin's Press, 1988): 63.

42. Thomas Ambrosio, "Congressional Perceptions of Ethnic Cleansing: Reactions to the Nagorno-Karabagh War and the Influence of Ethnic Interest Groups," *The Review of International Affairs* (forthcoming).

43. Mathias, "Ethnic Groups and Foreign Policy," 981.

44. "The Birth of an Arab-American Lobby," *The Economist*, 12 October 2000.

45. The classic statement of constructivism is Alexander Wendt's "Anarchy Is What States Make of It," *International Organization* 46 (1992): 391–425.

46. Ted Hopf, "The Promise of Constructivism in International Relations Theory," *International Security* 23, no. 1 (1998): 171–200.

47. At the time of writing, the "war on terrorism" has only involved Afghanistan militarily.

48. Dana Milbank, "In War, It's Power to the President," *Washington Post*, 20 November, A1.

49. David E. Sanger and Patrick E. Tyler, "Wartime Forges a United Front for Bush Aides," *New York Times*, 23 December 2001, A1.

50. Thomas E. Ricks and Steven Mufson, "In War on Terrorism, Unseen Fronts May Be Crucial," *Washington Post*, 23 September 2001, A3; Alexander Nicoll, "Stage Is Set for Extensive Use of Special Forces," *Financial Times* (London), 24 September 2001, 2.

51. Ron Martz and Moni Basu, "Who's Next on List? U.S. Treads Cautiously," *Atlanta Journal and Constitution*, 19 December 2001, A1.

52. Miles A. Pomper, "Adversity for Ethnic Lobbies," *Congressional Quarterly Weekly* 59, no. 41 (2001): 2558.

53. Phil Reeves, "Palestinian Leader Is Portrayed by Israel as 'Bin Laden Mark Two,'" *Independent* (London), 6 December 2001, 6.

54. Joseph Lieberman, "After Bin Laden, We Must Target Saddam," *Wall Street Journal*, 29 October 2001, A22.

Selected Bibliography

The following select bibliography cites books and articles that deal with the nexus between ethnic identity groups and U.S. foreign policy. It is divided into general works and those that address a specific group or conflict. For the edited volumes that deal exclusively with ethnicity/race and U.S. foreign policy (in particular, the edited books by Michael L. Krenn), the entire volume is cited, rather than individual chapters.

GENERAL

Ahrari, Mohammed E., ed. *Ethnic Groups and U.S. Foreign Policy.* Westport, CT: Greenwood Press, 1987.

Anderson, Benedict, "Exodus." *Critical Inquiry* 20 (Winter 1994): 327.

Christol, Hélène, and Serge Ricard. *Hyphenated Diplomacy: European Immigration and U.S. Foreign Policy, 1914–1984.* Marseille: J. Laffitte, 1985.

Clough, Michael. "Grass-Roots Policymaking: Say Good-Bye to the 'Wise Men.'" *Foreign Affairs* 73, no. 1 (1994): 2–7.

DeConde, Alexander. *Ethnicity, Race, and American Foreign Policy.* Boston: Northeastern University Press, 1992.

Dekmejian, R. H. and Angelos Themelis. "Ethnic Lobbies in U.S. Foreign Policy: A Comparative Analysis of the Jewish, Greek, Armenian and Turkish Lobbies." Occasional Research Paper no. 13. Athens, Greece: Institution of International Affairs, 1997.

Destler, I. M., Leslie H. Gelb, and Anthony Lake, "Breakdown: The Impact of Domestic Politics on American Foreign Policy." In *The Domestic Sources of American Foreign Policy: Insights and Evidence,* ed. Charles W. Kegley, Jr., and Eugene R. Wittkopf, 17–29. New York: St. Martin's Press, 1988.

Fuchs, Lawrence H. "Minority Groups and Foreign Policy." *Political Science Quarterly* 74, no. 2 (1959): 161–75.

Gerson, Louis. *The Hyphenate in Recent American Politics and Diplomacy.* Lawrence: University of Kansas Press, 1964.

Glastris, Paul, Kevin Whitelaw, Bruce Auster, and Barbra Murray. "Multicultural Foreign Policy in Washington." *U.S. News and World Report,* 21 July 1997, 30–35.

Glazer, Nathan. *We Are All Multiculturalists Now.* Cambridge, MA: Harvard University Press, 1998.

Glazer, Nathan, and Daniel Patrick Moynihan, eds. *Ethnicity: Theory and Experience.* Cambridge, MA: Harvard University Press, 1975.

Harrington, Mona. "Loyalties: Dual and Divided." In *The Politics of Ethnicity,* ed. Michael Walzer, et al., 93–138. Cambridge, MA: Harvard University Press, 1982.

Hollinger, David A. *Postethnic America: Beyond Multiculturalism.* New York: Basic Books, 1996.

Huntington, Samuel P. "The Erosion of American National Interests." *Foreign Affairs* 76, no. 5 (1997): 28–49.

Jones, Maldwyn A. *The Old World Ties of American Ethnic Groups.* London: H. K. Lewis, 1976.

Lahiri, Sajal, and Pascalis Raimondos-Møller. "Lobbying by Ethnic Groups and Aid Allocation." *The Economic Journal* 110 (March 2000): C62–C79.

Lauren, Paul G. *Power and Prejudice: The Politics and Diplomacy of Racial Discrimination,* 2d ed. Boulder, CO: Westview Press, 1996.

Lind, Michael. *The Next American Nation: The New Nationalism and the Fourth American.* New York: Free Press, 1996.

Mathias, Charles McCurdy, Jr. "Ethnic Groups and Foreign Policy." *Foreign Affairs* 59 (1981): 975–98.

Miller, John J. *The Unmaking of Americans: How Multiculturalism Has Undermined the Assimilation Ethic.* New York: Free Press, 1998.

Rogers, Elizabeth S. "The Conflicting Roles of American Ethnic and Business Interests in the U.S. Economic Sanctions Policy: The Case of South Africa." In *The Limits of State Autonomy,* ed. David Skidmore and Valerie M. Hudson, 185–204. Boulder, CO: Westview Press, 1993.

Said, Abdul Aziz, ed. *Ethnicity and U.S. Foreign Policy,* revised ed. Westport, CT: Praeger, 1981.

Schlesinger, Arthur M., Jr. *The Disuniting of America.* New York: Norton, 1992.

Schlesinger, James. "Fragmentation and Hubris: A Shaky Basis for American Leadership." *National Interest* (Fall 1997): 3–10.

———. "Hyphenating Foreign Policy." *National Interest* (Winter 2000–2001): 110–13.

Shain, Yossi. "Ethnic Diasporas and U.S. Foreign Policy." *Political Science Quarterly* 109, no. 5 (1994–1995): 811–41.

———. *The Frontier of Loyalty: Political Exiles in the Age of the Nation-State.* Middletown, CT: Wesleyan University Press, 1989.

———. *Marketing the American Creed Abroad: Diasporas in the U.S. and Their Homelands.* Cambridge, England: Cambridge University Press, 1999.

———. "Multicultural Foreign Policy." *Foreign Policy* 100 (1995): 69–87.

Smith, Tony. *Foreign Attachments: The Power of Ethnic Groups in the Making of American Foreign Policy.* Cambridge, MA: Harvard University Press, 2000.

Stanfield, Rochelle L. "Ethnic Politicking." *National Journal* 21, no. 52 (1989): 3096.

Uslander, Eric M. "All in the Family? Interest Groups and Foreign Policy." In *Interest Group Politics,* 5th ed., ed. Allan J. Cigler and Burdett A. Loomis, 365–86. Washington, DC: Congressional Quarterly Press, 1998.

———. "All Politics Are Global: Interest Groups and the Making of Foreign Policy." In *Interest Group Politics,* 4th ed., ed. Allan J. Cigler and Burdett A. Loomis, 369–89. Washington, DC: Congressional Quarterly Press, 1995.

Vidal, David J. *Defining the National Interest: Minorities and U.S. Foreign Policy in the 21st Century.* New York: Council on Foreign Relations, 1997.

AFRICAN-AMERICANS

Alston, Ona. "Promoting an African American Foreign Policy Agenda: A Municipal Strategy." *Urban League Review* 16 (1992): 45–57.

Challenor, Herschelle Sullivan. "The Influence of Black Americans on U.S. Foreign Policy toward Africa." In *Ethnicity and U.S. Foreign Policy,* revised ed., ed. Abdul Aziz Said, 33–62. Westport, CT: Praeger, 1981.

Dickson, David A. "American Society and the African American Foreign Policy Lobby: Constraints and Opportunities." *Journal of Black Studies* 27, no. 2 (1996): 139–51.

Klotz, Audie. "Norms Reconstituting Interests: Global Racial Equality and U.S. Sanctions against South Africa." *International Organization* 49, no. 3 (1995): 451–78.

Krenn, Michael L. *The African American Voice in U.S. Foreign Policy since World War II.* New York: Garland, 1998.

Longmyer, Kenneth. "Black American Demands." *Foreign Policy* 60 (Fall 1985): 3–17.

Morris, Milton D. "African Americans and the New World Order." *Washington Quarterly* 15, no. 4 (1992): 5–22.

Schraeder, Peter J. "Speaking with Many Voices: Continuity and Change in U.S.-Africa Policy." *Journal of Modern African Studies* 29 (September 1991): 398–406.

Walters, Ronald W. "African-American Influence on U.S. Foreign Policy toward South Africa." In *Ethnic Groups and U.S. Foreign Policy,* ed. Mohammed E. Ahrari, 65–82. Westport, CT: Greenwood Press, 1987.

Weil, M. "Can the Blacks Do for Africa What the Jews Did for Israel?" *Foreign Policy* 15 (1974): 109–30.

Weisbord, Robert G. *Ebony Kinship: Africa, Africans, and the Afro-American.* Westport, CT: Praeger, 1973.

ARMENIAN-AMERICANS

Aftandilian, Gregory L. *Armenia, Vision of a Republic: The Independence Lobby in America, 1918–1927.* Boston: Charles River Books, 1982.

Panossian, Razmik. "Between Ambivalence and Intrusion: Politics and Identity in Armenia-Diaspora Relations." *Diaspora* 7, no. 2 (1998): 148–97.

Paul, Rachel Anderson. "Grassroots Mobilization and Diaspora Politics: Armenian Interest Groups and the Role of Collective Memory." *Nationalism and Ethnic Politics* 6, no. 1 (2000): 24–47.

ASIAN-AMERICANS

Bernstein, R., and R. H. Munro. "The New China Lobby." In *The Domestic Sources of American Foreign Policy,* ed. E. Wittkopf and J. M. McCormick. Lanham, MD: Rowan and Littlefield, 1998.
Moon, Chung-in. "Complex Interdependence and Transnational Lobbying: South Korea in the United States." *International Studies Quarterly* 32, no. 1 (1988): 67–89.
Watanabe, Paul. Y. "Asian American Activism and U.S. Foreign Policy." In *Across the Pacific: Asian Americans and Globalization,* ed. Evelyn Hu-DeHart. Philadelphia: Temple University Press, 1999.
———. "Global Forces, Foreign Policy, and Asian Pacific Americans." *PS: Political Science and Politics* 34, no. 3 (2001): 639–44.

EASTERN EUROPEANS

Garrett, Stephen A. "Eastern European Ethnic Groups and American Foreign Policy." *Political Science Quarterly* 93, no. 2 (1978): 301–23.
———. "The Ties That Bind: Immigrant Influence on U.S. Policy toward Eastern Europe." In *Ethnicity and U.S. Foreign Policy,* revised ed., ed. Abdul Aziz Said, 97–120. Westport, CT: Praeger, 1981.
Kruszewski, Z. A. "The Polish American Congress, East-West Issues, and the Formulation of American Foreign Policy." In *Ethnic Groups and U.S. Foreign Policy,* ed. Mohammed E. Ahrari, 83–100. Westport, CT: Greenwood Press, 1987.

LATINO-AMERICANS

Arnson, C. J., and P. Brenner. "The Limits of Lobbying: Interest Groups, Congress, and Aid to the Contras." In *Public Opinion in U.S. Foreign Policy,* ed. R. Sobel. New York: St. Martin's Press, 1993.
Ayon, David, and Ricardo Anzaldua Montoya. "Latinos and U.S. Foreign Policy toward Latin America." In *Latin America and Caribbean Contemporary Record, vol. 5, 1985–1986,* ed. Abraham Lowenthal, 126–42. New York: Holmes and Meier, 1988.
Cohen, Isaac. "Hispanics and Foreign Policy." *International Journal of Public Administration* 23 (May–August 2000): 1311–39.
de la Garza, Rodolfo O. "U.S. Foreign Policy and the Mexican-American Political Agenda." In *Ethnic Groups and U.S. Foreign Policy,* ed. Mohammed E. Ahrari, 101–14. Westport, CT: Greenwood Press, 1987.
de la Garza, Rodolfo O., and Harry P. Pachon, eds. *Latinos and U.S. Foreign Policy: Representing the "Homeland"?* Lanham, MD: Rowman and Littlefield, 2000.

Fernàndez, Damiàn J. "From Little Havana to Washington, D.C.: Cuban-Americans and U.S. Foreign Policy." In *Ethnic Groups and U.S. Foreign Policy,* ed. Mohammed E. Ahrari, 115–54. Westport, CT: Greenwood Press, 1987.

Haney, Patrick J., and Walt Vanderbush. "The Role of Ethnic Interest Groups in U.S. Foreign Policy: The Case of the Cuban American National Foundation." *International Studies Quarterly* 43 (1999): 341–61.

Jones-Correa, Michael. "New Directions for Latinos as an Ethnic Lobby in U.S. Foreign Policy." *Harvard Journal of Hispanic Policy* 47 (1995): 47–87.

The Stanley Foundation and the Tomás Rivera Policy Institute. *Latinos, Global Change, and American Foreign Policy.* Claremont, CA: The Tomás Rivera Policy Institute, 1995.

Rendón, Armando B. "Latinos: Breaking the Cycle of Survival to Tackle Global Affairs." In *Ethnicity and U.S. Foreign Policy,* revised ed., ed. Abdul Aziz Said, 183–200. Westport, CT: Praeger, 1981.

Richardson, Bill. "Hispanic American Concerns." *Foreign Policy* 60 (Fall 1985): 30–39.

Robbins, Carla Anne. "Cuban-American Clout." *Foreign Policy* 88 (Fall 1992): 162–82.

GREEK-TURKISH-CYPRUS DISPUTE

Constas, Dimitri C., and Athanassios G. Platias, eds. *Diasporas in World Politics: The Greeks in Comparative Perspective.* London: Macmillan, 1995.

Hackett, Clifford. "Ethnic Politics in Congress: The Turkish Embargo Experience." *Ethnicity and U.S. Foreign Policy,* revised ed., ed. Abdul Aziz Said, 33–62. Westport, CT: Praeger, 1981.

Halley, Lawrence. *Ancient Affections: Ethnic Groups and Foreign Policy.* Westport, CT: Praeger, 1985.

Hicks, Sallie M., and Theodore A. Couloumbis. "The 'Greek Lobby': Illusion or Reality?" *Ethnicity and U.S. Foreign Policy,* revised ed., ed. Abdul Aziz Said, 63–96. Westport, CT: Praeger, 1981.

Watanabe, Paul Y. *Ethnic Groups, Congress, and American Foreign Policy: The Politics of the Turkish Arms Embargo.* Westport, CT: Greenwood Press, 1984.

IRISH-AMERICANS

Duff, John B. "The Versailles Treaty and the Irish-Americans." *Journal of American History* 55, no. 3 (1968): 582–98.

Guelke, Adrian. "The United States, Irish Americans, and the Northern Ireland Peace Process." *International Affairs* 72, no. 3 (1996): 521–37.

Maxwell, Kenneth R. "Irish-Americans and the Fight for Treaty Ratification." *Public Opinion Quarterly* 31, no. 3 (1967–1968): 620–41.

O'Grady, Joseph. "An Irish Policy Born in the U.S.A: Clinton's Break with the Past." *Foreign Affairs* 75, no. 3 (1996): 2–8.

Thompson, Robert J., and Joseph R. Rudolph, Jr. "Irish-Americans in the American Foreign-Policy–Making Process." In *Ethnic Groups and U.S. Foreign Policy,* ed. Mohammed E. Ahrari, 135–54. Westport, CT: Greenwood Press, 1987.

MIDDLE EAST DISPUTE

Bard, Mitchell. "Ethnic Group Influence on Middle East Policy—How and When: The Cases of the Jackson-Vanik Amendment and the Sale of AWACS to Saudi Arabia." In *Ethnic Groups and U.S. Foreign Policy,* ed. Mohammed E. Ahrari, 45–64. Westport, CT: Greenwood Press, 1987.

———. "The Influence of Ethnic Interest Groups on American Middle East Policy." In *The Domestic Sources of American Foreign Policy,* ed. Charles W. Kegley, Jr., and Eugene R. Wittkopf, 57–69. New York: St. Martin's Press, 1988.

———. *The Water's Edge and Beyond: Defining the Limits to Domestic Influence on United States Middle East Policy.* New Brunswick, NJ: Transaction, 1991.

Curtiss, Richard H. *Stealth PACs: Lobbying Congress for Control of U.S. Middle East Policy.* Washington, DC: American Educational Trust, 1996.

Glick, Edward B. *The Triangular Connection: America, Israel, and American Jews.* London: Allen and Unwin, 1982.

Goldberg, David H. *Foreign Policy and Ethnic Interest Groups: American and Canadian Jews Lobby for Israel.* Westport, CT: Greenwood Press, 1990.

Goldberg, J. J. *Jewish Power: Inside the American Jewish Establishment.* Reading, MA: Addison-Wesley, 1996.

Madison, Christopher. "Arab American Lobby Fights Rearguard Battle to Influence U.S. Mideast Policy." *National Journal* 17 (1985): 1934–38.

Sadd, David J., and G. Neal Lendenmann, "Arab American Grievances." *Foreign Policy* 60 (1985): 17–30.

Spiegel, Steven L. "Ethnic Politics and the Formulation of U.S. Policy toward the Arab-Israeli Dispute." In *Ethnic Groups and U.S. Foreign Policy,* ed. Mohammed E. Ahrari, 23–44. Westport, CT: Greenwood Press, 1987.

Trice, Robert H. "Domestic Interest Groups and the Arab-Israeli Conflict." In *Ethnicity and U.S. Foreign Policy,* revised ed., ed. Abdul Aziz Said, 121–42. Westport, CT: Praeger, 1981.

Tivnan, Edward. *The Lobby: Jewish Political Power and American Foreign Policy.* New York: Simon and Schuster, 1987.

WHITE IDENTITY

Doty, Roxanne Lyn. "The Bounds of Race in International Relations." *Review of International Studies* 22 (1993): 443–61.

Horne, Gerald. "Race from Power: U.S. Foreign Policy and the General Crisis of 'White Supremacy.'" *Diplomatic History* 23 (1999): 437–61.

Krenn, Michael L., ed. *Race and U.S. Foreign Policy during the Cold War.* New York: Garland, 1998.

———. *Race and U.S. Foreign Policy from Colonial Times through the Age of Jackson.* New York: Garland, 1998.

———. *Race and U.S. Foreign Policy from 1900 through World War II.* New York: Garland, 1998.

———. *Race and U.S. Foreign Policy in the Ages of Territorial and Market Expansion, 1840 to 1900.* New York: Garland, 1998.

Lemelle, Tilden J. "Race, International Relations, U.S. Foreign Policy, and the African Liberation Struggle." *Journal of Black Studies* 3 (1972): 95–110.

Weston, Rubin Francis. *Racism in U.S. Imperialism: The Influence of Racial Assumptions on American Foreign Policy, 1893–1946.* Columbia: University of South Carolina Press, 1972.

YUGOSLAV CONFLICT

Blitz, Brad. "Serbia's War Lobby: Diaspora Groups and Western Elites." In *This Time We Knew: Western Responses to Genocide in Bosnia,* ed. Thomas Cushman and Stjepan G. Mestrovic. New York: New York University Press, 1996.

About the Contributors

THOMAS AMBROSIO is an assistant professor of political science at North Dakota State University, having received his Ph.D. in foreign affairs at the University of Virginia (2000) and taught previously at the University of Virginia and Western Kentucky University. He has published *Irredentism: Ethnic Conflict and International Politics* (2001) and coedited *International Law and the Rise of Nations: The State System and the Challenge of Ethnic Groups* (2001). He has also published several journal articles and chapters in edited books and is embarking on a new project examining U.S.-Russian relations in the post-Cold War period. Ever since joining the faculty of the Department of Political Science at North Dakota State University in 2000, he has resided in Fargo with his wife Beth.

MICHAEL JONES-CORREA is an associate professor of government at Cornell University, having received his Ph.D. in politics at Princeton University in 1994 and taught at Harvard as an assistant and associate professor of government from 1994 to 2001. His research interests include immigrant politics and immigration policy, minority politics and interethnic relations in the United States, and urban and suburban politics. He is the author of *Between Two Nations: The Political Predicament of Latinos in New York City* (1998), and the editor of *Governing American Cities: Inter-Ethnic Coalitions, Competition, and Conflict* (2001). Jones-Correa has also written more than a dozen articles and book chapters, is currently completing a book that examines the renegotiation of ethnic relations in the aftermath of civil disturbances in New York, Los Angeles, Miami, and Washington, D.C., and is embarking on a new project on the increasing ethnic diversity of suburbs and its implication for local and national politics in the United States.

PAUL MCCARTNEY received his Ph.D. from the University of Virginia and is currently teaching at Rutgers University as a visiting professor. He is completing work on a book that uses the Spanish-American War to examine both the cultural dimensions of U.S. foreign policy and the relationship between U.S. foreign policy and the development of American national identity.

ABDULAH OSMAN, a native of Somalia, is currently a doctoral candidate in the Wayne State University political science department in Detroit, Michigan. His research interests include politics in sub-Saharan Africa, as well as peace and conflict studies.

RACHEL PAUL is a political scientist at the Ohio State University-Newark. Her research interests include identity politics, European politics, and U.S. foreign policy. She received her doctorate from Miami University in 1999.

CATHERINE V. SCOTT teaches in the political science program at Agnes Scott College in Decatur, Georgia. She is the author of *Gender and Development: Rethinking Modernization and Dependency Theory* (1995) and is currently working on a book on U.S. foreign policy after Vietnam.

FRAN SCOTT is currently a visiting assistant professor in the political science department at Texas A&M University. She received her Ph.D. in political science from Wayne State University in Detroit, Michigan, and currently does research in African-American politics and public policy.

YOSSI SHAIN is the 1999–2002 Goldman Visiting Professor of Government at Georgetown and former head of the political science department at Tel Aviv University. He has written numerous books and articles on international relations and comparative politics. His latest book is *Marketing the American Creed Abroad: Diasporas in the US and Their Homelands* (1999). He is now completing a book on kinship in international affairs.

PAUL Y. WATANABE is the codirector of the Institute for Asian American Studies and associate professor of political science at the University of Massachusetts Boston. He is the author of *Ethnic Groups, Congress, and American Foreign Policy: The Politics of the Turkish Arms Embargo* (Greenwood Press, 1984).

TAMARA COFMAN WITTES is the director of program at the Middle East Institute in Washington, D.C. She earned her Ph.D. from Georgetown University and is working on her book on symbols of security in ethnic conflicts.

Index